Triumph of The Will
How Two Men Hypnotised Hitler and Changed the World

DAVID LEWIS

PRESS

Falmer, Brighton

Cataloguing in Publication Data is available from the British Library

ISBN: 978-1-5136-4140-9

Photographs

Every effort has been made to fulfil requirements regarding copyright material. The author and publisher will be glad to rectify any omissions at the earliest opportunity. Please contact david@dredmundforster.info

Cover design by Goran J Tomic

TRIUMPH OF THE WILL

To my dear friend, partner and colleague Steven with love and gratitude for everything we have shared..

CONTENTS

ACKNOWLEDGMENTS

My research for this book, which took me to the United States, Germany, Austria, France, Switzerland and the Netherlands, was only possible thanks to the help of many individuals whose assistance I am pleased to acknowledge here.

My friend and colleague, the late Professor 'Rudy' Binion, not only granted me access to his extensive Forster archive but, with his charming French wife Elena, gave me hospitality at their delightful home outside Boston.

My German researchers: Eva Magin-Pelich MA, in Berlin and Jacqueline Holzer MA, in Austria. Their skill and dedication made it possible to unearth many previously unpublished documents and to obtain interviews with individuals who had never before disclosed what they know about the life and times of Edmund Forster. Their enthusiastic and tireless contribution made the lengthy research an enjoyable and exhilarating experience.

Edmund Forster's grandchildren, Arne Forster and Mechthild Mudrack, Marie Rose von Wesendonk MA (granddaughter of Edmund's brother Dirk), Pam Forster (widow of Dirk's son Vincent) and Dr Edmund Forster for their tremendous assistance and for kindly allowing me access to their extensive family archives and personal photographs.

Professor Dr Dirk Ropohl, University of Freiburg, for his assistance in contacting Edmund's surviving relatives. Michele Frouge-Noret of Librarie Thierry Corcelle (Paris) and Jill and Roger Bromiley (Amsterdam).

Dr Paul and neurologist Professor Anthony Zador of Cold Spring Harbour laboratory for providing me with information about the life and death of their relative Julius (Gyula) Zador, whose controversial research with the 'tilting table' while at Greifswald unwittingly contributed to Forster's fall from grace.

The Research Department at the Imperial War Museum, London, especially to Dr Terry Charman. Matthew Buck, researcher at Firepower, the Royal Artillery Museum, for advice on the use of gas in the First World War and to Major Tonie and Valmai Holt, authors of the invaluable guides to the battlefields of that war. Dr Sean Kelly, a neurophysiologist with an interest in nerve agents, was kind enough to provide expert advice on the effects of mustard gas and nicotine poisoning.

Frau M. Schumann, archivist at Ernst-Moritz-Arndt-Universität Greifswald; Herr W. Brose, curator of the Pasewalk Museum; Frau Neitzel, from the Greifswald town's archive; Pastor Hanke, the curator and staff of the Museum of Nonnenhorn, and Sheila Noble, senior librarian at the University of Edinburgh.

Icelandic historian Thor Whitehead and, to Dr Klaus Kroner, son of the late Dr Karl Kroner, for reliving the still-painful memories of his family's flight from Nazi persecution. I am also grateful for the helpful comments on early drafts of the book by Peter Hughman, Duncan Smith, Juliane Beard and Robb Lamb. To my brilliant editor Emily Cox for her wonderful work on the text.

As a professional psychologist rather than a historian, I approached writing this history of the Third Reich with trepidation. My sincere thanks go out to all who have helped me over the past fifteen years in researching and writing this book. If you have any further information or views on the lives of Edmund Forster or Erik Hanussen, please get in touch via the www.trumphofthewill.co.uk.

INTRODUCTION

This is the true story of an eminent German doctor and a Jewish psychic who transformed a purposeless drifter into one of the 20th century's most merciless tyrants.

Dr Edmund Robert Forster first met Hitler in October 1918 when he used hypnosis while treating him for hysterical blindness. Clairvoyant and media tycoon Erik Jan Hanussen, a Moravian Jew masquerading as a Danish aristocrat, used similar techniques to reinforce the dictator's belief in his own divine destiny.

Between them, these two men inadvertently and intentionally helped the Nazis into power and so changed the world forever.

Why I Wrote This Book

My interest in the little-known story of nerve specialist Dr Edmund Forster, and his role in creating one of the greatest monsters of the 20th century, began some thirty years ago. While researching an article on German psychiatry during the First World War for International History Magazine, I came across an article by Rudolph Binion, Professor of Modern History at Brandeis University. He described both Pasewalk, where Edmund Forster had practiced as a doctor, and the University at Greifswald, where he had been Professor of Neurology and Director of the Nerve Clinic. Since they were behind the Iron Curtain, his research was difficult and dangerous.

Fluent in German, French and Russian, Binion had become intrigued by the story of Edmund Forster after reading a then-classified 1943 United States Naval Intelligence report on an Austrian doctor named Karl Kroner. While living in Iceland as a refugee from the Nazis, Kroner had described to US Intelligence how, in 1918, Forster had treated Hitler.

Determined to discover more about these events, Binion took a year's leave from the university and, at no small risk to himself, penetrated the tangled communist bureaucracy to carry out original research at both Pasewalk and Greifswald. There he found transcripts of an internal investigation into Forster which resulted in the fifty-five-year-old's violent death. For reasons of security, these transcripts had been recorded using an archaic and almost-forgotten form of shorthand, making them unintelligible to anyone not versed in this long-abandoned code. He was able to track down two archivists in the Greifswald University Library who had worked there in Forster's time and were among the few people able to decipher the text. At his request, they produced a typescript, saving for posterity an invaluable historical document.

As a clinical psychologist and psychopathologist, I became intrigued by Forster's story and interested in learning more about his use of hypnosis to cure Hitler's blindness. While his unconventional treatment successfully restored the lance-corporal's sight, it ended catastrophically for both Forster and humanity.

In *Triumph of the Will*, I answer one of the 20th century's most baffling questions: What happened to transform Adolf Hitler from a purposeless drifter into a ruthless leader with the power to manipulate the minds of millions and change our world forever?

CHAPTER 1
HITLER LACKED THE PERSONALITY TO LEAD!

We all believe on this earth in Adolf Hitler, our Leader. We believe that this God has sent us Adolf Hitler so that Germany should be as a foundation stone in all eternity. - Hitler Youth poster, 1934[1]

September 7th, 1948, was an overcast day[2] that allowed only occasional glimmers of sunshine to penetrate the grime-smeared windows of Courtroom Number Two in Nürnberg's ancient Palace of Justice. From those windows, stretched out on either side of the Pegnitz River, could be seen the broken buildings of a once beautiful medieval city. Allied bombing had razed to the ground or opened to the sky more than six thousand of the picturesque, high-gabled houses with their steeply pitched roofs. Among the ruins, flanking its narrow streets, were the homes of Renaissance artist Albrecht Dürer[3] and the cobbler-poet Hans Sachs.[4]

Three years earlier, major Nazi war criminals had been tried in this medieval courthouse.[5] By 1946, their places had been taken the bureaucrats, who, through their dedication to the Party, had kept the wheels of government turning even as the Third Reich collapsed into rubble around them. In the oak-panelled courtroom, 49-year-old Robert Wasili Kempner, wearing the uniform of a US Army Captain, was questioning former German diplomat Fritz Wiedemann.

The only German-born Jewish member of the US prosecution team at the International Military War Crimes Trial, Kempner[6] had started his legal career during the twenties as an advisor to the Prussian police. After failing in an attempt to have the Nazi Party declared illegal, he sought to indict Adolf Hitler on treason charges and have him deported as an illegal Austrian immigrant. Not surprisingly, once the Nazis came to power, Kempner had been arrested and thrown into prison by the Gestapo. Released thanks to the intervention of influential friends, he fled to the United States. Two years later, he became Professor of Law at the University of Pennsylvania. Now, he had returned to his shattered home country, the only German-born member of America's prosecution team, to assist in the prosecution of Nazi officials who, in the words of United States Chief Counsel Justice Robert H. Jackson had 'created in Germany, under the '*Führerprinzip*', campaigns of arrogance, brutality, and annihilation as the world has not witnessed since the pre-Christian ages.'[7]

Kempner vs. Wiedemann

While Kempner came across in court as methodical but plodding, the same could not be said of the witness he was cross-examining. Fritz Wiedemann, despite his greyish pallor after four years in detention and an ill-fitting, prison-issued suit, dominated the courtroom with his confidence and air of authority. A professional soldier from the age of

nineteen, Wiedemann had graduated from the Munich
Military Academy shortly before the outbreak of war in
1918. In 1916, when a Regimental Adjutant with the 16
Bavarian Reserve Infantry Regiment, he met 27-year-old
lance-corporal Adolf Hitler for the first time and had been
distinctly unimpressed.

'Hitler did not cut a particularly impressive figure,' he
recalled. 'His posture was careless and his answers when
one asked him a question were always sloppy. He held his
head a little to the left and all these things made him look
very unmilitary.'[8]

At the end of the First War, Wiedemann bought a farm in
southern Germany and might well have remained a simple
farmer for the rest of his life had he not, in 1933, stage-
managed a meeting with Hitler at Munich station. This, as
he had hoped, led to an offer of employment as the Führer's
personal adjutant, a position he held until 1939 when he had
the temerity to question Hitler's determination to go to war.
Banished from Berlin, he went as Consul General to San
Francisco at his own request. American journalist Sidney
Roger, who met him frequently during his time in
California, remembers him as 'one of those tall, handsome
men, with a title like Baron so-and-so. (He) drove a super
expensive Mercedes Benz sports car and played polo. The
social upper crust of San Francisco went wild for him,
paraded him at their posh parties and were not fazed by the
fact that he flew the swastika banner over his residence.'[9]

At the end of June 1941, when the German consulates in
the USA were closed down, Wiedemann transferred to the
Chinese coastal city of Tientsin. In 1945, he asked the Swiss
consul to send a message to Lord Halifax, former British
Foreign Secretary and now British ambassador to the United
States. A week later, he was being interrogated by the Office

of Strategic Services (OSS) in Washington. Accepting that 'a number of unspeakable crimes' had been committed under the Nazi regime, he co-operated entirely with his interrogators.

'He offered character analysis of the Nazi leaders and advocated the death penalty for most former leaders still alive,' says historian Thomas Weber, '...detailing the workings of Hitler's chancellery in the 1930s and explaining why any protestations by German leaders and their underlings not to have known what was going on in the concentration camps were implausible.'[10]

The proceedings involving Kempner and Wiedemann, listed on the Court's schedule as Case Number 11, soon became known as the Wilhelmstrasse Trial, since all twenty-two defendants had worked for various Nazi Ministries. Among them was Otto Meissner, once State Secretary in the Presidential Chancellery and, in the words of Otto Friedrich, 'A factotum of such chameleon talent that he served in the same capacity under both Friedrich Ebert and Adolf Hitler.'[11]

Summonsed as a character witness for Meissner, Wiedemann had made a favourable impression on the judges. As he rose to start his cross-examination, Kempner knew he must try and discredit this impressive witness by branding him as Hitler's unrepentant disciple. With this in mind, he started by asking, 'You knew Hitler from the First World War when he was your messenger?'[12]

'Yes.'

'Can you tell us what this job entails?'

'A messenger has the assignment of collecting messages dictated by Regimental and Battalion staff and delivering them to companies. I believe the English expression is 'Dispatch Rider'.'

'Hitler was a lance-corporal, is that right?'

'Yes.'

'Can you explain why you did not consider him suitable for promotion?'

Wiedemann hesitated for a moment and then replied frankly, 'Hitler was an excellent soldier. A brave man, he was reliable, quiet and modest. But we could find no reason to promote him since he lacked the necessary qualities required to be a leader.'

Robert Kempner paused, savouring what he believed would be his moment of triumph. By attacking Hitler's leadership abilities, he hoped and expected Wiedemann would feel obliged to defend his former boss. By doing so, he would reveal a commitment to the Nazi cause that he was striving to conceal from the Tribunal. 'Put simply,' he said, 'Hitler lacked the personality to ever become a leader!'

Kempner expected to provoke an indignant denial. But to his astonishment, and the amusement of the court, Wiedemann's merely nodded in agreement, *'Genau das!'* (*Exactly so!*) was his curt reply.

This was spoken with such feeling that everyone in court, including the defendants, burst out laughing.

'Professor Kempner considered he had made a good joke,' Wiedemann recalled. 'Yet what he had said was perfectly true. When I first knew him, Hitler possessed no leadership qualities at all.'[13]

The Transformation of Adolf Hitler

In the chaos following the end of the First World War, there was no shortage of would-be despots in Germany. Men only too eager to seize power. Each one of them, whether from the far left or extreme right of politics, convinced that only they possessed the answers to their defeated nation's immense social and economic problems.

Hitler, no matter how spell-binding his oratory or passionate his self-belief, could never have achieved power without the thugs of Ernst Röhm's Storm Abteilung (S.A.) or Brownshirts; the organisational brilliance of Hermann Göring; the propaganda skills of Joseph Goebbels; the miscalculations of politicians such as Franz von Papen or the greed of industrialists like Hjalmar Schacht, Gustav and Alfred Krupp and Fritz Thyssen.

Even though National Socialism was a multi-headed monster, it would never have come to power but for the supremacy of one man's will.

'Will-power, latent and then deliberately cultivated, is what Hitler was about,' comments journalist Neal Ascherson. 'Hitler is the supreme product of the 'Age of Will' ... He cultivated his will-power as other boys cultivate their physical muscles – to the same end of acquiring forms of influence over others.'[14]

So where did his 'will' come from? What, in the words of the American historian Rudolph Binion 'wrought that change' and transformed a man who never rose above the rank of lance-corporal into one who British politician Lloyd George described as 'a born leader, a magnetic, dynamic personality with a single-minded purpose'?[15]

In this book, I will argue that it was not *his* will that transformed a purposeless drifter into one of the twentieth century's most powerful and ruthless despots, but the 'will' of two men whose names are now largely lost to history. The first was Dr Edmund Forster, an eminent and widely respected German academic and nerve specialist. The second was Erik Hanussen, a Moravian Jew who found fame and fortune in 1930's Berlin as a clairvoyant, media tycoon and Nazi supporter.

'More than any other single person, Hitler made the 20th century and largely created the world we live in today,' comments Frederick Spotts in his book *Hitler and the Power of Aesthetics*. 'He created a new world by destroying the old one. He ushered in the atomic age, decolonisation and the Cold War. Culturally as well as politically he finished Europe off as the centre of Western life. He left the world poorer by 16 million souls.'[16]

This is the story of how one man brought those cataclysmic changes about and how two other men helped him do so.

CHAPTER 2
THE HITLER OF NÜRNBERG

My Führer! ...we ...wait solely for your order and your order alone. And we, comrades, know only one thing: to follow the orders of our Führer and to prove that we have remained exactly the same – to be loyal only to our Führer – Adolf Hitler Sieg Heil! Sieg Heil![1] - Viktor Lutze, 1934

The fact that Wiedemann had dismissed Hitler's leadership abilities in Nürnberg was especially ironic. Neither Munich, where the Party was born, nor Berlin, from which the Nazis exercised their power, was as intimately linked to the National Socialists as this 11th-century city. Over a six-year period, it had not only played host to the Party's grandiose annual rallies but it was there, on September 15th, 1935, that the Nazis promulgated their infamous *Law for the Protection of German Blood and German Honour*. By expelling Jews from mainstream German society, this notorious law paved the way for *Einsatzgruppen* (death squads), concentration camps, gas chambers and the Holocaust.

Nürnberg had first attracted the attention of the Nazis in 1923 when Julius Streicher, a secondary-school teacher and anti-Semitic rabble-rouser, was searching for a suitable venue for their rallies. The city's location at the junction of seven main railway lines made it easy for party members to travel there from all over Germany. Furthermore, because the old centre was relatively compact, even the fledgling Nazi Party's modest membership could make an impressive show of strength as Storm Troopers paraded along the narrow streets and massed in the ornate squares.

Practicalities aside, the 11th-century city, with its steeply pitched roofs, narrow, winding cobbled streets and ancient bridges also provided the perfect backdrop against which to act out the Nazi's pseudo-mythological and romantic 'volkish' fantasies. It was in Nürnberg that the 19th-century poet Ludwig Tieck re-discovered German art and culture, and here, too, where the cobbler-poet Hans Sachs sang in one of Hitler's favourite operas, Wagner's *Die Meistersinger*, which speaks of the violence lurking in the heart of all men.

Captivated by its history and architectural delights, Hitler and the Party set about transforming Nürnberg into a citadel of National Socialist culture. On the south-east outskirts, they constructed a complex series of buildings and open-air arenas to provide dramatic backdrops for their annual rallies. These included three gigantic parade-grounds, each capable of holding around half a million people; the Märzfeld (one of a number of arenas in which military manoeuvres were held under public gaze) and the Grosse Strasse, a mile-long, hundred-yard wide paved area along which massive formations of troops and armoured vehicles could parade. They were, in the words of author Alan Wykes, 'gigantic melodramas glorifying the implacable monster of Nazism.' Ones in which 'no cheap theatricality was omitted nor expense...In a blaze of searchlights, framed by towering banners, fireworks and mock battle, thunderous martial music and mesmeric chanting drown rationality – but not the Führer's screeching, hate filled tirade.'[2]

In preparation for their rallies, which took place between 1923 and 1938, the Nazis erected a vast, tented city on the outskirts capable of accommodating two hundred thousand visitors from all over Germany. All aspects were meticulously planned with rules and procedures in place for everything from dealing with thunderbolts to unblocking latrines.

From 1929 onwards, every rally included the same key elements, each designed by the Nazis to mesmerise those present. A 'Cathedral of Light,' was created by using 130 anti-aircraft searchlights placed 12 metres apart and pointed skywards to surround spectators with vertical columns of white light. There were thundering Wagnerian overtures, stirring martial songs, multitudes of banners, streamers, flags and standards. There were hundreds of thousands of goose-step marchers in highly disciplined formations, torchlight processions, massive bonfires, and magnificent firework displays. Every major public building, and a majority of private homes, were festooned with huge flags, swastika banners and other Nazi insignia.

Against the backdrop of the Nürnberg stadium, its podium dominated by a gigantic swastika-bearing eagle, spectacles involving hundreds of thousands of the Nazi faithful reached their climax with the solemn 'consecration of the colours'. To a rendering of the Nazi hymn, the Horst Wessel marching song, new S.A. and S.S. banners and standards were carried forward to be reverently touched against the *Blutfahne* (Blood Banner), the tattered flag the

Nazis claimed had been soaked with the blood of those slain in Hitler's abortive Munich Putsch of 1923.

The stage-managed rallies were meticulously designed to create a mood of hysterical adoration among Hitler's followers. As the American journalist William Shirer noted in his *Berlin Diary*, 'Like a Roman emperor Hitler rode into this medieval town…past solid phalanxes of wildly cheering Nazis who packed the narrow streets…Tens of thousands of Swastika flags blot out the Gothic beauties of the place, the facades of the old house, the gabled roofs. The streets, hardly wider than alleys, are a sea of brown and black uniforms…a mob of ten thousand hysterics who jammed the moat in front of Hitler's hotel shouting: 'We want our Führer' …They looked up at him as if he were a Messiah, their faces transformed into something positively inhuman.'[3]

At the heart of the spectacle was Adolf Hitler, the divinely inspired leader and mesmerising orator with his intense blue eyes and brisk, aggressive gestures, working his magic on the masses and, through the use of repetitive rhythms of speech, generating in them an almost hypnotic state so they came away with 'shining faces and dreamy eyes.'

'No one in history has understood the basic principles of mass persuasion better than Hitler, and no organisation expended more labour and material in perfecting and using its techniques than did the Nazi Party during its turbulent and vicious life,' comments author Barrie Pitt. 'Every art, every subterfuge and contrivance was employed to hammer into the spectators and participants the message that Nazism was the only religion and Hitler its God.'[4]

'Nazi devotion took many forms,' observed Ernst von Weizäcker. 'Some tried to touch Hitler, as though he were endowed with thaumaturgic powers. Others built little domestic shrines to him. Widows sent him small gifts. A tubercular party member gazed at the Führer's portrait for hours 'to gain strength,'[5] schoolgirls painted swastikas on their fingernails, and a group of blonde maidens vowed to 'Heil Hitler' at the point of orgasm. 'There was only one thing for me,' explained one devout male believer, 'either to win with Adolf Hitler or to die for him.'[6]

Nowhere is the portrayal of Hitler as Germany's Messiah more vividly apparent than in the documentary of the 1934 Nazi Rally *Triumph of the Will*. While not director Leni Riefenstahl's first choice of title,[7] it perfectly describes Hitler's conviction that only through an unwavering faith in the ultimate and predestined triumph of his own will would Germany regain its former power and glory. Her film opens with a lyrical aerial sequence of cumulous clouds. These slowly disperse to reveal an aircraft flying over thousands of brown-shirted storm troopers marching in a seemingly endless procession. To a symphonic rendition of the Nazi anthem, the 'Horst Wessel March', the shadow of the aircraft appears as a black cross moving over the swarming masses. Riefenstahl is symbolically representing Hitler as descending from the heavens and bringing not merely military and political glory but a new religious order.

'The Führer was able to transmit this faith not only to his immediate followers most of whom, like Goebbels, allowed themselves to be mesmerised by him,' notes author Piers Brendon. 'He could also project his charismatic presence onto a wider screen. At such an apocalyptic moment, the power of his personality cult was overwhelming.'[8]

Hitler's power over his supporters was such that even with Berlin in flames around him, propaganda minister Joseph Goebbels could still proclaim, 'The times through which we are passing demand of a Leader more than vision and energy. They need a kind of toughness and endurance, of courage of heart and soul such as seldom appear in history, but when they do lead to wonderful achievements of the human spirit. To whom but our Führer could these words apply...Who but the Führer can show the way? If history tells of this country that its people never abandoned their leader and that their leader never abandoned his people that will be victory.'[9]

The Destruction of Nürnberg

It was because the medieval city so potently symbolised all that was most bestial and malign about Nazism that the Allies earmarked it, early in the war, for complete destruction. As a Bomber Command Intelligence report in 1943 makes clear, the medieval city was condemned to obliteration mainly because it represented 'a political target of the first importance and one of the Holy Cities of the Nazi creed.'[10]

The rallies of the twenties and thirties, just as much as the devastation and destitution which confronted the German people in the forties, bore witness to the hypnotic power of Adolf Hitler and his ability to manipulate the minds of millions. All that followed from his ascendancy to power in 1933 can be traced to the overriding will of that one man. Without his will to achieve political supremacy for himself and National Socialism, Hitler could neither have gained nor sustained his hold on power.

That Hitler genuinely believed himself guided and guarded by some divine power is apparent from his frequent references to providence and predestination. As early in February 1930, at a time when the Party's future remained uncertain, he confidently and presciently predicted 'the victory of our movement will take place...at the most in two and a half to three years.'[11]

On another occasion, he confided to an associate, 'The impossible will become possible, miracles will happen.'[12] Emerging unscathed from a serious car accident during the twenties, for example, he reassured his aides by saying they had no need to be concerned about his physical safety since it was impossible for anything to happen to him until his mission had been completed.

Once in power, his conviction that his every action was predetermined and therefore infallible only grew stronger. Nazi Foreign Minister Joachim von Ribbentrop once remarked on 'the absolute certainty' with which Hitler took major decisions on the basis that because his judgement was infallible a favourable outcome must be inevitable. [13]

Exactly when and where Hitler became possessed by this unshakeable belief in his divinely ordained mission is not in doubt. He often recounted how in 1918, while being treated for gas-induced blindness in a military hospital at Pasewalk, his historic mission as the 'people's deliverer' had been revealed to him supernaturally by means of 'ecstatic visions of victorious Germany'.

Although the notion of Hitler's 'ecstatic vision' was largely a Nazi myth – like so much else about his carefully reimagined life story – an event of great significance in his life did occur at Pasewalk.

It was here Hitler was hypnotised by neurologist Dr Edmund Robert Forster in an attempt to cure his psychosomatic blindness. While Forster's unconventional treatment succeeded, it also convinced him of his 'divinely inspired' mission to 'liberate the German people and make Germany great again'.

CHAPTER 3
A WOLF IS BORN

No change in childhood's early day,
No storm that raged, no thought that ran,
But leaves a track upon the clay,
Which slowly hardens into man. - Georges Romanes[1]

Adolf Hitler was born at 6.30pm on Easter Saturday, April 20th, 1889. It was in bedroom number 3 at the Gasthof-zum-Pommer in the little Austrian border town of Braunau-am-Inn. His father, Alois, was a burly, 51-year-old customs officer; his slightly-built mother, Klara, a 29-year-old farmer's daughter.

It was a gloomy and humid evening with low clouds, which, combined with the proximity to the River Inn, made the small bedroom dark and dank. By the time midwife Franziska Pointecker delivered Klara's baby son, the exhausted mother was soaked with perspiration.[2] But it was fear as much as the humid atmosphere and exertion of childbirth that caused Klara to perspire so freely during the long hours of delivery. In four years of marriage she had already lost three children, two sons and a daughter, under the age of two. Now Klara and Alois, who desperately wanted a family, had pinned all their hopes on this, their fourth child. Holding the squealing infant in her arms, she vowed that no matter what sacrifices entailed, this baby boy would grow to manhood.

At 3.15pm on April 22nd, Easter Monday, the infant was baptised by the parish priest, Father Ignaz Probst. He was christened Adolphus, meaning 'noble wolf', a name he came to consider symbolic of his personality. Early in his political career he adopted the pseudonym 'Herr Wolf'; he named his war headquarters in Eastern France *Wolfsschluchut* (Wolf's lair), that in East Prussia *Wolfschanze* (Fort Wolf) and his temporary base inside Russia *Werewolf. Werewolf* was also the name chosen for the group of resistance fighters trained to operate behind Allied lines after the invasion of Germany between 1944 and 1945. His favourite dogs were that most wolf-like of breeds, the German shepherd and his favourite, Blondi, shared his last hours with him in the *Führerbunker* deep beneath the Chancellery. Albert Speer observed, 'The German shepherd probably played the most important role in Hitler's life: it was more important than even his closest associates.'[3]

As he splashed Holy Water onto the baby and admitted him to the Catholic faith, Father Ignaz could hardly have regarded the youthful Klara and her middle-aged husband Alois as two of the Church's most devout followers. The brawny customs official, who described himself as a 'free-thinker', was frequently involved in heated attacks on clerics and religion. Apart from getting married or attending burials and baptisms, the only time he attended church was on the birthday of Emperor Franz Joseph of Austria-Hungary.

Even less commendable, from the priest's point of view, must have been Alois' private life which, characterised by promiscuity and adultery, had long been a local scandal. In the late 19th century, Braunau-am-Inn retained the character more of a village than a town and, as in every small community, the private affairs of its citizens were very much a matter of public discussion.[4] Not that the gossip was without foundation. By the time Adolphus was born, his twice-married father had not only taken a bride twenty-three years his junior, but a woman closely related to him by birth. It was also rumoured, probably with justification, that he also kept a mistress in Vienna.

Although the townsfolk were always polite and respectful, a respect Alois pompously demanded in view of his official Government position, relationships with his neighbours were formal rather than friendly. When, a few years after Adolf's birth, he was promoted to the rank of Customs Officer Grade 1 and transferred to Passau, a paper manufacturing town with a population of around 16,000, neither he nor Klara can have regretted the change.

Not only did Alois regard his promotion as a well-deserved reward for his more than thirty years of loyal service to the Austro-Hungarian State but a fitting conclusion to the life of a poor village boy who, through his own efforts, had made something of himself.

The Boyhood of Hitler's Father

Alois was born burdened by the stigmas of illegitimacy and poverty. In 1836, his mother, Maria Anna Schicklgruber, a 42-year-old unmarried farmer's daughter, became pregnant. Her outraged parents ordered her out of the house. It was only through the kindness of a villager in the nearby hamlet of Strones that when Alois was born, on June 7, 1837, he was delivered in a cottage bedroom rather than an open field. A weakly child who was not expected to live more than a few hours, he was baptised the same day by the Döllersheim parish priest. Somehow, he survived and in spite of the family's poverty contrived to flourish.

In 1842, Maria Anna married Johann Georg Hiedler or Hütler (the spelling of the name varies), a spendthrift journeyman miller so idle that he scarcely did a day's work in the five years between their marriage and Maria Anna's death in 1847 at the age of fifty-two. During those years she struggled to provide for both her indolent husband and child and the family gradually sank into destitution. With their furnishings sold around them, Johann Georg was forced to sleep in a cattle trough. Following the death of his wife, the erstwhile husband disappeared from the scene, not to reappear in Alois' life for another thirty years. The abandoned five-year-old would have been in desperate straits but for his uncle Johann von Nepomuk. Unlike his indolent younger brother, Johann von Nepomuk was a hardworking and prosperous farmer in the nearby village of Spital. Although he provided his nephew with board and lodging, Alois' childhood was an unhappy one with Johann making it clear he had no prospect of inheritance.

Thirty years later, Johann Georg Hiedler came back into his son's life and had Alois' birth legitimised by producing a legal document showing him as the young man's father. The local parish priest, Josef Zahnschirm, altered the records by scratching out the remark: 'Male, illegitimate' and then filling in the name 'Georg Hiedler' in the previously blank space under 'Father'. He also noted, 'It is confirmed by the undersigned that Johann Georg Hiedler, whose name is here entered as Father, being well known to the undersigned did accept paternity of the child, Alois, according to the statement of the child's mother Anna Schicklgruber.'[5]

Alois celebrated his legitimacy by subtly distancing himself from both Johann von Nepomuk Hütler and Georg Hiedler, by combining both their surnames into a third variation on the spelling. Henceforth, he and his family would be known as Hitler.

Early in Hitler's political life, researchers and journalists – friends and foes alike – set about trying to establish the truth of his father's paternity; there was a rumour circulating that Hitler's grandfather was not Johann Georg Hiedler but a wealthy Jew. Some hinted he might even be a member of the Rothschild family who lived in Vienna. A more likely candidate, however, was a Jew from the town of Graz named Frankenberger for whom Anna Maria worked as a cook. In the early twenties, this rumour was used by Hitler's opponents at home and abroad, both those outside and within the Nazi Party ranks in an effort to damage his career.

In October 1933, the London Daily Mirror published a photograph which purported to show the tombstone of Hitler's paternal grandfather in the Jewish cemetery in Bucharest. A copy was forwarded to S.S. chief Heinrich Himmler and found its way into the rapidly growing file which he was keeping on his Führer. This document dated August 4th, 1942 survives in the Federal Archives and carries the handwritten instruction 'Please send here, Reichsführer wishes to retain.'

Even Hitler appears to have had doubts about his grandfather and, in late 1930, asked his lawyer Hans Frank to investigate matters. Shortly before he was hanged for war crimes in Poland, Frank wrote, '(Hitler) showed me a letter which he described as a 'disgusting piece of blackmail' on the part of one of his most loathsome relatives (his nephew William Patrick Hitler) and said that it concerned his, Hitler's, antecedents.'[6]

In the letter, William Patrick Hitler threatened to tell the newspapers that his Uncle was part Jewish. In the event, he did write an article on the subject for *Paris Soir* and went on a pre-war lecture tour of the United States.

At Hitler's request, Frank made some investigations and claims to have discovered that the Frankenbergers' paid Maria Anna an allowance to raise her son and that there were letters showing a relationship between the family's nineteen-year-old son and their cook.

'Hence the possibility cannot be dismissed that Hitler's father was half Jewish as a result of the extra-marital relationship between the Schicklgruber woman and the Jew from Graz. This would mean that Hitler was one-quarter Jewish.'[7]

But if the 'Jew from Graz' was not Alois' father, who was? One candidate is the work-shy jobbing miller Johann Georg. While this is certainly possible, it seems more likely to have been his brother, the apparently benevolent Johann Nepomuk, who had raised Alois from the age of five. The significance of Alois legitimisation's lies in the change of surname this brought about. From January 6th, 1877, when the new name was registered at the government office in Mistelbach, Alois Schicklgruber was able to officially call himself *Hitler*. As Adolf Hitler's personal photographer, Heinrich Hoffmann, dubbed 'the court jester of the Third Reich' by the Führer's inner circle, once commented while the masses would enthusiastically bellow 'Heil Hitler!' they might have been less inclined to yell 'Heil Schicklgruber!'

At the age of thirteen, Alois left home to 'better himself'

and – like his son almost half a century later – travelled to Vienna to seek employment. There he became apprenticed to a bootmaker and worked in this trade for five years while studying at night classes to make up for his lack of education. He was successful and, at the age of eighteen, entered government service as a clerk with the Inland Revenue. Within nine years, the hardworking and ambitious young man had achieved the position of Probationary Assistant in the Customs Service. In 1873, having already had one affair which led to the birth of an illegitimate son, Alois wed Anna Glassl-Hörer the widowed daughter of an inspector in the Imperial tobacco monopoly, fourteen years his senior. The marriage brought him considerable financial benefits; his bride came with a generous dowry from her father and for the first time Alois was able to enjoy a life of some comfort and employ a housemaid. Two years later, he was promoted to assistant inspector and transferred to Braunau-am-Inn.

The following year, obviously feeling he had 'bettered himself' sufficiently to return home, Alois travelled to Spital and stayed with his 'foster father' Johann von Nepomuk. In the neighbouring cottage lived Johann Nepomuk's daughter, her husband and their three daughters. The eldest, Klara Pölzl, was a slim, dark-haired girl of sixteen who immediately caught Alois' roving eye. He persuaded her to return with him to Braunau as his new maid and share their rooms at the Gasthaus Streif. These lodgings were located conveniently close to his customs post at the Austrian end of the great iron bridge spanning the River Inn.

Working in the Gasthaus Streif's kitchens was a 21-year-old cook named Franziska 'Fanny' Matzelsberger, and within a few weeks of their return from Spital she had become Alois' mistress.

When she learnt of his affair, Anna immediately walked out and asked for a judicial separation which was granted in 1880. No sooner had she left him had Alois invited Fanny Matzelsberger to take her place. She agreed on the condition that the attractive young maid, Klara Pölzl, was sent back home.

On January 13th, 1882, Fanny Matzelsberger gave birth to a son named Alois after his father. When some fifteen months later, on the April 6th, 1883, Anna Glassl-Hörer died of tuberculosis, Alois wasted no time in marrying Fanny. Two months after the wedding Fanny gave birth to her second child, a daughter, christened Angela. But by now Alois was already sleeping with several other local women and having bitter rows with Fanny over her refusal to allow Klara Pölzl to take up residence with them again. Not long after their wedding, Fanny was diagnosed as suffering from tuberculosis and sent to a sanatorium, giving Alois the opportunity to invite Klara to return to Braunau. She gave up a job in Vienna to look after him and the children from his marriage to Fanny – two-year-old Alois Jnr and ten-month-old Angela.

In August 1884, only a few months after her twenty-third birthday, Fanny Matzelsberger, like Anna Glassl-Hörer, died from tuberculosis, and was buried in the small country church at Ranshofen, the same parish in which she had been married only a year before.

Alois wanted to marry Klara, who was by now pregnant, straight away but there was a problem. According to his revised birth certificate, his father was the brother of Klara's grandfather. The closeness of this blood tie meant that the relationship between Alois and Klara was prohibited under the consanguinity laws of the Catholic Church. If, as seems likely, Johann Nepomuk and not Johann Hiedler was Alois' true father, the blood tie was even closer. Had they suspected this it seems improbable the Church would have allowed them to get married. In practical terms, this would have made little difference since the couple was already living together and Klara was four months pregnant.

Alois petitioned for a Papal dispensation. Father Kostler, the priest who was asked to deal with Alois' request, was initially reluctant to agree; he lectured Alois on the dangers posed to their children by so incestuous a relationship. But when Alois bluntly informed him that not only was Klara pregnant but they intended to have several more children whether or not the Church granted them a dispensation, Kostler sent their request to the Bishop of Linz who in turn forwarded it to the Vatican. Within three weeks the dispensation had been granted and on January 7th, 1885, Alois married his young and heavily pregnant bride. Alois, who was on duty at the customs post, insisted that the ceremony be held at the unusual hour of 6am and returned to work immediately afterwards.

Five months after the wedding, Klara gave birth to her first son they christened Gustav. In September 1886 she had a daughter, Ida, and sometime during 1887 another son Otto. All three died from diphtheria, Otto when only a few months old, Gustav and Ida before their third birthdays.

The Boyhood of Adolf Hitler

A bright and energetic child, Adolf's relationship with his father was turbulent and often violent. The same qualities of self-reliance and ambition which had enabled a poor and illegitimate boy to rise above his humble origins also made him an obstinate and cantankerous parent.

'At home,' notes the historian B.F. Smith, 'he was more than a formidable character. He was master, and he impressed this fact upon every member of the household. He alone had raised the whole lot of them and he demanded the obedience and respect that he felt they owed him...The old man's dominance made him a permanent object of respect, if not awe, to his wife and children. Even after his death his pipes still stood in a rack on the kitchen shelf, and when his widow wished to make a particularly important point she would gesture toward the pipes as if to invoke the authority of the master.'[8]

Whenever Alois was away from home on a posting to Linz, meek and submissive Klara strove to maintain discipline by warning Adolf and his older step-brother Alois Jnr of the severe punishment that awaited them on their father's return if they behaved badly. It was no idle threat. At the age of sixteen, he wrote, 'Then comes, poor man, his wife and heals his bottom with thrashings.'[9]

In 1942, discussing the fate of a prisoner he had handed over to the Gestapo for 'interrogation', he remarked, 'Had I, myself, received in one fell swoop all the thrashings I deserved (and had had) in my life I should be dead!'[10]

In March 1894, while Alois was still away from home, Klara gave birth to her third son, Edmund. A year later, Alois returned and the family was reunited in a new home at Lambach-am-Traun. On May 1st that year, Adolf began attending a primary school attached to Lambach's ancient monastery and run by the local Benedictine monks. Overawed by the splendour of the Catholic mass and captivated by the beauty of church music, he took singing lessons and joined the choir. For some years he was attracted to the church as a career, convinced that the priestly vocation was the 'highest and most desirable ideal'.

In 1900, Adolf transferred to the *Realschule* in Linz to which he took an immediate dislike. From being a lively and high-achieving primary school pupil, the eleven-year-old changed into an apathetic and lazy student. His first end of term report describes his moral conduct as no more than 'adequate' and application to his studies as 'erratic'. Alois, perhaps recalling the difficulties created by his own lack of education, demanded his son work harder at school, an exhortation he typically hammered home with a thrashing.

On June 25, 1895, with forty years' service behind him, Alois retired from the Customs Service vowing to spend the remainder of his life running a small holding and keeping bees. In December 1902, he developed a chest cold and spent several days in bed but at the start of the New Year he appeared to have recovered and on Saturday January 3rd went to see a neighbouring farmer about buying some apples. It was a bitterly cold morning and, on the way home, he started feeling unwell so called at the Gasthaus Steifler for a glass of wine. Before the landlord could pour it, Alois collapsed and was carried into a back room and laid on a table. The pot boy was sent to fetch a doctor but moments later the old man haemorrhaged and choked to death on his own blood. He was buried two days later in the cemetery opposite his house. The local newspaper, *Linz Tagepost*, published a lengthy obituary that began, 'We have buried a good man – that we can rightly say about Alois Hitler, Higher Official of the Imperial Customs, retired, who was carried to his final resting place today.' The writer went on to observe, 'The harsh words that sometimes fell from his lips could not belie the warm heart that beat underneath the rough exterior.'

Hitler wept as the coffin was lowered into the grave but he can hardly have been devastated by the old man's death since not only did it free him from the endless arguments and frequent beatings but also meant he only needed to share the affections and attention of Klara with his young and slightly backward sister Paula.

In September 1904, he started the fourth form in the Senior Secondary School at Steyr, an industrial town some twenty-five miles from Linz. He shared lodgings with another boy of the same age and, according to this lad's recollections, spent much of his spare time shooting at rats as they scampered across the gloomy courtyard below their window. At Steyr, while he remained rebellious and surly, his school work showed some signs of improvement. A pencil sketch made by one of his classmates depicts Adolf as a slim fifteen-year-old with a high, receding forehead, prominent nose and jutting chin; appearing to be prematurely old and far from well.

With money from the sale of the cottage and Alois' pension, the family was comfortably off and Klara was able to buy her son all the elegant clothes he demanded. The teenager took pride in his appearance and liked to stroll through the town swinging a small black cane. Not that he dressed smartly to attract others; while other men of his age might have sought out male companionship or started relationships with girls, Hitler seemed to have made no attempts to strike up a friendship with other boys. He saw himself as being above such mundane desires. Apart from dressing up and parading around the neighbourhood, his major passion, and one in which Klara was able to indulge him generously, was attending opera. It was while at such a performance, in November 1904, that he met a young man around his own age who was to become his closest, and only, friend.

Hitler Meets Kubizek
August 'Gustl' Kubizek, a rather naive youth nine months

Hitler's senior, worked as an apprentice in his father's upholstery workshop in Linz. Although his days were spent surrounded by dusty sofas and tattered armchairs doing a job he loathed, Kubizek was no ordinary tradesman. He played the violin and piano, lived only for music and had ambitions to study at the Vienna Conservatoire and become a conductor. All his spare cash and every free moment were spent playing music or at the Linz opera house where he could afford only the cheapest tickets which permitted the holder to stand in one of the gangways. The most sought-after position was beside one of the two ornate pillars holding up the Royal Box since these provided a convenient support for one's back and a clear view of the stage. By missing his supper and racing to the opera house from work, Kubizek usually managed to gain one of these prime standing locations.

One night, he arrived to find another young man occupying his favourite spot in the auditorium. Later he recalled that moment, 'Half annoyed, half surprised I glanced at my rival. He was a remarkably pale, skinny youth about my own age, who was following the performance with glistening eyes.... we took note of each other without exchanging a word. But in the interval of a performance some time later we started talking as, apparently, neither of us approved of the casting of one of the parts. We discussed it together and rejoiced in our common adverse criticism.'[11]

According to Kubizek, their friendship developed through a shared love of music. Just how close that friendship was remains open to question. Although Kubizek gives the impression of being deeply fond of his often-moody companion, Hitler's feelings are a good deal less certain. For him, the main attraction of their relationship seems to have been his companion provided a receptive audience.

'Our characters were utterly different,' Kubizek recalls, 'I was a quiet, somewhat dreamy youth, very sensitive and adaptable and therefore always willing to yield. Adolf was exceedingly violent and highly strung.'[12]

He was also extremely possessive and jealously guarded the intimacy of their relationship. On one occasion when he attended the funeral of his violin teacher, Heinrich Dessauer, Hitler insisted on tagging along despite never having met Dessauer and knowing no one at the service. 'I can't bear it that you should mix with other young people and talk to them,' he explained. [13]

When not going to the opera or concerts, they spent hours walking together in the countryside while Hitler talked endlessly about his ambitions, philosophy and plans for their future together. His friend would listen patiently and attentively to the diatribe without making any attempt to contradict or disagree. This unconditional acceptance of his views and unquestioning obedience to his commands were what Hitler expected and it appears Kubizek had no objection to a passive role in their relationship, since 'it made me realise just how much my friend needed me.'[14]

On occasions, the vehemence of his friend's oratory surprised and startled him, 'These speeches, usually delivered somewhere out in the open, seemed to be like a volcano erupting. It was as though something quite apart from him was bursting out from him... again and again I was filled with astonishment at how fluently he expressed himself, how vividly he managed to convey his feelings, how easily the words flowed from his mouth when he was completely carried away by his own emotions... This to me was something new, magnificent... I had never imagined that a man could produce such an effect with mere words.'[15]

As Rudolph Binion comments, 'This unctuous book was originally intended for the Nazi archive, and it shows. It mostly can't be confirmed, and his (Kubizek's) Linz townsman Franz Jetzinger in his book *Hitler's Youth*, demolished lots of the yarns.'[16]

Hitler's Failure and Klara's Fate

Klara had agreed to her son sitting the entrance examination at the Academy of Fine Arts and, in May 1906, he paid his first brief visit to Vienna. He sent Kubizek a scenic card depicting the Karlsplatz, writing that he had arrived safely, was going to the opera but felt homesick already, 'Although I find everything very beautiful I am longing for Linz.'

On October 1st and 2nd, Hitler sat the test on which all his dreams depended. Although the examination had the reputation of being a formidable trial for any young artist, he was confident of his success. On the first day, candidates had to create two paintings from a list of 48 subjects, including a number of Biblical themes; *The Expulsion from Paradises* and the *Return of the Prodigal Son*. Although a third of the 113 candidates failed, Hitler passed. The next hurdle was a presentation of original work to the selection board. In this, Hitler, along with 55 other hopefuls, was unsuccessful. The *Malschule* archive in the *Akademie* carries the notation 'too few heads' suggesting that his portfolio may have included too many street and architectural pictures and not enough portraits or life drawings to demonstrate sufficient overall ability. Bitterly disappointed, Hitler asked for and was granted an interview with Sigmund L'Allemand Rector of the Academy. He advised the young man to abandon any idea of becoming an academic painter and concentrate on architecture instead. Hitler took up this suggestion and applied to the Architectural School for a place, later explaining that this rejection was due to a lack of a Gymnasium diploma.

In January 1907, Klara, whose health had been poor for months, visited Dr Eduard Bloch. The Jewish doctor had trained in Prague and served in the Austro-Hungarian Army Medical Corps before starting his practice in Linz. Bloch was probably neither more nor less competent than any other provincial doctor of that period and he had a reputation as a 'friend of the poor' since he kept their bills as low as possible and even treated them for nothing in cases of real need. During his examination, the doctor found a cancerous tumour in Klara's left breast and a further malignant growth in the lining of her lungs. He advised an immediate operation and, four days later, she was admitted to the hospital of the Sisters of Mercy on the Herrenstrasse where surgeon Karl Urban removed her breast during an hour-long operation. On leaving the hospital, early in February, Klara was weak and found the stairs to their third-floor apartment more than she could manage, so that summer the family moved into three small rooms on the ground floor at 9 Blütengasse in the suburb of Urfahr.

As his mother's health deteriorated, Hitler begged Bloch to ease her suffering and prolong her life. On October 22nd, he began using an old form of treatment long since abandoned by most doctors. Almost daily, he bound strips of gauze impregnated with the powerful antiseptic Iodoform around Klara's raw and wasted body. Later, as Klara's agony increased, Bloch administered morphine by injection. But within days, whatever pain she was in from her ulcerating wounds must have been overwhelmed by the agony of iodoform poisoning. She developed a raging thirst, but could not drink without retching because the iodoform in her mouth made everything she ate or drank taste poisoned. On reaching her brain, the drug produced increasing giddiness, hallucinations and insomnia. Research carried out in the twenties indicated that death from repeated treatment usually occurred within twenty days of the treatment starting.

Perhaps because of her desperate will to live and protect her son, Klara managed to endure the pain for over a month, 'She was more concerned about what would happen to her family than she was about her approaching death,' recalled Dr Bloch. 'She made no secret of these worries or about the fact that most first thoughts were for her son.'[17]

Meanwhile, Hitler had become her devoted nurse. The boy who had been too idle to get up in the morning now worked tirelessly to bring his mother whatever comfort he was able. He moved her bed into the kitchen, which was warmer, and slept on a couch to be at her side during the night. He did all the cleaning and cooking. Each morning he would discuss the day's meals with his mother, asking what she would like and trying to encourage her appetite.

At 2 o'clock on the morning of December 21st at the age of forty-seven, Klara died. Her last thoughts were for her son and her last words to Kubizek, who visited her on December 19th concerned his future.[18]

When Klara was buried beside her husband in the little cemetery at Leonding, Hitler broke down, remaining beside the grave long after the other mourners had left, as if unable to part from his mother even in death. Adolf spent a dismal Christmas with his sister before returning to Vienna in 1908 to seek his fortune in the big city. Klara's medical bills and funeral arrangements had eaten into his inheritance. Based on Bloch's records, Rudolph Binion[16] has calculated the cost of her medical treatment at 359 crowns, only slightly less than the 'hard polished wooden coffin with metal corners'

Hitler had ordered for her burial. Despite these expenses, Hitler could afford to live in modest comfort despite making no attempt to find work or earn some money. He rented a room at 29 Stumpergasse and in February 1908 wrote to Gustl, his preferred name for Kubizek, suggesting they share it.

Living with Adolf

August persuaded his parents to let him give up the upholsterer's trade to study music at the Conservatoire and at 6am on February 23rd, 1908, he arrived at Vienna station to be met by his elegantly-dressed friend. Hitler's shoes were highly polished, his suit carefully pressed and he carried an ivory handled stick beneath one arm. He greeted Gustl warmly and helped carry his baggage to their apartment which, although located only a few blocks from the architectural glories of the Imperial Palace and the Ringstrasse, might just as well have been located on a different planet.

Stumpergasse was a narrow alley flanked by grey tenement blocks and small shops selling shoddy goods to the district's predominantly working-class population. With increasing concern, Kubizek followed his friend through an arched entrance into a dank courtyard, up twisting stairs lit by a flickering gas mantle and down a gloomy second-floor corridor flanked by a dozen brown painted doors. Hitler stopped in front of number 17, unlocked it and ushered his friend into a dingy kitchen. Dismayed by the size and dirtiness of the dimly-lit, three-room apartment, Kubizek received a further shock when Hitler cheerily informed his friend they would be sharing with their elderly Polish landlady, Maria Zakreys. They would have a single room furnished with two narrow iron beds, old chairs and a shabby table. A guttering kerosene oil lamp filled the room with smoky light and stench.

When he protested that, as a music student, he must have sufficient space for the grand piano he proposed to rent, Hitler agreed they would move if they could find somewhere more suitable. With limited resources, their search turned into a depressing round of grubby tenements in unprepossessing streets. The problem was finally solved when they persuaded Frau Zakreys to exchange rooms with them in exchange for increased rent. The piano was hired and installed, leaving just sufficient space for Hitler to pace up and down in the manner he claimed was essential for thinking.

Despite the widely-held belief that Hitler lived in abject poverty during his years in Vienna, a myth he assiduously promoted for political reasons, the death of his mother did not immediately plunge him into destitution. Research suggests that, in 1908, his monthly income from legacies was around 83 crowns, comprising the 58 crowns he had, since the age of eighteen, received from his father's estate and 25 crowns orphan's pension, plus small and irregular amounts gained through the sales of his pictures and drawings. As their lodgings cost only 10 crowns a month, of which Kubizek paid half, Hitler's was able to purchase tickets for the operas and concerts they attended nightly as well as private art tuition and materials.[19]

Within a few weeks, their lives settled into a familiar pattern. Kubizek would rise early to attend the Conservatoire while his friend stayed in bed until late in the day and then spent fine afternoons wandering the streets of Vienna and marvelling at the buildings. After training at the Academy of Fine Art, his ambition was to become an architect. In order to pass the examination, at his second attempt, he took private lessons from Viennese sculptor and art teacher, Rudolf Panholzer.

For many months, the two young men got along well enough with Hitler even sketching out the design for a house they would one day share, planning their lives together in meticulous detail. Each would have a separate room and work area, Kubizek for his music practice, he for his drawing and painting. They would be looked after by a housekeeper and dress exactly alike. Every summer, Hitler informed his friend, they would travel around Germany studying architecture and listening to opera. This plan depended on his winning the lottery which he was certain would happen imminently. When he failed to do so, Hitler became furiously angry, screaming that it was a fraud against honest men.

Anger at the unfairness of life was to become an ever-present feature of his existence which he regarded, in the words of his early German biographer Konrad Heiden, as a 'desperate struggle against the city, the Fatherland, (and) the world which has not recognised the artist-prince in him.'[20]

In spite of Gustl's easy-going nature, their life together became increasingly fraught. Hitler would fly into sudden tempers and for days on end Kubizek could do nothing right. The situation finally grew so bad that August began to worry that his mother's death had unbalanced him mentally. He filled his time with extravagant and never completed projects, scribbling down ideas, writing endless poems and composing music.

In October, Hitler reapplied to the Academy. This time he had chosen his portfolio of pictures with more care and included much of the work painted under Panholzer's tuition. It was almost certainly good enough to win him a place, but on this occasion, Hitler did not even get through to the selection board, being failed after the first day's painting examination. Did this rejection indicate, as many have claimed, that Hitler was without talent? The view of many modern art critics is that, while limited in his abilities, he was by no means as bad as has been claimed. His pictures of buildings are generally considered good – his lifelong passion was for architecture – but his rendering of people far less accomplished. When figures were included in paintings of buildings he usually failed to get the proportions correct and this was one of the reasons for his second and final rejection.[21]

In June 1908, Kubizek was called up for six months compulsory military service. On his return to Vienna in November, he found Adolf had disappeared from their lodgings without leaving any forwarding address. Landlady Maria Zakreys could only tell him that Hitler had packed his bags, paid the rent due and walked out. Kubizek was not to see his friend again until thirty years later when, in 1938, he rode through Vienna 'like a triumphant Caesar'.[22]

Their failure to meet is surprising given that Hitler had only moved a few blocks away to a slightly larger room in the Felberstrasse near the Western station. The most likely explanation for his sudden move and reluctance to meet his former friend is Hitler's failure to gain a place in the Academy. Typically, he dealt with the problem by avoiding it, preferring to walk away from their friendship rather than suffer the embarrassment of admitting his rejection.

This rejection and the abandonment of his only friend in the world was just the start of his troubles. Over the next months he would be transformed from a modestly wealthy young man into a homeless vagrant living rough on the pitiless streets of Vienna.

Descent into Destitution

With his inheritance spent, Hitler was reduced to existing on his orphan's allowance of 25 Crowns and compelled to move to ever-dingier lodgings until he became what was known as a *Bettgeber*, the name given to a slightly superior vagrant who had the price of a bed or couch in some cramped and dirty lodging. In the spring of 1909, a relative of Frau Zakreys saw him queuing outside a convent soup kitchen and thought how pathetic it was that a young man who had always been so particular about his appearance should now look so dirty and ragged.

When the weather turned cold, Hitler was forced on at least a few occasions to seek shelter in one of the city's six notorious doss houses. Discipline was strict in these dark and filthy places with talking or smoking strictly forbidden; anyone coughing or snoring was instantly tossed out on the street to make room for one of the other derelicts curled up on the pavement outside. No matter how cold or wet the day, all the men would be turned out first thing in the morning and not allowed back in before 7pm.

Inmates were given a bowl of thin soup and a slice of hard bread before attempting to get some sleep while sitting bolt upright, huddled together on hard wooden benches with only women and children permitted to lie down on the floor. A concession which investigative journalist Ernst Kläger, who dressed as a tramp to investigate conditions in such places, commented with heavy irony was only to be expected in 'a century devoted to child welfare.'[23]

Another establishment sandwiched fifty people into one diminutive hallway and a small room adjoining. Shreds of blankets and sheets served as cover and one needs little imagination to evoke the stench of such a hell... Filth, disease, agony of spirit and degradation of body were the most obvious by-products of these supremely ugly habitations.[24]

It was the lowest point of Hitler's life. Poverty had transformed him into an unshaven derelict, a thin and bedraggled 20-year-old habitually dressed in a long, filthy, louse-ridden coat. Years later, reflecting on his life in Vienna, Hitler was to write in *Mein Kampf* (My Struggle), 'I owe it to that period that I grew hard and I'm still capable of being hard.'[25]

Meeting Reinhold Hanisch

A chance encounter provided the first step back to respectability. One night in the dormitory, Hitler met up with a former peddler by the name of Reinhold Hanisch, also known as Walter. At his insistence, Hitler sought paid work for the first time in his life, initially by shovelling snow in the streets – the freezing cold and lack of warm clothing soon put paid to that job – and then by carrying passengers' luggage at the Western station. In January 1910, Hanisch wangled their transfer to a superior hostel, the 'Home for Men' at 27 Meldemannstrasse. Completed in 1905 under the patronage of the Emperor Franz Joseph I Jubilee Foundation for Citizen's Housing and Welfare Institutions, the well-designed building was a hostel for single working men who earned less than 1,500 crowns a year.

According to Josef Greiner, who claimed to have known Hitler well, he arrived at the Home looking like a tramp with 'neither shirt nor under draws they had simply worn out. The coat Adolf wore was an old-fashioned salon model...its sleeves were ravelling and the lining was but a fragment of its original self. Grease and dirt were ground into the fabric, harmonising with the grey trousers and the disintegrating shoes. Only the young man's cultivated voice offset the dubious impression he made with his sunken and pale cheeks, his hurried manner, and his dirty rags.'[26]

As the hostel was not intended for those who had sunk beyond social redemption, the Director, Johann Kanya, almost refused him admittance. Greiner claims he persuaded Kanya to lend him 50 Crowns against the security of a watch which he loaned to Hitler so he could purchase better clothes. His version of events has been attacked by historians who point out they could not have met at the 'Home for Men' during the period he claims since Hitler was still living at 29 Stumpergasse. However, his confusion over dates does not necessarily mean everything else was an invention.

His transfer to the 'Home for Men' marked a crucial step up the ladder to respectability. Each lodger had his own sleeping cubicle which allocated him precisely 4 metres of floor space and 12 metres of breathing space. Each was furnished with an iron bed covered with a horsehair mattress and a pillow bolster, two sheets, a double blanket and bolster cover on top and a chamber pot beneath it. Clothes were hung on a rail beside the bed. There was no other furniture.

Cleanliness was insisted upon and the home was well-equipped with a washroom and showers. Outside the washroom was a disinfectant chamber in which lice-ridden clothes could be treated. In order to shower, a guest had to pay ten hellers for a towel and a bathing apron; nakedness in the shower rooms was forbidden. The rooms were closed off during the day, but those residents who did not have a job to go to, or were on holiday, could sit in the lounge, a reading room or a writing room. Only chess, dominos and checkers were permitted and these too could be stopped if they led to noisy arguments. Spirits were forbidden on the premises and, if a man became drunk, he might be refused wine and beer as well. It was an austere, monastic-like institution much in demand during the cold winter months because it was warm, comfortable and provided cheap but nourishing food.

With great reluctance, and only under relentless pressure from Reinhold Hanisch, Hitler wrote to his half-sister Angela asking for money. By return of post came a sympathetic letter and 50 crowns, some of which Hitler used to buy materials as he had once again started painting and drawing. Most of his art was taken from photographs rather than life, not through lack of ability – the pictures and sketches he made during the First World War show he was a competent draughtsman – but because the warm reading room was a much more comfortable place to work than the streets. After appointing Hanisch as his salesman, Hitler soon began not only selling his pictures but obtaining commissions from advertising agencies. He was, however, a poor worker, so lazy and easily distracted that deadlines were frequently missed and promised pictures never delivered.

'He spent hours in the reading room of the Home for Men paying no attention to the unfinished drawing in front of him,' says Konrad Heiden, 'wildly brandishing his ruler, and roaring speeches at the astonished audience. Sometimes he made a deep impression, sometimes people simply laughed at him, and then Hanisch would have to console the weeping boy in the evening. When the shouting grew too loud, the porter rushed up and ordered quiet, threatening to throw the disturber out; then Hitler would pull down his arms and crouch over his drawing like a model child. He was always quiet and well-behaved when the other was clearly the stronger; in Vienna, he acquired a wild fear of the police which he never lost.'[27]

Their partnership ended in a quarrel and a lawsuit when Hitler went to the police and accused Hanisch of embezzlement. Hanisch countered, claiming Hitler had injured him and prejudiced his clients through laziness and megalomania. The court found against Hanisch who was sent to prison for a week.

On May 24th, 1913, after three years at the 'Home for Men', Hitler packed his case and carried it down to the station bound for Munich. As the train pulled out of the *Westbannhof* that spring morning, he had few regrets about leaving Vienna where he had experienced, he says in *Mein Kampf*, 'the saddest time of my life.'

By abruptly leaving the city, he was not just escaping an existence which had become intolerable but avoiding the most awful fate that could imagine ever befalling him – conscription into the Austro-Hungarian Army!

CHAPTER 4
THE FORSTERS OF NONNENHORN

Do not bow your heads. Do not know your place. Defy the gods.
You will be astonished how many of them turn out to have feet of
clay. - Salman Rushdie, Step Across This Line[1]

Conrad and Elise Forster, Dr Edmund Forster's
grandparents, owned and ran a lucrative wine trading
business in Nonnenhorn on Lake Constance. Their company
had been founded almost a century earlier by Johann Georg
Forster. A shrewd and energetic entrepreneur, he travelled
the country securing contracts with major wine traders in
most of the larger cities. By 1795, the business was
prospering to such an extent that Johann purchased a
vinegar factory and added it to his trade in wine and spirits.
His son Conrad left school while still a teenager to work in
the family business. When Johann died unexpectedly in
1834, the twenty-year-old was knowledgeable enough to
manage the business and run it so successfully that two

years later he felt sufficiently financially secure to marry and start raising a family.

His chosen bride, Elise Schnell, the daughter of a wealthy Lindau merchant, was two years his junior. Once married, the couple wasted no time in starting what was to become a large family, although their first two children, Johann Jakob born in 1837 and Johann Conrad who arrived a year later, both died in infancy. By the time Franz Joseph was born on April 6th, 1844, Conrad and Elsie had become wealthy and respected members of Nonnenhorn's community and were building an elegant, three-storey house that still stands today.

Despite his affluence and bourgeois respectability this tall, imposing man with his bushy black beard and penetrating gaze did not epitomise all those inward-looking and narrow-minded social attitudes that Germans derogatively labelled as *Biedermeier*.[2] Not only did the heart of a revolutionary beat beneath his sober attire but when the occasion arose he unhesitatingly risked his freedom for a just cause and, in doing so, played a significant role in the early history of the United States.

In 1848, when Conrad was thirty-four, the March Revolution[3] plunged the country into turmoil. Triggered initially by discontent among intellectuals and students at their lack of personal freedom, their revolutionary zeal swiftly spread to the working classes. While educated Germans were protesting at the authoritarian nature of the regime, workers had a more basic reason for dissent – many were starving to death. The combined effects of rapid industrialization, urbanization and increases in population had caused hundreds of thousands to live in abject poverty with even the hardest working families unable to lift themselves above subsistence level. The widespread ownership of land by the aristocracy and church meant that in rural areas, where eighty percent of the population still lived, pitifully low wages kept agricultural labourers in a state of permanent servitude and squalor.

Four years earlier, a minor uprising by destitute Silesian weavers had been savagely crushed by the army and protests about 'starvation wages' met with the retort 'then eat grass.' Crop failures in 1847 led to famine, soaring unemployment and riots. After these had been ruthlessly suppressed by the military an uneasy peace followed until March the following year when the Revolution occurred. In Prussia, King Friedrich Wilhelm IV decided, against the advice of his ministers and generals that the best way to control a revolution was to lead it. Accordingly, he agreed to almost all the protestors' demands, including a written constitution, free parliamentary elections and the abolition of press censorship. These early achievements, however, proved a false dawn.

Dogged by a lack of organisation and the conflicting aims of different leaders, who included Karl Marx,[4] the revolutionaries proved no match for a determined State. Within twelve months the idealists had been routed, its leaders were on the run and the general population was too disorganized to continue the struggle. As military authority was re-established, thousands of Germans, many of them the most highly educated, chose emigration with most of them settling in the United States. A strong supporter of the Revolution, Conrad had formed the *Märzverein* (March Association) in Nonnenhorn and, with the backing of seven other prominent local businessmen, sent two resolutions to the Bavarian King Max II pleading with him to accept a new constitution. The King's response was to dispatch six hundred soldiers to occupy Nonnenhorn and stamp out any smouldering discontent. Within a year, the garrison was firmly established with regular street patrols and random house-to-house searches for fleeing revolutionary leaders.

The Story of Carl Schurz

One of the best known and most rigorously hunted of these leaders was twenty-year-old Carl Schurz[5], a former student at Bonn University. After almost a year of living underground in Berlin, he managed to reach Nonnenhorn where Conrad concealed him in the firm's wine cellars while devising a plan to smuggle him across the lake to Switzerland. The already hazardous situation was made even more dangerous when an informant tipped off the authorities that Carl Schurz was being hidden somewhere in the town. The garrison Commander gave orders that every house was to be thoroughly searched and both the fugitive and those harbouring him arrested. Because the Commander did not receive this tip-off until late in the afternoon he decided to wait until first light the following day before starting the search. The delay gave Conrad an opportunity to pass a message to his fellow townsfolk asking them to invite the soldiers into their homes that evening and provide them with more than generous hospitality, including ample supplies of Nonnenhorn's excellent wines. He extended a similar invitation to the garrison's officers and a long night of riotous drinking ensued. Cask after cask of his choicest vintages were broached and bottle after bottle of his finest Schnapps poured down thirsty throats. By dawn, every one of the six hundred soldiers and their officers were too busy sleeping off the biggest hangover of their lives to conduct the intended search. With the entire garrison sprawled in a drunken stupor, Conrad was able to row Carl Schurz the fourteen kilometres across Lake Constance to freedom. This escapade is still remembered in Nonnenhorn and, in 1984, they commemorated their leading citizen's guile and courage with a four-act play *'Die Flucht'* (The Flight).

With the March Revolution no more than a distant memory, Conrad returned to the profitable if mundane business of trading wine and raising his children. By his early fifties, Conrad Forster had become Nonnenhorn's most prominent citizen, serving as Bürgermeister from 1869 up to his death on 23rd January 1878, as well as representing his community on the Regional Council. He was instrumental in setting up the town's fire service and helped run the Lake Constance Railway. Today, his is still fondly remembered in Nonnenhorn which has a street named in his honour.

Unlike some self-made men, Conrad was a strong believer in the German middle-class ideal of *Bildung*; the acquisition of worth through self-development and culture. Eager for his children to receive the schooling he had been denied he encouraged all his sons and daughters to study hard. It quickly became apparent that Franz Joseph was more than merely clever, he was brilliant. Realising that such ability demanded a higher level of education than could be found in Nonnenhorn, Conrad and Elise sent him more than one hundred miles away to live with relatives while he studied at the Gymnasiums of Augsburg, Munich and Leipzig. Their confidence in his precocity proved to be fully justified when, in his final exams, eighteen-year-old Franz Joseph achieved the highest marks of any student in Germany. His reputation as a scholar thus assured, he had no difficulty in gaining acceptance as a medical student at Munich University and, thanks to a generous allowance from his parents, was able to move into comfortable rented accommodation in a five-storey house at 13 Sonnenstrasse.

The Medical Career of Franz Joseph

Within four years he had qualified as a doctor of medicine, surgery and obstetrics. After qualifying, he worked for a time as an assistant to one of Germany's most eminent physiologists, Professor Karl von Voits, whose studies of metabolism laid the foundations for modern nutritional science. During over a decade of research, Voits had been able to provide an accurate measurement of the number of calories humans use when either active or resting and he laid the bases for present-day diet regimes. Voits' research so fascinated Franz Joseph that he abandoned his earlier ambition to become a physician and decided instead to make his career in the field of nutritional research.

Before he could take that step, however, the Franco-Prussian war of 1870 broke out and the 26-year-old immediately volunteered as a battalion doctor with the 12th Royal Bavarian Infantry Regiment. He saw action in the battles of Sedan, Coulmiers, Orleans, Loignay-Pomry and Beauganey and was awarded the Military Order of Merit for his courage under fire. He also gained a reputation among officers and troops both for his bravery under fire and his humanity in the treatment of patients. One example that illustrates his generosity of spirit occurred after his assistant was killed during the Battle of Sedan. Franz Joseph requested another aide, preferably somebody with knowledge of French, and the regiment sent him a doctor named Johann Faist. To their mutual astonishment, the men immediately recognised one another. Not only were they both from Nonnenhorn, but had been friends at primary school. Later, when Faist was taken seriously ill and had to be invalided home, Franz Joseph wrote asking his father to care for him and provide a bottle of good wine and a hearty meal each day until he had made a complete recovery.

On leaving the army he returned to Munich where, in 1874, he applied for and received his Habilitation,[6] an essential post-doctoral qualification for anyone wanting to lecture at a university.

He had maintained a close friendship with his older sister Anna Juliana, who was married to eminent Munich architect, August Voit. One evening, during a dinner at the couple's Munich apartment, Anna introduced Franz to her husband's 23-year-old cousin Wilhelmina 'Mina' Emilie Louise von Hösslin. It was love at first sight for both of them and they were soon seeing each other regularly, despite their courtship initially facing strong opposition from Mina's patrician parents.

While Franz Joseph was a brilliant young doctor, a decorated officer and an academic, he was also the son of a tradesman. In the rigidly hierarchical society of 19th century Germany this was as much a barrier to marriage as it would have been in class-conscious Victorian England. Another barrier was the fact that while the von Hösslins, who came originally from Holland, were staunch members of the Dutch Reform Church, the Forster's were Catholic.

Faced with such a daunting challenge some young men might have bowed to the inevitable but Franz Joseph, like his father, was not one to meekly resign himself to disappointment. Instead, he embarked on a relentless campaign to charm and reassure her parents which, after two years of tactful persistence, finally succeeded in winning their consent. The condition was that Franz Joseph should bring up his children in the Dutch Reform Church. He had no objection because his religion was not especially important to him and because like most German males of the period, he regarded the upbringing of the children entirely the responsibility of his wife.

On October 3rd, 1876, Franz and Wilhelmina married in Munich and the following year his academic career was assured when, as a still youthful lecturer of thirty-three, he was appointed Professor of Physiology at Munich's Central Veterinary School. On July 28th that same year, their first child, a daughter christened Margarethe Francisca Augusta, always known to the family as Gretchen, was born and on September 4th the following year the couple had their first son, Edmund Robert. Both children were delivered by Franz Joseph himself in the family's spacious fourth-floor apartment at 73 Lindwurm Strasse Munich; a broad, tree-lined avenue whose tranquillity was disturbed only by the occasional rattle of passing trams and steady click of hoof beats as horse-drawn carriages clattered over the cobbles.

Lindwurm Strasse, Munich in the 1890's

The following year, through the influence of his wife's family who were in contact with influential members of the Dutch government, Franz Joseph was offered the Directorship of the new and still uncompleted Hygiene

Institute in Amsterdam. By the summer of that year, the Forsters were comfortably settled into a gracious five-storey house overlooking a canal on Nicholaas Witsenkade. Already a fluent Dutch speaker, Mina helped her husband master the language and ensured her children were raised to be fluent not only in German and Dutch but also in French and English.

Within a year of moving to Amsterdam, a second daughter, Geertruida Hermine Emma, was born only to die four months later. The following year saw the birth of their second son Arne Waldemar Hermann and 1884 that of their fifth and final child Eduard Dirk Conrad Walther Forster.

Wilhelmina Forster with, (left to right) Edwards, Arne, Geertruida and Dirk in Amsterdam.

Franz Joseph's time was fully occupied in supervising the completion of the Hygiene Institute which was situated amidst trees and gardens on the banks of a canal within a short cab ride from the centre of Amsterdam. Once it was operational, he worked even harder to build an international research reputation both for the Institute and himself. In addition to achieving practical advances in the fields of human and animal health, he co-edited a learned journal, the *Archiv für Hygiene* which published papers on the hygienic aspects of nutrition especially in relation to milk and meat.

Hygiene Institute in Amsterdam

In 1883, he was elected a member of the German Academy of Science; in 1884, to the Dresden Academy of Sciences; and in 1886, to the Scientific Department of the Royal Academy of Sciences in Amsterdam. In 1893, the Dutch government awarded him the *Ritter des Ordens vom Niederländischen Löwen* for outstanding services to his adopted country. Founded in 1815, this order is not only the Netherlands' oldest civil decoration but also its most prestigious, given only to those who have given service to society of a very exceptional nature.

Three years after receiving this award, Franz Joseph left Holland for Strasbourg to become Director of the city's Hygiene and Bacteriological Institute. In 1903, he was appointed its Rector, a position he held until his death seven years later. At the end of July 1898, he and his wife travelled to Scotland where he was awarded an honorary Doctor of Laws by the University of Edinburgh; he was one of nineteen eminent medical men from many parts of Europe to be honoured by the faculty. Had he been invited to the subsequent ceremony on November 29th that year, Franz Joseph would have found himself sharing the platform with Lord Kitchener of Khartoum – the British general who was to play a prominent role in recruiting soldiers during the First World War.

By his mid-sixties, Franz Joseph Forster, admired and respected by his colleagues and adored by his wife and children, had achieved the pinnacle of his academic career.

Professor Franz Joseph Forster in his laboratory

A portrait shows him to have been portly and plump-featured, with receding grey hair and a thick, curling white moustache. While his steel-framed pince-nez glasses, formal black morning coat and high-collared shirt convey the serious demeanour expected of a Herr Doktor Professor, his dark eyes are kind and the edges of his mouth appear on the point of twitching into a smile. It is clear from all the accounts of his life that the unknown portrait photographer had perfectly captured the rare blend of warm humanity and rigorous scientific objectivity that characterised his wise and generous nature. All his children remained close to him, constantly writing letters and sending postcards home to keep their parents informed of everything that was happening to them and to ask for advice and assistance.

During the final months of his life, Franz Joseph was able

to look back not only on his own considerable scientific achievements but also on the academic success of his sons, especially that of Edmund who had consistently gained the highest marks in all subjects during his school career. He died, aged sixty-six, in Strasbourg on October 12th, 1910, just over a week after his twenty-fourth wedding anniversary.

CHAPTER 5
JOURNEY INTO MIND

The selection procedure for those embarking on a career in medicine discriminates in favour of...the sort of people who will be good at passing medical exams and can be relied upon to behave in a way deemed appropriate for members of the medical profession. -
Garth Wood [1]

In the year of Edmund's birth, Russia was fighting with Turkey and the British, who had allied themselves with the Turks, sent troops to Gallipoli. At the London Pavilion, music hall artist, the Great MacDermott [2], sang, 'We don't want to fight, but by jingo if we do, we've got the ships, we've got the men, we've got the money too!'

The word *Jingoism*, to describe expressions of belligerent nationalism, entered the English language. It was to provide the leitmotif for Edmund's turbulent life and violent death.

A Dutch Education

In part, Franz Joseph's readiness to work in Holland may have been due to his distaste for Germany's education system. His aversion to Germany's rigid, militaristic schooling was shared by many intellectuals, including Albert Einstein. In his book, *Before the Deluge,* Otto Friedrich quotes the views of one elderly German, for whom the way children were educated at that time faithfully reflected the cultural and social mores of the period:

'You must remember that the basic questions were not intellectual questions. The basic questions involved the development of character. I remember, for example, one day when we got a barrel of apples, and our governess always made us eat the bad ones first, the wormy ones, so that no apples would be wasted. And since we were only allowed to eat one apple a day, the good apples went bad while we ate the bad ones, and so most of the apples we ate had worms in them. But that was supposed to develop the character. And I remember that when I went to have my tonsils out, there was no talk of anaesthetic or anything like that. The doctor just stared at me for a long time, and then he said, 'Are you a brave German boy or are you a coward who cries because of a little pain?' Of course, I had to say I was a brave German boy, and not a coward, and so he took his long shears and reached into my mouth and cut out my tonsils. And I didn't cry.'[3]

With memories of his own school days fresh in his mind, the gentle and enlightened Franz Joseph felt a sense of relief that his own sons would be able to experience Holland's more liberal approach to education where independent thinking rather than unquestioning obedience was more widely encouraged.

From the age of six to twelve, Edmund, Arne and Dirk attended the Dutch-German School in Amsterdam and from

July 1890 to June 1896 the prestigious Gymnasium located in a building of imposing if austere architectural grandeur.

Amsterdam's German-Dutch school

Edmund, who consistently gained the highest marks in all subjects while in school, was a headstrong, stubborn and argumentative extravert with a quick temper that he made little attempt to control and a readiness to take risks by rebelling against authority whenever he considered the rules arbitrary or unreasonable. He spoke his mind without considering the consequences and showed little patience either with those who stayed silent in the face of injustice or expressed opinions he regarded as stupid or dull. In his view, all such conflicts involved a battle of the wills and since he considered his own will-power superior to that of anyone else, the idea of defeat or surrender never entered his mind. This, not surprisingly, brought him into regular conflicts with the school authorities. On one occasion, he became so angry with the philosophical opinions of one of his teachers that he struck him over the head with a salami sausage and was suspended for the remainder of the term.[4]

While disapproving of his rebellious nature, Edmund's teachers also recognised his original and painstaking approach to problem solving and the eagerness with which he confronted unfamiliar intellectual challenges. He was, in the eyes of both his parents and teachers, 'brilliant and outstanding'.

Dirk, although no less intellectually capable, lacked his older brothers creative daring and innovative thinking. Where Edmund was sociable, confident and extravert, Dirk was quieter and far more introspective. Cautious and dutiful, he preferred to guard his tongue and obey the rules rather than risk incurring anyone's disfavour, a habit he retained to the end of his life. An inveterate diarist from an early age, his entries reveal the extent to which he considered every action in terms of their likely consequences for himself rather than their effects on others. There are constant references to 'I did this…' or 'I felt that…' and he kept copious notes about his own thoughts and feelings about every event in his life.

Forster's third son, Arne, lacking his brothers' quick intelligence and had to work especially hard to keep up with their reputation for scholastic brilliance. While Edmund was a practical young man and Dirk a diligent conformist, Arne was a dreamer fascinated by romantic literature and often seeming to live in a fantasy world of his own.

At the age of eighteen, Edmund took his first steps to becoming a physician when he was accepted by the medical school at Strasbourg's Kaiser Wilhelms University where his father was a Professor. It was an intellectual journey that would take him into one of medicine's most recent and least understood of specializations – neurology. He would spend the rest of his life attempting to make sense of that most impenetrable of all medical mysteries – disorders of the human mind.

After completing his first year at Strasbourg, he spent the next six months at the University of Munich living in comfortable, modest, lodgings funded by his parents. At the start of the last century, many students lived a peripatetic existence, moving from one place of learning to another in search of the most eminent lecturers or suitable topics. At the completion of each semester they would produce a 'workbook' which, when signed by their lecturer, served as an 'educational passport' enabling them to move between universities without prejudicing their final degree.

In what were virtually daily post cards to his mother, which he wrote mainly in Dutch, Edmund reveals an enthusiasm for student life combined with the naïve uncertainty and parental dependence of a young man let loose in a big city for the first time, 'I like it very much,' he assured them in one card. 'There is always so much to do and see. I went hiking and love the beautiful landscape. Can you please send me a bicycle and also a list of the people I should visit? I went to see Professor Bollinger and his wife, but she was unwell and could not receive me. Do you think I should call on them again?'[5]

Once his studies in Munich were completed, he returned to Strasbourg where he completed his degree on July 21st, 1901, passing his final exams with an equivalent of a present-day upper-second-class degree.

Among the Strasbourg lecturers who significantly influenced Edmund's later attitudes towards the treatment of mental illness, two names particularly stand out: Karl Fürstner, his Professor of Psychiatry who had conducted pioneering research into the relationship between brain tumours, hysteria and accident neuroses, and physiologist, Richard Ewald, who by means of delicate operations on pigeons had made significant advances in the scientific understanding of the role played by the semi-circular canals in controlling head movements.

Edmund's interest in and talent for delicate experimental work in the laboratory are demonstrated by his choice of final year research project. In this study, supervised by Professor Ewald, he examined the effects of electricity on the actions of nerves and muscles. The fact that muscles can be stimulated by passing an electric current through them had been known since 1791 when Luigi Galvani published an essay describing how, by means of an electrostatic machine, he was able to make the muscles of a dead frog twitch vigorously. But Edmund's breakthrough was to devise a method by which it was possible to apply these currents to individual nerves and muscles rather than, as had been done previously, to groups of them. This was a significant achievement demanding not only intellectual rigour but considerable manual dexterity in precisely positioning the hair fine microelectrodes into individual muscle spindles and nerve fibres.[6]

Under the influence of mentors, like Fürstner and Ewald, Edmund was encouraged to take a strictly mechanistic view of brain function and psychiatric illness. In his book, *The Myth of Neurosis*, Garth Wood writes of a tendency in medical education 'to emphasise the scientific method, which results in many doctors being ill at ease with, and therefore inclined to disregard, that which cannot easily be measured or inferred from measurement.' He goes on to point out that such doctors tend to be 'conservative, conformist people who tend to believe in scientific solutions to the problems of the people who approach them. The medico-biological attitude is second nature to them, and because they may have little first-hand experience, in their own well-ordered lives, of the type of life problem that is frequently brought to them, they may have much sympathy for it, but little understanding of it.'[7]

Edmund and Dirk in military uniform

Edmund Joins the Army

While still a medical student, Edmund had joined the Field Artillery Regiment No 15 as a part-time volunteer and in August 1901, with his medical studies completed, he followed in his father's footsteps by volunteering to become a military doctor with the First Naval Division at the Kiel Naval Hospital in north-east Germany as well as at the

Royal Shipyard. It was there that he got his first taste of real medicine on the wards, writing to his parents, 'Yesterday, I did my first surgery. I cut off a tumour of a man and vaccinated seven children and therefore have to be definitely called a benefactor of humanity!'[8]

After leaving military service in early 1902, Edmund took a course in tropical medicine before signing on as a ship's doctor aboard the Suevia, a small, 6,000-ton cargo and passenger liner owned by the Hapag-Lloyd Line operating on the company's Far East Service.[9] On the February 24th, he wrote to his parents from Hamburg, 'Right now, I am looking for malaria parasites in mosquitoes at the Institute of Tropical Medicine. I will start my journey to Japan on 10th.'[10]

On Monday 10th March, with twenty-two first-class passengers and a crew of forty, the Suevia steamed out of Hamburg bound for Rotterdam, Port Said, Penang, Singapore, Hong Kong, Yokohama and Kobe on Honshu, Japan's main island. The first few days at sea were rough and Edmund, while trying to help seasick passengers, found himself being violently sick himself. By the time they reached Port Said, however, he had found his sea legs and began to enjoy himself thoroughly. At each port, he spent his shore leave visiting hospitals, talking to doctors about tropical diseases and examining patients. He was also punctilious about sending cards home, most commercial but some featuring his own delicately executed water colours of places of interest.

One of the many hand painted postcards sent home by Edmund

By late October, he was back in Europe to take up his new appointment as a clinical assistant in the Pathological Institute at the University of Geneva under Professor Frederick Zahn. Although Edmund found the pathology interesting, he was eager to move into the field that had fascinated him from his days as a student under Professor Fürstner at Strasbourg – the study and treatment of nervous diseases and mental disorders. He loathed Geneva and his postcards home became an almost unending grumble about the cold and rainy weather and his lodgings: 'My accommodation is terrible and I am really fed-up with the food they serve at the pension. I am already looking forward to reasonable fodder!'[10] He was also depressed by the tastelessness of his surroundings. Shortly before Christmas in 1902, he wrote home apologetically, 'I could not find any presents for you. It is impossible to find anything worthwhile here as everything is unbelievably crude and bourgeois.'[11]

After a year, it was with a sense of relief he was able to

transfer to more congenial surroundings at the University of Heidelberg. Here, in one of the most prestigious research centres in the Wilhelmine Empire, he studied under Germany's most notable psychologist, Emil Kraepelin. As a student, Kraepelin had worked with Wilhelm Wundt, the 'father of experimental psychology'. While Professor of Psychology at Leipzig University, Wundt established the Institute for Experimental Psychology, the world's first psychological laboratory. Before long, this Institute had not only become a Mecca for any doctor in Europe with an interest in psychology but a model for all other laboratories. Edmund could not have had a more knowledgeable or experienced teacher of experimental psychology than Kraepelin who encouraged his students to carry out psychological experiments on their patients. While he found such studies of some interest, Edmund's strictly materialistic viewpoint left him unsympathetic towards psychological research and dubious of his professor's main call to psychiatric fame. Like many of his fellow psychiatrists and neurologists, he regarded the professor's classification of mental illness as being based far more on speculation than objective evidence.

Mechanical Minds

Neurology, the medical specialisation to which Edmund dedicated his professional career, was a new science. In the year of his birth the words 'neurology', 'neurological' and 'neurologist,' were not in general use by European doctors.[12] Even by the time he qualified, neurology was neither widely-recognised nor seen as ranking much higher in status than that most despised of all medical specialisations – psychiatry. Diagnosis was frequently unscientific and the methods of treatment neither sophisticated nor reliable.

Sedation in the form of the opiates, hyoscine and digitalis had been used by asylum doctors since the mid-19th century to put the mad to sleep for a while in the hope that, on awaking, they would somehow be cured. One widely used sedative was methylene blue, originally developed for use as a commercial dye but later discovered to be a potent sedative in the treatment of the mentally ill. Apart from drugging their patients, if only to calm down the violently deranged, the only other widely-used form of treatment was electrotherapy.

By the middle of the 19th century, administering electric shocks was one of the few types of non-invasive physical treatments for nervous disorders and it was, as a result, widely advocated and even more widely used. As late as the 1880's, Freud declared regretfully, 'My therapeutic arsenal contained only two weapons, electrotherapy and hypnotism…'[13]

From Heidelberg, Edmund was sent not to Berlin's Charité hospital, as he had hoped, but to the Clinic for Neurology and Mental Illness at Halle University. From May 1904, he worked there as clinical assistant to Professor Carl Wernicke. Wernicke, the most famous of all his mentors, was in his mid-fifties when the two first met. As the author of *The Aphasic Syndrome* (*Der Aphasische Symtomencomplex*), a landmark study of speech disorders he had published in 1874 at the age of only twenty-six, he enjoyed a formidable international reputation. While Forster had been out of sympathy with Kraepelin's views on diagnosing mental illness through clinical observation, Edmund found his new professor's opinions far more to his liking.

Wernicke regarded neurology and psychiatry as inseparable and emphasised that even though it might not always be clear what was happening in the brain or nervous system of a mentally ill patient, this was no reason for abandoning a materialistic approach.

Although he enjoyed the stimulation of working with Wernicke, whom he found to be an excellent teacher, Edmund missed the comforts of family life and returned to his parents' home in Strasbourg whenever possible. Following one such visit in April 1905, he wrote wistfully to his father, 'It is still winter here, no leaves on the trees and no flowers. The journey was fine, but I have so few things to do here that I could have stayed longer in Strasbourg. I have obtained some French statistics on psychosis. Wernicke has sprained his ankle and doesn't work in the clinic but is in a good mood.'[14]

Not that all his trips to see the family were harmonious – his quick temper and impulsive frankness often led to rows with his younger brother Dirk, who was training to become a lawyer, usually over women, their different tastes in literature or music.[15]

On May 19th, his family rejoiced when Edmund learned that his Habilitation had been accepted. His clarity of thought and painstaking attention to detail can be judged from the report on his thesis by one of his two external examiners Professor Ziehen from the Medical Faculty at the Royal Friedrich-Wilhelms University of Berlin.

'In his extremely extensive and carefully assembled review of the literature,' Ziehen noted, 'the author sets out to demonstrate, following Wernicke, that 'Anxiety Psychoses' is not in itself a disease. While this proof is neither as complete nor as certain as the author believes it to be he has moved a long way towards resolving the question.'[16]

Edmund Fights a Duel

At Halle, which, like Geneva he found 'absolutely boring

and tasteless', Edmund's impetuous nature and outbursts of temper landed him first in a duel to the death and then in prison. Writing about the event to his father, he explained with casual insouciance, 'I was involved in a student's duel in the summer, and although no one was injured the police got to learn about it and we were sentenced to three months in prison. Of course, I told Wernicke about it who was very nice and who advised me to sort matters out by taking a holiday. I have therefore taken a four-week temporary leave of absence from the 15th March onwards, as we will probably have our sentences reduced, and will then come to Strasbourg where I will serve my sentence in the Fort. It is boring, but cannot be changed. Maybe I will run out of money, then I will write again and you can send me some more. All the best to everybody, Edmund.'[17]

The fact that Edmund was even permitted to take part in a duel is a measure of the progress which this grandson of a wine merchant had made up the hierarchical German social ladder. From a position so low on the social ladder no 'gentleman of honour' would have demeaned himself by agreeing to engage him in a duel, to the more elevated status of an officer and a professional. As a contemporary duelling code puts it: 'Those may be considered gentlemen who, be it through birth, through self-acquired social position, or as a result of completed studies, raises himself above the level of the common honourable man and by dint of one of the aforementioned can be treated as an equal with the officer.'[18]

While prohibited under the German penal code of 1871, duelling was still widely acknowledged as the only legitimate means whereby an *Ehrenmann* (man of honour) might defend that honour in the face of insult. For the *Ehrenmann*, life was of far less importance than safeguarding one's honour through a physical demonstration of courage, will and moral superiority. In 1907, Maximilian Beseler, the Prussian Minister of Justice, had told delegates to Prussia's upper chamber, 'Our duel rests not only on injured honour but also indirectly on the fact that the masculinity of the injured is attacked and that the offended seeks restoration of his questioned masculinity in the duel. It is impossible to find punishment wherein it would be expressed that the impugned masculinity is once again recognised.'[19]

During a 1912 debate about revisions to the archaic duelling code, for example, one commentator had exalted in the fact that 'the German people sees in bravery, thank God, the highest purpose of man', while even those in favour of abolition recognised that 'courage is an essential prerequisite of honour. Cowardice is as little compatible these days with the concept of honour as earlier.'[20]

Exactly what led Edmund to be drawn into a duel and whether he was the instigator or recipient of the challenge is not known. Given his impulsive nature and quick temper it is possible he offended one of his colleagues by using one of three categories of insult deemed sufficient to provoke a duel. These ranged from a slight or curse, for instance being called a *Schwachkopf* or imbecile, to the most serious involving a blow or slap to the face, although even this could be symbolic rather than physical. 'The violation of another's physical integrity was considered so reprehensible that even a threatened blow was regarded as an extreme offence,' notes author Kevin McAleer in his definitive study of German duelling customs at the turn of the last century. 'Gentlemen would spare themselves the exertion by stating simply: 'Consider yourself slapped!''[21]

Participants and supporters of duelling could be found throughout the professional classes, especially among army officers. In the Kaiser's Germany, military officers such as

Edmund and Franz Joseph before him were considered the measure of all things. In the words of author Isabel Hull, 'The standards of the officer corps were basically the standards of the nobility tightly focused and made more explicit.'[22]

Edmund's light-hearted attitude towards an affair that might, under different circumstances, have resulted in a long term of imprisonment is explained by that fact that in 19th-century Germany, provided its codes had been strictly adhered to, duelling was considered a legitimate means of defending the honour of oneself or one's family. When the outcome was an injury, no matter how serious, those involved were unlikely to face more than a two-month sentence. Even when a duel ended in death, the surviving participant was unlikely to serve more than two years behind bars.

Edmund Moves to the Charité

His time at Halle ended abruptly in September 1905 when Wernicke was killed in an cycling accident in the Thuringian Forest. Within a couple of months of the Professor's death, however, Edmund's professional prospects brightened considerably when Karl Bonhoeffer, the newly appointed director of the Charité's Nerve Clinic, offered him a post as a junior doctor. It was the position he had long been hoping for and 27-year-old Edmund accepted without hesitation. Within the month, he had moved into hospital-run lodgings at 20-22 Schumannstrasse,[23] which was to be his home for more than a decade.

Apart from his military service during the First War, he worked at the Charité for the next twenty years, rising steadily through the medical hierarchy until by 1918 he had achieved the status of assistant professor and Consultant.

Although by nature a blunt and outspoken individual who could sometimes be overbearing, Edmund, like his father, was a humanitarian who saw it as his duty to restore patients to full health. In pursuit of this goal he could be unorthodox and reckless in the expression of his opinions. Two traits that would determine the way he treated Hitler for blindness and his own violent end.

CHAPTER 6
HITLER GETS CALLED UP

I had so often sung 'Deutschland über Alles' and shouted 'Heil'… that it seemed to me almost a belated act of grace to be allowed to stand as a witness in the divine court of the eternal judge and proclaim the sincerity of this conviction.[1] - Adolf Hitler, *Mein Kampf*

Hitler's abrupt departure from Vienna was caused by fear of being imminently conscripted into the Austro-Hungarian army and having to serve alongside 'Jews and Czechs'. It was not that he feared fighting or was opposed to being a soldier, to the contrary, as the world raced towards war, following the assassination of Archduke Franz Ferdinand by eighteen-year-old Gavrilo Princip, Hitler rejoiced:

'To me those hours seemed like a release from the painful feelings of my youth,' he wrote. 'Even today I am not ashamed to say that, overpowered by stormy enthusiasm, I fell down on my knees and thanked Heaven from an overflowing heart for granting me the good fortune of being permitted to live at this time. A fight for freedom had begun, mightier than the earth had ever seen; for once Destiny had begun its course, the conviction dawned on even the broad masses that this time not the fate of Serbia or Austria was involved, but whether the German nation was to be or not to be.'[2]

On August 2nd, he joined other excited citizens who swarmed around the Feldherrenhalle, (Hall of the Warrior Chiefs) in Munich's Odeonplatz to listen to the declaration of war on Russia. Standing at the window overlooking the square, surveying the crowd through the wire-frame viewfinder of his camera, was a young Munich photographer named Heinrich Hoffmann. As the mob cheered their approval for the announcement, Hoffmann pressed his shutter release and preserved the scene for posterity. Some ten years later, he was to extract that photograph from his files and carefully study the hundreds of faces with a magnifying glass. By chance, he found the man he had sought – his patron and friend Adolf Hitler, to whom he had become personal photographer. Hoffmann enlarged that portion of the negative and, after Hitler grew in political prominence over the next few years, sold tens of thousands of copies of what was to prove one of the most popular and widely reproduced photographs he ever took.[3] Hitler is bare-headed and pressed in on all sides by soberly dressed Munich citizens sporting straw hats and bowlers, many waving excitedly. His face, like many in that crowd, is transfixed with excitement. At last, he was to be given a chance to prove himself and his fervent German nationalism in battle. 'As a boy and a young man,' he later wrote, 'I had so often felt the desire to prove at least once by deeds that for me national enthusiasm was no empty whim.'[4]

Hitler Joins the List

On his arrival at Munich, with just 80 crowns in his pocket, Hitler walked up the Schleissheimerstrasse, one of the long, narrow streets leading from the station. Spotting a handwritten notice offering a room for rent to a 'respectable gentleman' in a ground floor window at No 34, he climbed the stairs and knocked on the door of a tailor named Josef Popp. Popp and his wife owned an apartment on the second floor of the sombre, grey-stone building and rented rooms on the floor above. Since Hitler liked the room and Popp considered him suitably 'respectable' a deal was struck. Within an hour of arriving in the city, Hitler was settling into the modest lodgings where he would live for the next twelve months, spending most of the time alone in his room writing, sketching and painting.

On January 19th, Hitler, accompanied by a Munich police officer, called at the Austro-Hungarian Consulate where he made a statement asking to be excused from military service on the grounds of ill-health. Pale and thin after several weeks of destitution in Vienna, he evidently aroused the sympathy of the consular official who wrote to the Linz authorities: 'From the observations made by the police and the impression gained in this office, it would seem that the excuses put forward in the enclosed letter are entirely in accord with the truth. It would also seem that this man is suffering from a complaint which renders him unfit service.... As Hietler (sic) seems very deserving of considerate treatment, we shall provisionally refrain from handing him over as requested and have instructed him to report on January 25th without fail to the Special Conscription Panel in Linz.... Hietler will therefore proceed to Linz unless you feel that the circumstances described above and his lack of funds justify his being allowed to report in Salzburg.'[5]

Desperate not to be conscripted into the Austro-Hungarian army, Hitler resorted to every delaying tactic he could muster. On August 3rd, he sent a petition to King Ludwig III of Bavaria asking his permission, as an Austrian, to join a Bavarian regiment. The following day, he says a document arrived by messenger at his lodgings, 'With trembling hands, I opened the document - my request had been approved.... My joy and gratitude knew no bounds.'[6]

A fortnight later, Hitler reported for service at Munich's Elisabeth School, headquarters of the 16 Bavarian Reserve Infantry Regiment, known as the List Regiment after its commander, Colonel Julius von List. On September 8th, the Colonel welcomed Hitler and his fellow volunteers with a warning that, 'The regiment, whose men for the most part are untrained, is expected to be ready for mobile deployment within a few weeks. This is a difficult task... but not an impossible one... With God's blessing, let's begin our work for Kaiser, King, and the Fatherland!'[7]

Enrolled as *Kriegsfreiwilliger* (volunteer) number 148, he was handed his kit and transferred to the Oberwiesenfeld Barracks where the training was poor and the equipment in short supply. Having run out of helmets, Hitler and his comrades were given oilcloth hats with a grey cotton cover to give the appearance of a military helmet. Not only did these offer no protection but even worse, they could be confused from a distance for British helmets.[8] As a consequence, several soldiers were injured or killed by 'friendly fire' once the fighting had started.

While they spent much of their time marching and drilling, basic firearms training was so limited that just prior to their first engagement when they were issued with the new bolt-action Mauser Gewehr 98 rifles, none of them had any idea how to use them. As a result, in action they were as much at danger from each other as the enemy. The List Regiment, as these deficiencies in equipment and training make clear, ranked low in the priorities of the Bavarian army.

En Route for France

In late September, the List moved to Lechfeld, a town on the confluence of the Lech and Danube some seventy miles from Munich, for a final period of training and on October 21st, entrained for the front. As the crowded troop train steamed slowly northwards carrying thousands of enthusiastic, inexperienced young soldiers to the war, for the first time many saw the subject of their patriotic song *Wacht am Rhein* (Watch on the Rhine). A private in the List recalled dawn on October 22nd as the train ran alongside the great German waterway, 'I remember as if it were yesterday, how it just struck us all to see the sun drawing up the mist from the river and unveiling before our dazzled eyes that splendid statue of Germania which looks down from the Niederwald.' Overwhelmed by patriotic fervour, they started to sing the '*Wacht Am Rhein*': 'Be undismayed, dear country mine: Firm stands and true the watch - the watch on the Rhine.'9

Hitler was 25-years-old when he arrived in Flanders, a quiet and solitary young man whose only notable characteristic was the speed and enthusiasm with which he obeyed every order. In his kitbag, he had included a sketching pad, paints and an architect's T-square so when off-duty he held himself apart from the others painting and drawing. Even in the heat of battle, he remained cool enough to observe and record with an artistic eye every moment of the action, as is apparent in the long and detailed letter he wrote on January 27th, 1915, to Ernst Hepp, a Munich lawyer who in 1913 had advised him over his call-up papers.

After describing the tedious train journey to Lille, he went on, 'We spent the night in the courtyard of the Bourse, a pretentious building which has not yet been completed.... the next day we moved into a billet, a huge, glazed hall. There was no shortage of fresh air since nothing was left but the iron ribs...the thunder of the guns was gradually growing louder. Our column moved forward like a gigantic snake. One of our howitzer batteries was in position just behind us and every fifteen minutes a couple of shells went sailing over our heads into the darkness. They made a coughing, whistling noise and then we'd hear, far off, two dull crumps. We all of us listened for them. After all, we'd never heard anything like it before...then a rat-tat-tat coming nearer and nearer and soon the shell bursts came so thick and fast that they merged into one continuous roar.'[10]

As a front-line soldier, Hitler could hardly be faulted but his officers could find nothing in his solitary and unsociable personality to indicate he had any talent for commanding or inspiring others. Instead, they put his readiness to obey orders without question to the best use they could by making him a Company runner or *Meldeganger*.

Hitler's Narrow Escapes

His first experience under fire during the First Battle of Ypres almost ended in serious injury when a bullet ripped his sleeve. In the skirmish, three of his companions were killed and one was badly wounded. It was the first of his many narrow escapes. A few weeks later, four company commanders arrived at the dug-out where Hitler and some companions were sheltering from the shelling. They ordered the men into the trenches so they could use the bunker for a conference. Hardly had the troops left when the bunker was destroyed by a direct hit which killed all within. On yet another occasion Hitler was sitting in a trench with a group of men when an 'inner voice' warned him to move away. A few moments later a shell landed in the trench killing or seriously injuring everybody in the group. Once again, Hitler was not even scratched.

Each evening, Hitler was sent to Brigade headquarters at Bapaume through a gauntlet of shell fire and bullets. His route lay between blazing buildings and he would often return to the trench with his clothes singed on his back. 'Our numbers got fewer and fewer,' recalled his fellow runner Ignaz Westenkirchner. 'The stunning din in the air never let up for one moment. All was the wildest uproar of death by shot and shell and cannonade. The thing grew unendurable, not to be believed. It took six runners to get a message through, three pairs set out on the off chance that one man, perhaps, might succeed.'[11]

In a 1932 affidavit, used by Hitler in a libel action against a newspaper which had accused him of wartime cowardice, his former commander Lieutenant-Colonel Engelhardt described him as an 'exceedingly brave, effective and conscientious soldier.' Colonel Spatny, his commanding officer, recalled how 'Hitler set a shining example to those around him. His pluck and his exemplary bearing throughout each battle exerted a powerful influence on his comrades and this, combined with his admirable unpretentiousness, earned him the respect of superiors and equals alike.'[12]

One must bear in mind these endorsements were written after Hitler had risen to political prominence by officers if not eager to please the Nazis, then certainly did not think it prudent to displease them!

On October 7th, 1916, almost two years to the day after he

arrived at the Front, Hitler was wounded for the first time. An urgent dispatch had to be taken to an especially dangerous sector of the line and Hitler, together with another runner, a tall, phlegmatic private named Ernst Schmidt, immediately volunteered. Schmidt, like Hitler, had gained a reputation for coming through the heaviest bombardments unscathed and, since the mission was considered so hazardous, both men were sent with identical messages in the hope that at least one of them would get through. As they sprinted from cover across a patch of flat land, a British grenade exploded only yards away. Both men flung themselves flat but, on this occasion, Hitler proved a fraction too slow and splinters ripped into his left thigh. He spent the next two months recovering from his wounds in a hospital at Beelitz near Berlin. Discharged on December 3rd, he was ordered to report to the 4th Company, 1st Replacement Battalion of the 16th Reserve Infantry Regiment in Munich. To his disgust, he found that civilian morale in the Bavarian capital was poor. 'Anger, discontent, cursing wherever you went,' he noted sourly, 'the general mood was miserable: to be a slacker passed almost as a sign of higher wisdom, while loyal steadfastness was considered a symptom of inner weakness and narrow mindedness.'[13]

Apart from a short leave between September 30th and October 17th, 1917, Hitler remained at the Front for the rest of the war, seeing action in Flanders, Upper Alsace and at Arras. He never seems to have had the slightest doubt that Germany would somehow, against all the odds, emerge victorious. In July 1918, he saved the life of a wounded company commander when he dragged him out of range of an American artillery bombardment and not long after that prevented German guns from accidentally firing on their own advancing infantry by carrying a vital message to the rear. On August 4th, he was awarded the Iron Cross First Class, ironically on the recommendation of Hugo Gutmann. Gutmann was the Regiment's highest-ranking Jewish officer, an embarrassing fact that was carefully erased from the records after Hitler had come to power.[14]

As the last of General Ludendorff's five spring offensives ground sputtering to a halt, in July 1918, General Ferdinand Foch, the first commander in chief of the Allied armies in France, launched the successful French counterattack. Three weeks later, in the early hours of August 8th, General Sir Henry Rawlinson's Fourth Army joined the battle and, supported by five hundred tanks, Australian and Canadian troops broke out of the trenches and retook miles of territory in the first day, creating such panic among the demoralised German troops that sixteen thousand surrendered almost immediately. For Hitler, as for Germany, the Great War was about to come to an inglorious conclusion.

CHAPTER 7
MEDICINE GOES TO WAR

We've now got to the point where nervous illness represents the most important medical category and in our province the nervous hospitals are practically the only ones that are always full. -
Robert Gaupp[1]

The declaration of war in August 1914 was greeted on all sides by a euphoria so obsessively delusional that German psychiatrists regarded it as a mental illness they named *Mobilisation Psychosis (Mobilmachungspsychose)*. Most German doctors, in common with the majority of the population, believed a few months of exhilarating action at the Front would see their young men as not merely victorious but mentally, physically and morally renewed by combat.

Public and professional opinion was united in the belief there was no better cure for 'nerves dried up and languishing in the dust from years of peace' than the battlefront and the 'mighty healing power of the iron bath (*Stahlbad*)'[2] which would restore the nation to its former imperial glory. This view was forcefully articulated by Walter Fuchs, a military doctor, who described war as 'the only means by which we, as a nation, can be saved from physical and psychological lethargy and emasculation which are relentlessly threatening.'[3]

As Berlin neurologist Kurt Singer, who served in a hospital close to the Western Front, put it, 'Will and obedience are ultimately determined by the intactness of the nervous system. Therefore, psychiatry plays a major role in the war, next to the main areas of medical activity: surgery, internal medicine and hygiene. It separates out the ill from the healthy. It prevents the will of an individual, when led astray, from contaminating those around it. Its task is important because mental disorders, when they remain unrecognised, are dangers for the many, for those fit for combat, and for the basic principle of military organisation, which is discipline.'[4]

Within hours of the Kaiser's announcement of war, Edmund had boarded a train to Kiel, three hundred miles away on the North Sea coast, to take up an appointment as auxiliary doctor at the Kiel-Wik naval hospital. His military training and extensive medical experience meant it was only a matter of weeks before thirty-six-year-old Edmund was promoted to senior assistant doctor and then, on November 14th, to a nearby officers' training school. In February 1915, he was promoted to Marine Medical Officer and posted to Marine *Lazarette* No 2, based at Bruges in north-western Belgium as a consultant in the neurological department.

Once in Bruges, Edmund discovered the optimism, still prevalent in Germany, was fast disappearing among front line doctors. In the wards, he found himself treating men whose minds rather than bodies had been destroyed by the war. Without having suffered any physical injury, some were partially blind, or deaf, or dumb, or mute, or incoherent through stutters and stammers. There were patients who, incapable of speaking, could only give voice to an eerie, rhythmic, barking; others were paralysed, lacked all co-ordination, or plagued by tics and tremors. There were soldiers whose limbs were contorted by violent seizures or bent at an acute angle, a condition known as Camptocormia.

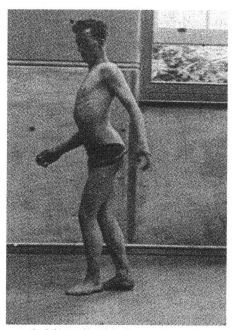

Soldier disabled by hysteria

Nothing in his training or experience had prepared him for this endless parade of disabled and disordered men flooding his wards.

There was, for Edmund, nothing metaphysical or non-material about the brain, no ghost in the machine and no aspect of the human mind that could not be reduced to an electro-chemical manifestation. A genuine mental illness, he believed, was always the result of physical damage, or changes to the brain and, or, nervous system. Hysterical patients, no matter how severe or distressing their disability, were either consciously malingering or unconsciously feigning. If the former, they were cowards to be dealt with firmly and severely; if the latter, weaklings whose disabilities were due to a failure of the will. A quality which, in 1911, German psychiatrist Robert Gaupp, had described as 'the highest achievement of health and strength, embodying such sublime and essential masculine virtues as stoicism, calmness, discipline, and self-control.'[5]

These beliefs, combined with Edmund's authoritarian personality shaped his approach to the hundreds of hysterically disabled soldiers he dealt with in the years ahead. Rather than sticking to a 'one size fits all' therapy, Edmund adapted it to match the patient's personality. With some he played on the soldier's feelings of guilt at abandoning his comrades to the dangers of the trenches while they 'shirked' in a comfortable hospital bed. With others, he threatened punishment for insubordination unless they immediately 'gave up' their hysterical disabilities. With most he employed his forceful personality to intimidate them back to health.

'With a little bit of will-power you could perform your duties,' he would admonish sternly. 'I know only too well that... not everyone has the same amount of will-power and that is why you are being treated here for a while. Not because you are poorly, but because you have been badly brought up and have no will-power. This will-power of yours [has] to be strengthened.'

While some of his colleagues viewed these methods as unorthodox, they also admitted that he not only brought about rapid cures but even earned the thanks of his patients, with those to whom he had been the most abusive later expressing the greatest gratitude.

Battlefields of the Mind

The war being capable of destroying men psychologically as well as physically should not have come as the surprise it did. More than four decades earlier during the Franco-Prussian War of 1870, German military medical officials, including Edmund's father Franz Joseph, had for the first time been required to keep casualty statistics. These showed that even during this year-long campaign more than three hundred had been diagnosed as suffering from a serious mental disorder.

During the Russo-Japanese War of 1904 to 1905, Russians had, for the first time in any conflict, established a psychiatric hospital to treat mentally ill soldiers. Within a few weeks, scores of men were being treated for health problems including hysteria, epileptic reactions, alcohol-induced psychosis, nervous exhaustion and what would today be termed post-traumatic stress disorders.

Yet, despite such well-documented evidence, the medical establishments on all sides were caught unawares by the scale of the mental health disaster unfolding before them. By the winter of 1917, war neuroses had risen to the point of parity with physical injuries up from 14 percent in 1914 to 45 percent three years later. 'Their number has grown and grown,' Gaupp reported late in 1917. 'Scarcely is one nervous hospital opened than it fills up and space must be found somewhere else.'[6]

The Problems of Treating Hysteria

While cases of hysteria among soldiers had occurred

86

throughout military history, its widespread appearance among troops within months of the start of the First War was totally unexpected. At first, in the words of historian Robert Whalen, the German medical profession responded as if the disabled soldiers had been the victims of some 'colossal industrial accident.'[7]

Scientifically-orientated doctors such as Edmund Forster initially attributed their difficulties to a condition known as the 'railway brain'. This quaint diagnosis arose from observations of railway accident survivors made during the 1880s by Hermann Oppenheim, Germany's most eminent neurologist. While apparently uninjured, these victims frequently displayed symptoms such as tremors, tics, stutters and partial paralyses identical to those now present among the soldiers. Oppenheim concluded that even though no physical injuries could be identified in such patients, the tremendous force of impact between two speeding trains had nevertheless produced tiny injuries to their brain or nervous system. Although invisible even under a microscope, it was these minute injuries, he argued, that produced their signs and symptoms. Once war began, he further proposed that the relentless artillery bombardments, the explosions from bombs, mines and grenades and the trauma of being buried alive were producing the same undetectable lesions in the brains and nervous systems of soldiers.

His ideas were eagerly taken up by both the medical and military authorities who, for reasons of patriotism, were reluctant to believe that these disabilities could indicate mental breakdown. Military doctors firmly believed their duty was to return every soldier they treated, whether their injuries were physical or mental, to the battlefields as swiftly as possible. 'In attempting to meet these goals,' argues historian Mendelssohn-Bartholdy, 'they not only borrowed from the methods of efficient industrial production, but dealt increasingly with soldier-patients as objects or resources to be efficiently utilised in an impersonal and mechanised system.'[8]

An Electric Cure

In 1903, while working at Heidelberg's nerve clinic, a psychiatrist named Fritz Kaufmann had watched in awe as a young girl suffering from hysteria made an immediate and complete recovery after the clinic's director, Wilhelm Erb, subjected her to a 'merciless' ten-minute burst of electric current accompanied by strong verbal commands. Twelve years later, in the overcrowded wards of Mannheim's nerve clinic, he recalled this experience and decided to try using the same procedure to create an 'assembly-line' method for treating neurotic soldiers. He publicised his method, also known as *Zwangsverfahren* (coercive processes) and *Gewaltsuggestionsmethode* (method of violent suggestion) in a series of lectures and demonstrations, as well as in an influential paper published in the *Münchener Medizinische Wochenschrift* of July 1916.

Fritz Kaufmann (2nd left) with medical colleagues, 1918

Describing his experiences at Kaufmann's hands, one patient wrote, 'The current was switched on. At first, I had a prickly feeling, which suddenly burst into intense pain ... I heard someone yelling, 'You must listen now,' and the doctor kept talking at me, 'Only uneducated people suffer from such conditions. How will you cope with your stutter in society?' The appeal was to my self-respect and my sense of honour.'[9]

Kaufmann insisted that for his treatment to succeed, strict military discipline must be enforced throughout the hospital. Doctors should always emphasise their rank and bark out commands as if on the parade ground. As Paul Lerner comments, 'Analogous to war itself (the approach) was conceived of as a battle of wills between doctor and patient, and in his contest with the doctor, the patient had to understand that he could not win.'[10]

Treatment ended only once the hysterical condition had been completely eliminated. To terminate it prematurely, Kaufmann warned, ran a risk of making the condition intractable and permanent. Whilst claiming a high degree of success for his electric-shock treatment, Kaufmann admitted that, although cured, his patients were never fit enough to return to the front line. His method was also directly responsible for the deaths of at least twenty patients.

Faced by this unending influx of hysterical soldiers, German doctors not only enthusiastically adopted the same approach but embellished it with variations of their own devising. In Bonn, neuropsychiatrist Heinrich Bickel modified the amount of electric shock the patient received by increasing both the current used and the time for which it was applied – at treatment number six it lasted for twenty minutes – so the amount of pain involved grew steadily more intense from one session to the next.

Doctors became, in the words of historian Paul Lerner, 'Judge, teacher, and disciplinarian...[able] to exercise a decisive influence over the fates of thousands of soldiers...they supervised the creation of a set of institutions and facilities over which they had complete control. Doctors used their newly achieved control and authority over the patient to promote medical views of German manhood, which were based on duty, obedience and, most of all, productivity.'[11]

It was not until towards the end of the war that protests and resistance by patients – in one instance leading to a full-blown mutiny – became so widespread and well-publicised that electric therapy was finally prohibited by the medical authorities. But even before then, some psychiatrists were unwilling on either medical or ethical grounds to administer electric shocks.

Hypnosis and Hysteria
The most benign alternative treatment for hysteria was hypnosis and one of its most effective practitioners was Dr

Max Nonne, a Hamburg neurologist. Yet his decision to attempt hypnosis, which he had learned while a medical student in Nancy many years earlier, came about more by chance than from any initial faith in the procedure.

Max Nonne

In October 1914, he was asked to treat a lieutenant, recently evacuated from Flanders, who appeared to have been struck dumb. Suspecting the young officer's muteness was psychological rather than physical in origin, but with no clear idea how to proceed, Nonne decided to attempt hypnosis, something he had never previously used on a hysterical patient and which he seriously doubted would have much effect. To his astonishment, no sooner had he placed the man in a trance and instructed him to talk did his patient immediately regain the power of speech.[12]

This initial success encouraged Nonne to use hypnosis on a regular basis, usually with equally favourable results. Mindful of his professions' undisguised hostility to hypnosis, he was initially reluctant to publicise this form of treatment. Before long, his often dramatic successes led him to reconsider this decision and as word of his accomplishments became more widely known, psychiatrists and neurologists started clamouring to be taught his secrets. While cautioning that not every patient could be cured instantly and admitting that with some it was necessary to 'slave away for hours', Nonne also insisted that in a majority of cases, treatment was both simple and speedy. He even claimed that *Blitzheilung* or 'split-second cures' frequently occurred.[13]

Nonne was soon in demand as a speaker and toured Germany addressing psychologists and doctors in Munich, Berlin, Metz and Koblenz. With the instincts of a born showman, his hour-long presentations were part clinical lecture and part pure theatre. While demonstrating his skills from the platform he would not only instantly cure soldiers suffering from paralyses, tics, tremors, stuttering and stammering but by using hypnotic suggestion, make those previously cured reproduce their original symptoms with 'photographic fidelity.' In 1917, he had a 16mm film made to illustrate his lectures with previously cured patients being re-hypnotised to exhibit their original symptoms. A copy of this sixteen-minute-long documentary still exists and creates a sensation of almost surrealistic voyeurism. Under the harsh white glare of the camera lights and against a stark black backdrop, we watch as anonymous German soldiers, wearing only underpants, tremble and jerk like grotesque puppets in the flickering silence. Abruptly, Max Nonne appears beside them, a tall and ghostly apparition in a long white coat. He places his hands on their shuddering bodies, gently massages the twitching limbs, whispers in their ear or snaps his fingers and suddenly, as if he had broken an evil spell, the trembling ceases and the terrible twitching stops.

After he had successfully demonstrated hypnosis to a group of high-ranking military doctors, the authorities accepted its merits and scores of physicians from all over Germany were sent to Hamburg to learn his methods. Despite Nonne's bold claims and dramatic demonstrations, however, most found the hypnosis, at best, unreliable; recent research shows success rates ranged from 20 percent to 70 percent[14] and it was often a complete waste of time. As a result of these frequent failures, many doctors came to believe that not everyone could be hypnotised, but this is untrue. Given sufficient time and effort, anybody can be put into a trance and failure to induce an altered state of consciousness mainly occurs when therapists use the same 'script' for each person.

'This sometimes happens when conducting research into hypnosis because it ensures every subject receives a more or less identical treatment,' explains leading British hypnotherapist Dan Jones. 'Unfortunately, because everyone is different, this 'off-the-peg' approach won't work. To be effective hypnotherapists must tailor their procedure to the individual needs of clients in order to enable them to enter a trance in their own way.'[15]

According to Max Nonne, success depended on following four essential rules. First, and most critical, is the therapist's confidence in the procedure. Any doubts, even if only subconscious, will always have a negative effect on their ability to hypnotise the patient. Second, patients have to make themselves entirely subordinate to the hypnotist's will. Third, the surroundings in which the hypnosis takes place are important. Finally, there is the need to mould the induction to precisely meet the needs and expectations of the patient. A doctor who meticulously followed Max Nonne's procedure but failed to match the individual needs and expectations of each patient would likely fail.

The Rise of Neurasthenia

The term 'neurasthenia' (literally 'nerve weakness') had been coined almost fifty years earlier by George M. Beard, a New York neurologist, in an 1869 paper for the *Boston Medical and Surgical Journal*. In the same year, a psychiatrist from Kalamazoo by the name of Van Deusen used it in a different journal. Possibly due to their unequal social status – a big city doctor with a rich, private clientele versus a 'hick from the sticks' – it was Beard rather than Deusen who received national and international acclaim for this discovery. Indeed, so famous did the East Coast physician become that in France the condition was commonly referred to as 'la maladie du Beard'.

According to Beard, everyone possesses a finite amount of 'nerve force' which is gradually depleted through constant use, just as a battery runs down faster the more its energy is consumed. In two books, *A Practical Treatise on Nervous Exhaustion (Neurasthenia)* and *American Nervousness*, published towards the end of his life, Beard expounded his belief that neurasthenia, which he described as 'the soil from which all mental illnesses spring', resulted from 'the complex agencies of modern life; steam power, the periodic press, the telegraph, the sciences, and the mental activity of women.'[16]

Those at greatest risk from this 'disease of civilisation' were, in his opinion, not the poor and socially deprived but the wealthy elite whose miseries had previously remained unstudied and unrelieved, 'Life in the technologically transformed, urbanised, industrialised world of the late Nineteenth Century may not have had any discernible effect on the dull-witted or uneducated, but it was enough thoroughly to exhaust the more refined, civilised portion of the population. The disease could thus be a sign of either moral laxity or extreme moral sensitivity.'[17]

As psychiatrist Tom Lutz points out, 'The wide swathe of symptoms made the diagnosis so widely available, and the theory of exceptional refinement and sensitivity made it so attractive – attractive both to those in elites who felt threatened by cultural change and those upwardly mobile persons who associated nervous feelings with new or desired status positions - that an epidemic was the result.'[18]

Although Beard considered neurasthenia to be an exclusively American disease, his concept of an enfeebled nervous system was warmly received in continental Europe and rapidly taken up by French and German doctors. In France, the enthusiasm for his ideas was so great that by the early 1900s one French doctor sarcastically suggested that 'everything could be explained by neurasthenia, suicide, decadent art, dress and adultery.'[19]

Only in Britain did doctors remain largely unimpressed and uninterested. During a visit to England in 1880, Beard had come under sustained criticism from several eminent physicians and the British Medical Association showed no interest in further investigating his findings. Their main objection, also voiced by some American physicians, was that 'neurasthenia' was too vague a term to have any clinical merit and was scarcely more than a way of describing a 'mob of incoherent symptoms borrowed from the most diverse of disorders.'[20]

By contrast, in Germany this vagueness was regarded as a benefit rather than a drawback. As one psychiatrist commented, '[it] managed to explain subjective bodily symptoms in terms of objective physical disease, thus removing any suggestion of the patient's own part in them and enabling German men to preserve an ethos of fortitude.'[21]

For moralists, neurasthenia offered further evidence against all they most disapproved of in modern life, from artistic decadence to masturbation and from the emancipation of women to industrialisation. For social reformers, it provided a powerful argument against the inner-city slums and sweatshop factories which psychiatrists such as Robert Gaupp had warned showed an 'extraordinary fruitfulness' when it came to producing illnesses of all kinds.[22]

Finally, because the wealthy were said to be at greatest risk, neurasthenia helped to ensure doctors in private practice enjoyed an endless supply of affluent clients clamouring to have exhausted nervous energy expensively recharged. Not only was Beard's theory swiftly adopted by German psychiatrists, but so too was the standard cure, developed by another North American neurologist, Silas Weir Mitchell from Philadelphia. For female patients, he advised complete rest and a milk diet, while male sufferers were prescribed rest, fresh air or a foreign cruise. The men, apparently, did not need any additional milk.

The Rise of the Womb

For military doctors who found the notion of neurasthenia unhelpful when attempting to staunch the relentlessly rising tide of mentally disabled soldiers, a second and far more ancient diagnosis was open to them – hysteria. Named from the Greek *hysteron*, for womb, physicians in ancient Greece believed this organ was 'the cause of a thousand ills'. Its convulsions '(excited by the emotional disturbance transmitted through the nerves) spread by sympathy to the head and chest and arouse a centre of vitality which deprives the other parts of the body of vital force.'

Many German psychiatrists saw the cause of hysteria as a failure of the will. In 1904, Karlsruhe physician Willy Hellpach described the 'will' as the 'A to Z of hysteria'[23] while neurologist Alfred Goldschieder contended, 'The activity of the will is raised to the highest conceivable level through love of Fatherland, through mutual example and not least through camaraderie, which melds superiors and subordinates into a single mass of will.'[24]

Given such beliefs, it is not surprising that when confronted by disabilities for which they were unable to find any physical cause, German psychiatrists, Edmund Forster among them, attributed them variously to a *Willenssperrung* ('inhibition of the will'); *Willensversagung* ('failure of the will') or *Willenshemmung* ('an arrest of the will').

This perception of the 'will' as a sublimely masculine quality, one which Swiss psychiatrist Otto Binswanger believed 'purified and fortified our minds'[25] exerted a baleful influence over the treatment of hysterical soldiers during the First War. German military psychiatrists and neurologists saw their duty as patriots, officers and physicians to act in accordance with the official policy of the German Psychiatric Association. This stated they should 'never forget that we physicians have now put all our work in the service of one mission: to serve our army and our Fatherland.'[26]

In pursuit of this policy, doctors were given licence to devise and practice virtually any treatment, however extreme, they believed might remove the hysterical disorder and return the soldier, if not to the battlefield then to some other form of employment helpful to the war effort, as speedily as possible. While many of those they devised now appear needlessly brutal and highly unethical, Edmund Forster and his colleagues reflected a general consensus among European psychiatrists that there was no such medical condition as 'hysteria'. As the eminent French psychiatrist Jean-Martin Charcot cautioned his students, 'Bear well in mind – and this should not exact too great an effort – that the word…means nothing.'[27]

As a result, soldiers diagnosed as 'hysterics' were viewed not merely as having 'inferior nervous systems' or 'degenerate brains,' but as 'threatening to national unity' since 'strength of will' had become synonymous with obedience. With no clear understanding of the physical basis of either neurasthenia or hysteria, there was no consensus for how best to treat it. The result was that it was left largely to the inclinations and aptitudes of individual psychiatrists and neurologists to devise their own forms of therapy.

The Hysteria Hospitals

By 1917, with overcrowding in general hospitals rapidly becoming unmanageable, the German War Ministry authorised the 'creation of special sections for this type of patient' and opened sick bays or *lazarettes* in remote areas all across Germany. For patients, this meant it was usually impossible for them to receive visits from family or friends. While undoubtedly adding to the patients' loneliness and misery, such isolation was, as the authorities were concerned, both medically and politically desirable. Doctors in both Germany and England believed it essential to separate mentally and physically disabled soldiers to prevent the spread of hysterical symptoms. In the words of Gordon Holmes, a psychiatrist based at the National Hospital for the Paralysed and Epileptic in London, 'Hysteria spreads by suggestion from one person to another and has got to be dealt with in no uncertain fashion. Otherwise the best army in the world finds itself in hospital.'[28]

Gordon Holmes, the son of an Anglo-Irish landowner who had studied medicine at Frankfurt University and spoke fluent German was to an uncanny extent Edmund Forster's *doppelganger*. Colleagues of the two men described them in almost identical terms as 'restless, indefatigable, investigator(s) with a practical, down to earth, mind and no interest in the major, metaphysical questions of life.' Edmund and Gordon each had a bedside manner that was brusque and took a similarly authoritarian approach both to patients and colleagues.

Ben Shephard, in his book *A War of Nerves*, describes Gordon Holmes as, 'Much loved by some students for his warm and impulsive nature, he was terrifying when angry and had been known to lift up an erring student by the scruff of the neck to twist an arm 'to emphasise a fault in (a) clinical description'... (he had) fought with most of his colleagues and come to blows with some.' He might equally well have been describing Edmund Forster.

Doctors favoured smaller units since these enabled them to get to know their patients better and exercise greater control than was possible on the wards of a large general hospital. The emphasis on rural locations was based on the belief that treatments would be faster and more effective if administered away from the corrupting influence of big cities, places many doctors regarded as breeding grounds for the neuroses they were treating. Military discipline in hysteria hospitals was as strict and as rigorously enforced as on the parade ground. As the staff openly admitted, the purpose of such a severe regime was to make hospitals so disagreeable that the injured soldiers would be encouraged to 'come to their senses' and return to the front line as soon as possible. 'The soldier must have the feeling that all in all nowhere is as nice as in the field,' wrote Willy Hellpach in 1915, 'despite all the dangers and the stresses, and nowhere is as unpleasant as in the hospital station, in spite of its security and safety.'[29]

'The patients were not abused,' insisted psychiatrist Karl Ponitz, 'but their stay in the station was certainly not made into paradise.'[30]

Given this approach, it is unsurprising that the authorities sought to keep what was happening within *lazarettes* as well hidden as possible from the civilian population. They worried that not only would the often grotesque spectacle presented by the mentally disordered casualties undermine national morale but that their treatments would lead to public outcry.

Under pressure from commanders and in their sincere belief that hysteria was another name for malingering, even humane and well-intentioned physicians behaved in ways that made the years of the First War among the darkest in modern psychiatric history.

CHAPTER 8
GAS ATTACK

Poor devils... their eyes bandaged, led along by a man with a string while they try to keep to the duckboards. Some of the after-effects are as extraordinary as they are horrible - the sloughing of the genitals for example.
- Dr Harvey Cushing[1]

On October 15th, 1918, while stationed near the small Belgian town of Wervicq-Sud on the River Lys, Hitler was blinded by British gas. In the German edition of *Mein Kampf*[2] he takes just 132 words to describe this momentous event. The English translation is eighteen words longer, but remains almost as concise:

'On the night of October 13, the English gas attack on the southern front before Ypres burst loose. They used Yellow-Cross gas, whose effects were still unknown to us as far as personal experience was concerned. In this same night, I myself was to become acquainted with it. On a hill, south of Wervick [*sic*], we came on the evening of October 13 into several hours of drumfire with gas shells which continued all night more or less violently. As early as midnight, a number of us passed out, a few of our comrades forever. Towards morning I, too, was seized with pain which grew worse with every quarter hour, and at seven in the morning I stumbled and tottered back with burning eyes; taking with me my last report of the War. A few hours later, my eyes had turned into glowing coals; it had grown dark around me.'[3]

This succinct description has for some eighty years[4] been widely accepted as an accurate version of the events that left Hitler blinded and in pain for almost a month.[5] Yet his account is inaccurate in two respects: the first trivial, the other of considerably greater significance.

First, the minor error – Hitler got the date of the attack wrong. The attack occurred on the morning of the 15th October, not the 13th as he states. Given the frenetic conditions under which he had lived during his last few days on the front line, his physical and mental exhaustion prior to the attack and his parlous health immediately after it, such minor confusion is hardly surprising. When dictating his memoirs to Rudolph Hess while in Landsberg Prison, he had no access to military or medical records and had to rely solely on his memory.

The more crucial error lies in his description of the gas as 'Yellow-Cross', or mustard gas. After four years of fighting, March 1918 brought an end to trench warfare and the start of fluid battle lines. Gas now became an important means of taking out enemy artillery, incapacitating machine-gunners and demoralising the enemy infantry prior to an attack. Poisoning large tracts of ground prevented whole sectors from being reinforced while simultaneously harassing and demoralising opponents by injuring them at times they least expected it.

At the end of September 1918, the 16th Regiment was dug-in to well-established positions on high ground overlooking the River Lys, south of Ypres. As I explained previously, Hitler's duties as a *Meldeganger* mainly consisted of carrying messages between regimental headquarters and forward trenches on Paul Bucq Hill, one of the highest pieces of ground in the area. To the north-east of Paul Bucq Hill was the gutted town of Wervicq, whose tumbled buildings and rubble-filled streets were dominated by a shell-scarred church spire. In 1914, the pro-German Swedish explorer Sven Hedin visited Wervicq and described how 'a large part of the population has remained and makes a curious picture in these quaint old streets where German kitchen wagons stand steaming and smoking at quiet street corners.'[6] Four years later, the little town, which remained in German hands until the final weeks of the war, had been transformed into a deadly trap for any enemy troops with concealed machine-gun posts and camouflaged sniper positions at every corner.

Spread out along a ten-mile front facing the 16th Regiment, on the opposite bank of the Lys, the British 30th Division awaited orders to attack. Both sides knew these could not be long in coming; for one thing, the marshy river basin was, in the words of the divisional historian, 'no place to spend the winter.'[7] Military planners knew only too well that within a few weeks, rains would make any assault across the waterlogged ground and swollen river more hazardous and costlier in lives. Not only that, but the British lines were vulnerable to enemy artillery fire, being 'overlooked beyond Wervick [sic] church spire by the higher ground south of the River Lys, Paul Bucq hill most obviously but behind again were Roncq and Mont Halluin,' noted a 30th Division officer, 'the Roncq church spire possessing a most valuable and comfortable observation place for the enemy.'[8]

The Battle of Courtrai

On October 13th, the day before the start of what would become known as the Battle of Courtrai, the intelligence officer of the 6th Brigade Royal Garrison Artillery noted in his diary, 'Six inch batteries carried out BB gas [i.e. mustard gas] concentrations on Busbecqu [east of Wervicq] and battery positions were harassed. At 7.30 p.m. we carried out a gas concentration . . . mustard gas shells were used for the first time.'[9]

Before dawn the following morning, German front-line troops heard the unmistakable sound of British soldiers assembling for an attack. One of the messages Hitler carried that night was a request from forward officers for an artillery bombardment of the British lines. Although this was carried out, the German gunners, firing blind in the darkness, could only lay down their barrage on positions identified during the previous day by observers in the spires of Wervicq and Roncq. The British, who had noted the fall of shells and had evacuated the areas concerned, suffered few casualties among the assembling troops.

German soldiers under gas attack

At 5.30 on what promised to be a sunny morning, soldiers from the 90th and 21st Infantry Brigades swarmed from their trenches and advanced through the early morning mist along a 3,500-yard front towards the river Lys. With no cover in the featureless valley basin, the artillery barrage that started exactly three minutes before jumping off time was of vital importance. The official historian of the 30th Division notes, 'It was, for the division, the last big barrage of the war.... (It) was as good as any under which the division had advanced. It came down along and in front and behind the Lys with all the cumulative fury of four years of war – machine gun bullets, shrapnel, smoke, gas, thermite[10] and high explosive – the smoke shells from the field guns were particularly blessed by the infantry advancing as close as they could to the curtain they made, for save on the extreme left where it was thinnest, it hid them from what defensive fire the enemy was able to bring to bear.'[11]

With an already demoralised enemy no longer prepared to sacrifice themselves in what they now perceived to be a lost cause, the British troops rapidly gained ground. In the first few hours, hundreds of Germans including one officer who gave himself up fully prepared for captivity with a packed lunch and his servant surrendered. Two hours after the attack had started, British forward patrols were entering Wervicq and clearing out the snipers and machine gun positions.

As the German army fell back in disarray, Hitler's final few hours of battle proved especially hectic and dangerous. It was with considerable relief that early on the morning of October 15th, he and some of his fellow messengers gathered around the smoky stoves of field-kitchen, hastily set-up in an abandoned concrete gun emplacement, for their first meal of the day. Ignaz Westenkirchner described what happened next, 'Not long after they had started eating artillery fire began and before the men fully realised what was happening blasting grenades mixed with gas grenades were raining down, one gas grenade detonated with the well-known dull thump immediately in front of the army kitchen and the old gun-emplacement respectively. The cook screamed 'gas alert' but it was too late. Most of the comrades had already inhaled the devilish mixture of the Yellow-Cross grenades (*Gelbkreuzgranate*) and stumbled away coughing and panting. They hardly made it back to the bombed-out house in whose cellar they had been living when they began to lose their eyesight and the mucous membranes in their mouths and throats became so inflamed that they were unable to speak. Their eyes were terribly painful; it was as if red-hot needles had been stuck into them. On top of that their eyes would no longer open, they had to lift their eyelids by hand only to discover that all they could make out were the outlines of large objects. Six of them, among whom was Adolf Hitler, scrambled to the assembly point for casualties, where they lost contact with one another due to their blindness... Hitler ended up in Pasewalk in Pomerania. The war had ended for all of them.'[12]

When speaking to the pro-Nazi writer Heinz A. Heinz, however, Westenkirchner described the same incident rather differently, 'We were in the neighbourhood of Commines; dazed and bewildered with the ceaseless flash and thunder of explosives... On the night of October 13th-14th the crashing and howling and roaring of the guns was (*sic*) accompanied by something still more deadly than usual. Our Company lay on a little hill near Werwick, (*sic*) a bit to the south of Ypres. All of a sudden, the bombardment slackened off and in place of shells came a queer pungent smell. Word flew through the trenches that the English were attacking with chlorine gas. Hitherto [we] hadn't experienced this sort of gas, but now we got a thorough dose of it. About seven next morning Hitler was dispatched with an order to our rear. Dropping with exhaustion, he staggered off...His eyes were burning, sore, and smarting – gas – he supposed, or dog weariness. Anyhow, they rapidly got worse. The pain was hideous; presently he could see nothing but a fog. Stumbling, and falling over and over again, he made what feeble progress he could...The last time, all his failing strength was exhausted in freeing himself from the mask...he could struggle up no more...his eyes were searing coals...Hitler collapsed. Goodness only knows how long it was before the stretcher bearers found him. They brought him in, though, at last, and took him to the dressing-station. This was on the morning of October 14th (sic) 1918 – just before the end. Two days later Hitler arrived in hospital at Pasewalk, Pomerania.'[13]

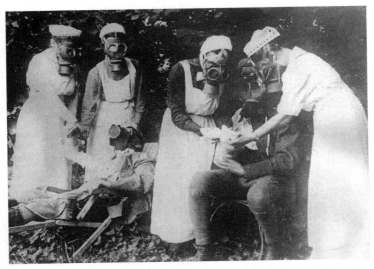

German nurses treating gas injured soldiers at Front

Here are three versions of the same event. Hitler's in *Mein Kampf* and Westenkirchner's two versions. Which is most likely to be correct?

Was the gas, as stated by Hitler and confirmed by Westenkirchner in one of his accounts, Yellow-Cross (the German name for mustard gas) or as Westenkirchner later claimed, chlorine? In the account given to Heinz A. Heinz in 1934, he is mistaken both about the date of the gassing (night of October 13th-14th) and the time taken (two days) to travel between Flanders and Pasewalk. The more important question is whether he was correct in identifying the gas used as chorine rather than Yellow-Cross.

When it comes to determining the true cause of Hitler's blindness the gas involved is of the utmost significance. Had Hitler been exposed to mustard gas, there could well have been physical damage to his eyes that would have required several weeks of hospital treatment. Indeed, the interval of approximately one month between the attack on October 15th and his complete recovery by November 19th is more or less what would be expected in such a case. In an analysis of three hundred patients with moderately severe sight loss due to mustard gas, British doctors found that 72 percent had regained their sight at the end of a month.

If, however, Hitler had been blinded by some other type of gas then, depending on the extent of his exposure, the effects might have been expected to disappear from somewhere between a few hours and a few days. Before we examine these conflicting claims in more detail, a review of the various gases used by the military will help us understand the nature and extent of Hitler's injuries in October 1918. As we will see, while some cause serious and permanent physical damage, others are more benign and transitory.

Gases in World War I

The idea of using gas to kill, disable or harass the enemy had first been suggested during the Crimean War sixty years earlier. Lord Thomas Cochrane, a young naval officer, devised a plan to produce lethal gas during the siege of Sebastopol by burning five hundred tons of sulphur and allowing the prevailing wind to suffocate the Russians. The British government rejected his idea both on grounds of its inhumanity and because they believed it contravened the laws of civilised warfare – a view later formally endorsed by The Hague Convention of 1907.

In Germany, research leading to the first military use of gas was conducted by Fritz Haber, a Jewish chemist employed by Berlin's Kaiser Wilhelm Institute. Despite an explosion in mid-December 1914 that killed his assistant Dr Otto Sackur, Haber continued his work and enabled the German Army to launch the first poison-gas attack on the Western Front in the spring of 1915. It had been used against the Russians on the Eastern Front three months earlier, but severe weather conditions had neutralised its effects. The first German gas attack to produce significant casualties and so demonstrate the military effectiveness of mankind's first weapon of mass destruction, occurred at 5.30pm on April 22nd, 1915.

Observers to the north of Ypres noticed 'two curious greenish yellow clouds on the ground on either side of Langemarck in front of the German line. These clouds spread laterally, joined up, and, moving before a light wind, became a bluish white mist, such as is seen over water meadows on a frosty night.'[14] Wafted by the breeze, the cloud drifted lazily along the ground and, moments later, flooded over and into the enemy trenches with horrific consequences. 'Choking, coughing, retching, gasping for breath, and half blinded, it is no wonder that the troops were seized with terror at the enemy's expedient and gave ground, stumbling back through heavy shell fire in their efforts to find some escape from the deadly fumes.'[15]

With an estimated 7,000 soldiers injured and 350 killed, French troops from the 45th (Algerian) and 87th (Territorial) divisions fled in terror opening a four-mile gap in the lines directly before Ypres. 'In the face of gas, without protection, individuality was annihilated,' comments C.R.M. Cruttwell, 'the soldier in the trench became a mere passive recipient of torture and death. A final stage seemed to be reached in the whole tendency of modern warfare to depress and make of no effect individual bravery, enterprise and skill.'[16]

Gas attacks tended to be made at night or in the early hours of the morning when atmospheric conditions were most suitable and the darkness and confusion made it far harder for troops to know when the assault had started. As a result, the psychological impact produced by fear and uncertainty soon became almost as debilitating as the gas itself. Indeed, as the war progressed 'gas, which had initially been proposed as a means of enabling breakthroughs to be made in the wake of the gas cloud or as a means of retaliation, was being advocated on the grounds that it incapacitated troops, lowered fighting efficiency, caused panic, depressed morale and, by attrition, wore down the enemies' manpower. This applied especially in view of the war weariness and physical exhaustion of the troops.'[17] Once the lethal potency and military advantages of gas warfare had been demonstrated, the Allies raced to catch-up.[18]

Germany's lead in gas warfare had come about not because they were less moral than their enemies, but rather because of higher manufacturing capacity for the industrial dyes on which gas-warfare chemistry is based. Great German chemical works such as the *Badische Anilin und Sodafabrik* at Ludwigshafen, the *Bayer Company* at Leverkusen and the *Griesheim-Elektron Chemische Fabrik* possessed matchless research and development facilities for satisfying military demands. The British, who had neglected their synthetic-dye industry, possessed little or no commercial expertise in producing the precursors of organic poisons. Within a year of the attack at Ypres, however, chemists at a newly-opened laboratory at Porton Down in the south-west of England, chosen due to the countryside's similarity to the ridges east of Ypres, had developed a range of potentially useful gases.[19]

Similar research and development facilities were also constructed in Germany and France around the same time. Their products fell into one of several categories according to their medical effects. They included two types of tear gas – benzyl bromide and xylyl bromide – and nine lung irritants, including chlorine and phosgene. The Allies identified these different types of gas by means of coloured stars, with Red Star for chlorine and Yellow Star for a mixture of 70 percent chlorine and 30 percent chloropicrin, a combination with the dual advantages of being even more immediately incapacitating and potentially lethal. By far the most widely used, however, was White Star, a powerful lung irritant made up of 50 percent chlorine and 50 percent phosgene. By the middle of 1916, this had become what Major General C.H. Foulkes, commander of the Royal Engineers' Special Gas Brigade, called 'the chemical mixture of choice - the 'workhorse' gas.'[20]

Even more terrifying were the paralysing gases such as hydrocyanic acid and sulphuretted hydrogen. These acted directly on the nervous system to cause death within seconds. The fourth gas category comprised 'sternutators', so called because they induced sneezing (*sternutation* is its medical name), as well as an intense burning and aching pain in the eyes, nose, throat and chest, accompanied by nausea and great depression. This was only used by the Germans, and, while effective even in low concentrations, its symptoms rapidly disappeared once the soldier left the poisoned area.

Mustard Gas

A latecomer to the battlefield, ßß-dichlor-ethyl-sulphide was a vesicant agent (one causing blistering) whose properties had first been described by Victor Meyer in 1886. The Germans referred to it as Yellow-Cross, from the yellow double-cross or Lorraine-cross markings used to identify these shells. The French knew it as Yperite because it was first used by the Germans at Ypres. The British called it either ßß gas, from the first two Greek letters of its chemical name, or colloquially, HS (Hun Stuff). It was probably best known, however, as mustard gas because of its faint odour reminiscent of either mustard or garlic, depending on its impurities. The gas burns any part of the body it touches, especially the face and hands because these are usually unprotected by clothing, together with the armpits, groin, genitalia and inner thighs because these are moist.

A unique feature of mustard-gas poisoning and the one that sets it apart from other battlefield gases is the slow rate at which its effects develop. 'Only a few of the men who were gassed died at once. Many of the men felt perfectly well after the bombardment [and] marched back with their companions on relief, under the impression that they had got through the affair satisfactorily. Several hours elapsed before they reported sick. The fatal course of the delayed illness was particularly striking.'[21]

From between two and forty-eight hours after exposure, the symptoms gradually developed and intensified. The horrendous nature of these injuries was graphically described in the *Official History of the Great War*: 'The most important pathological changes to be found in the human body after exposure to mustard gas are those in the respiratory tract...The destruction of the membrane may have proceeded to such an extent that the whole area of the trachea and the larger bronchi are covered by a loosely adhered false membrane or slough of a yellow colour several millimetres thick. Occasionally the slough on the trachea and larger bronchi can be separated as a whole and removed giving the appearance of a cast of the bronchial tree. Such a cast has been coughed up during life... The skin exhibits all stages of burn from the primary erythema, which is the first manifestation of the cutaneous irritation, up to the final stage of deep burn with necrosis and sloughing of tissues. The eyes share in the general inflammation of the skin, and exhibit all the stages of an acute conjunctivitis, from the early chemosis up to an ulcerative keratitis.'[22]

Its high boiling point (mustard gas is mostly a liquid at room temperature) makes it extremely persistent. Once shelled, an area would remain dangerous for hours or even days as the poisonous fluid either slowly evaporated or was broken down by the elements. In April 1918, it was used so extensively during the shelling of Armentieres that the gutters ran with it and no German troops were permitted to enter the town for two weeks. It was a gas completely unlike any other Allied soldiers had previously experienced. 'Up to this date they had been accustomed to associate 'gas' with violent irritating or choking sensations, and many, under the impression that the gas was not strong enough to hurt them, omitted to wear their helmets or keep them on for long enough, nor did they yet grasp that the ground in the vicinity of a burst was heavily contaminated by the poison and continued to be a source of danger long after the bombardment had ceased.'[23]

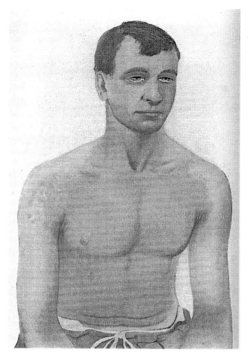

Mustard Gas victim from WW1 medical manual

British researchers had first tested the gas in the summer of 1916. While the Commander-in-Chief, Sir Douglas Haig, had been eager to employ it the British government refused to sanction the use of a substance which, on the basis of the injuries it produced in laboratory animals, they considered barbaric. The German military, free from the control of their civilian leaders, deployed the gas for the first time at Ypres on the night of July 12th-13th 1917, fourteen months ahead of it becoming generally available to British troops. [24]

Following the British 30th Division's successful attack across the River Lys on October 14th and with the rapid advances into enemy-held territory, it might be imagined that its use might decrease. Furthermore, as the countryside around Wervicq still contained many civilian noncombatants, this too might have inhibited Allied commanders from its widespread use. Major General Foulkes commented that as 'the battle zone intruded more and more into areas hitherto behind German lines... the presence of great numbers of French civilians remaining in these areas retarded even localized gas activity on the British front.'[25]

However, in the view of Matthew Buck, a researcher at Firepower, the Royal Artillery Museum, 'The war was characterised by frequent errors in planning, not necessarily due to indifference or incompetence on the part of the planners but to the very imperfect communications technology available during this period. This made it extremely difficult to provide appropriate or timely responses to constantly evolving battlefield situations. 'Mustard' was often used on the flanks of attacks precisely because of its persistent nature – flanks which may have changed as the operations developed. It is thus not beyond the bounds of possibility that mustard gas would have been used by the Allies in these attacks, whether appropriate or not. I would even go so far as to suggest that it was a general characteristic of this war, where operations depended so much on fixed plans which often proved inappropriate to the actual development of events that errors were to be expected. Mustard gas was also a relatively new munition as far as the British were concerned, and prized for its effectiveness.'[26]

Even if we assume the Allies ceased using mustard gas after their preliminary artillery bombardments on the night of October 13th-14th, which indisputably included a large number of such shells, Hitler could still have been exposed to gas fired from much closer range by one of two gas-firing mortars – the Stokes[27] and the Livens.[28]

Between October 1st 1918 and the end of the war on November 11th, mustard gas attacks led to an estimated twelve thousand German casualties. The question is, was Hitler among them?

Blinded by Mustard Gas?

Ignaz Westenkirchner's unequivocal statement that 'chlorine' had been used might appear to tip the balance of probabilities away from the use of mustard gas. Unfortunately, he is not always the most reliable of witnesses. In one account, for example, he claims that the gas attack took place both 'in the early morning' and 'during the evening meal', while his apparent mention of 'chlorine' may simply be a mistranslation from the German.

Hitler's own testimony is similarly flawed. In *Mein Kampf*, Hitler clearly stated, 'As early as midnight, a number of us passed out, a few of our comrades forever.' Not only do German military records show the British attack occurred early in the morning of October 15th but Hitler's version is contradicted by the known effects of mustard gas over such a short period of time.

Westenkirchner makes a similar error in his other account, claiming that the warning 'gas alert' came 'too late', that the victims were 'coughing and panting' immediately and that they 'hardly made it back to the bombed-out house [before] they began to lose their eyesight. . . [and] were unable to speak'. This description of events is incompatible with the medical effects of mustard gas. Furthermore, it is unlikely that anyone present, including the cook, would have known if this gas had been used in the attack. Not only is its faint mustard smell typically masked by the more pungent odour of high explosive but because it rapidly destroys the victims' sense of smell, troops poisoned in this way rarely had any immediate knowledge of what had just happened to them.

But if it wasn't mustard gas, what did produce the incapacitating effects Hitler and Westenkirchner described?

The only other gas whose symptoms closely match their descriptions are the lung irritants and here the most likely candidate, because the British used it so freely, is White Star. The odour of a mixture of chlorine and phosgene is, as one might imagine, immediately apparent and its medical effects are virtually instantaneous. According to the *Official History of the Great War*, 'Even in concentrations as low as two in a million these gases had an immediate and violently irritating action on the eyes, causing a profuse watering of the eyes and so much pain that it rapidly became impossible to keep them open.'[29]

Other symptoms include coughing, choking and panting with severe irritation of the mouth and throat making speech all but impossible. Exposure can also result in a loss of consciousness and even rapid death through asphyxiation; eight out of ten fatalities occurred within twenty-four hours of exposure. Once removed from the source, however, many victims quickly recovered, certainly as far as their eye problems were concerned, and except in the most severe cases suffered no serious consequences later in life.

The same cannot be said for exposure to mustard gas sufficient to cause blindness. Here, although by no means inevitable, the risk of respiratory damage is high. Given that Hitler's weak lungs were serious enough to keep him away from school and probably led to him being declared unfit for military service in 1913, he would appear to have been especially vulnerable. As his post-war lifestyle clearly demonstrates, however, he experienced no trouble in breathing even at high altitudes. During the 1920s, he spent much of his time in Berchtesgaden located 1,700 feet above the sea on the Untersberg. Here he thrived in air so thin and cold that no one suffering from a serious lung weakness could have endured it. 'I lived there like a fighting cock,' he told associates in 1942. 'Every day I went up to the Obersalzberg, which took me two and a half hours walking there and back.'[30] The strength and stamina of his lungs were also evident in his ability to address large audiences unaided by microphones or loudspeakers.[31]

Gas Poisoning and Mental Breakdown

We know that once the Allies had made the decision to supply mustard gas to their troops, it was used liberally and enthusiastically. But while thousands of troops suffered from the appalling effects of mustard gas[32] even more fell victim not to gas but their own imaginations.

Post-war analysis of medical records suggests that up to half of all gas casualties came into this category. 'With men trained to believe that a light sniff of gas meant death, and with nerves highly strung by being shelled for long periods and with the presence of not a few who really had been gassed, it is no wonder that a gas alarm went beyond all bounds,' says author Denis Winter. 'It was remarked as a joke that if someone yelled 'gas' everyone in France would put on a mask. Two or three alarms a night was common. Gas shock was as frequent as shellshock.'[33]

In 1918, for example, significant numbers of American troops who had been warned about the dangers of gas without having any experience of it complained about having been gassed without presenting any 'symptoms or physical signs suggesting that they had actually inhaled any form of poison gas in amounts sufficient to be harmful.'[34]

This was equally likely to be true in the case of German

troops who were first exposed to mustard gas when the French used it in June 1918. With troops taken completely by surprise, the attack spread such consternation that hundreds of casualties, with real and imagined injuries, flooded aid centres where doctors frequently had great difficulty in correctly identifying those who were alleging or feigning gas poisoning.

After 1917, gas partly usurped the role of high explosive in bringing to a head a natural unfitness for war as poisoning was often 'an expression of trench fatigue, a menace when the manhood of the nation had been picked over.'[35] This problem was so widespread that doctors were obliged to lay down stringent rules regarding the treatment of those who were deliberately faking their symptoms and others, like Hitler, who without any conscious attempt to deceive had developed hysterical blindness. These included clear instructions that all patients alleging gas poisoning were to be observed for between 24 and 48 hours. This was to be done in the medical inspection rooms of units, bearer companies, field hospitals, or, in mild cases, in collecting stations with a view to sending the men back to their units if possible. They were specifically not to be admitted to either local or field hospitals, nor to gas casualty stations (*Gaskrankenstation*). Only patients in whom there were unequivocal signs of gas poisoning could be treated like other casualties of war.

Hitler's medical dockets and military records make no mention of a specific gas, simply stating that it was gas poisoning. For example, '*gasvergiftet*' (gas poisoned) from the Oudenaarde doctors; '*Gasvergiftung*' from those at Pasewalk; *l[eicht] Verwundet-Gasvergiftung* (lightly wounded, gas poisoning) from the 16th Regiment's casualty list and similarly on numerous other contemporary documents.[36]

From where, then, does the widely held and reported but erroneous notion that Hitler was blinded by mustard gas originate?

The answer is from his own brief account of the incident in *Mein Kampf*. Was this a deliberate attempt to deceive, to safeguard the truth that far from being seriously injured in the British attack, he had suffered a mental breakdown?

While this can hardly be excluded, given the duplicity at which he and his propaganda experts were so adept, a more likely explanation is that Hitler genuinely but mistakenly believed himself to have been the victim of mustard gas rather than White Star poisoning. What is apparent from his medical records was the exposure was brief and the injuries to his eyes minimal.[37] According to Thomas Weber, 'The quantity of gas was so small that it would not even had necessitated an extended stay in an army-hospital.'[38]

That was the conclusion of doctors who examined him at the Oudenaarde hospital following his transfer from the Linselle aid station. After twenty-four hours observation, they had no hesitation in sending him for treatment. Not, he must have been bewildered to discover, to their well-equipped hospital in Brussels with the rest of his gassed comrades, but to a remote *Lazarette* (clinic) in the town of Pasewalk not far from the Polish border.

The doctors gave him no explanation as to why he was being separated from the soldiers he had fought alongside for four years. Nor was he told the *Lazarette*'s true purpose. It was not, as he may have believed, a place where doctors healed broken bodies but a specialist nerve clinic where neurologists and psychiatrists sought to mend broken minds.

CHAPTER 9
THE SHOOTING HOUSE

*The key to hypnotism is suggestion. The subject, left to himself,
does nothing. The hypnotic state may then change to normal sleep
and he will awaken ...always open to suggestions ...but quite
incapable of acting on his own initiative.* - Hypnotism G.H.
Estabrook[1]

Although never a stylish dresser,[2] when Adolf Hitler
emerged from the gloom of Pasewalk station into bright
sunshine[3] early that October morning in 1918, he looked
more like a homeless vagrant than a proud soldier of the
Kaiser. An ill-fitting hospital uniform rendered even more
shapeless by five nights on the train from Flanders hung in
folds from his emaciated frame. The gauntness of his pale,
exhausted features was accentuated by the drooping black
moustache beneath his long nose. His piercing blue eyes,
which would one day enrapture female followers, were

covered by a soiled dressing. Blinded, he shuffled uncertainly behind an orderly, grasping the man's shoulder with one hand while hesitantly brushing the air around him with the other.

Pasewalk railway station 1914

According to his medical notes, the lance-corporal had been exposed to poison gas on October 15th[4] during a British assault on German lines at Wervicq-Sud in Northern France. Soon afterwards, his 'eyes had turned into glowing coals; it had grown dark around me.'[5]

Hermann Heer, one of the soldiers who had been less seriously affected by the gas led them all to the nearest casualty clearing centre where the doctors sent the majority of the injured men to the well-equipped hospital outside Brussels. The one exception was Adolf Hitler. He was packed off to Pasewalk, a Pomeranian town not far from the Polish border some six hundred miles away.

With their army in retreat and thousands of seriously

injured soldiers urgently needing transport back to Germany, such a decision might seem a waste of scarce recourses. The doctors had no choice in the matter. Despite Hitler's swollen eyelids and his plaintive insistence that he had been blinded by the gas, they had no hesitation in diagnosing his blindness as due not of a physical injury but a mental breakdown.

He was, they agreed, suffering from what is termed *hysterical amblyopia*. They did so only with reluctance since such a diagnosis branded him as being either weak-willed or a coward seeking to escape front line dangers. 'The suspicion will always be there that the patient is in fact malingering,' Hanus Grosz and J. Zimmerman comment in their book *Aetiology of Hysteria*. 'The final distinction between hysterical blindness and malingering is almost impossible to make.'[6]

Hitler's medical chit signed by a Front Line doctor on 15ᵗʰ October 1918

From Oudenaarde, Hitler was transferred to an ambulance train collecting wounded soldiers at Ghent station. Loading the wounded with stretchers having to be manhandled carefully through the open windows of congested carriages, was a slow process. It was late that night before the train steamed out of the station and Hitler began his long journey to Pasewalk. Unable to move through the crowded train, without a nurse or orderly to guide him, he spent most of the journey slumped on the hard, narrow seat struggling in vain to sleep, aware only of the burning pain in his eyes and the cacophony of cries, groans and screams from the wounded men surrounding him.[7]

With lengthy delays in Berlin and Hanover to discharge some of the wounded men, it took him five days to reach his final destination. Once there, he was led through its arched and creeper-covered exit and helped onto one of a number of horse-drawn ambulances drawn up in the chestnut tree shaded yard.[8]

Inside the Shooting House

In 1914, on the basis of its remoteness and excellent rail links with the rest of Germany, the military had selected the 12th Century walled town of Pasewalk on the River Ücker[9] as the location for constructing small clinics or *Lazarettes*. In all, they requisitioned seven properties including a school, a hotel and some large private houses for conversion. The most unusual was the *Schützenhaus* or Shooting House. This mainly single-storied, grey stone building with a three-storey addition at one end and a timber-framed annex at the other was situated on the south-east fringes of the town. Surrounded by extensive grounds, the *Schützenhaus* had views across open fields to the Pasewalker forest in one direction and, perhaps less encouragingly for its patients, the *New Friedhof* cemetery in the other.

The Shooting House in 1914

A former brick factory, the Shooting House had been purchased in September 1859 by Christian Darling, a local businessman and entrepreneur. He converted it into a restaurant and bar surrounded by what his advertising leaflets described as 'attractively laid out gardens.'[10] A few years later, he added an indoor rifle range, from which the building derived its name, together with a stage for variety entertainment.

This unusual combination of a restaurant, bar, meeting rooms, rifle range and music hall theatre proved so popular that the *Schützenhaus* was among the first premises in Pasewalk to have a telephone, Pasewalk 363, on which to take bookings. A poster advertising one of its shows performed at 8pm on Thursday January 24th, 1907, lists among the popular songs being performed such sentimental ballads as *Dear Granddad* and *War and Peace* with two eerily prophetic numbers *The Devil Laughs Aloud* and *You Can't Do Anything About it!*

In a 1913 advertisement, landlord Johannes Thom proclaimed, 'I recommend my friendly hostelry with its garden, large room with a stage, shooting range etc. for Clubs and private hire. Good food and beverages with courteous service.'[11] A few months after this notice appeared, the hostelry was requisitioned by the military for conversion into a *Lazarette* specialising in the treatment of hysterical disorders. The restaurant, offices, shooting range and music hall were turned into wards with beds for around thirty patients, cared for by a staff of fifteen doctors, nurses and orderlies under the command of Dr Wilhelm Schroeder.

On admittance, Hitler was bathed, issued with a clean hospital uniform and allocated a narrow, iron-framed bed in one of the five small wards. The following day his eyes were examined by Dr Karl Kroner, a forty-year-old Jewish physician whose knowledge of the effects of gas poisoning was both professional and personal.[12]

While serving as a doctor with the Third Husaren Cavalry Regiment, Kroner had seen action on the French front at Verdun and Sedan and had been promoted to Colonel General before being gassed and temporarily blinded in 1917 during an engagement for which he was later awarded the Iron Cross 1st Class. Invalided out of the army, he returned to Berlin and started work as a clinician specializing in internal medicine and nervous diseases while, like Edmund Forster, remaining on call as a consultant to a number of military sick bays including those at Pasewalk.

Kroner confirmed the original diagnosis that Hitler's

blindness was due not to physical damage caused by Mustard Gas by a result of what doctors termed 'conversion hysteria'. In this intense anxiety is 'converted' into specific symptoms. Typically, these involve the loss of a physical function.

Dr Karl Kroner 1918

He recommended the patient be handed over to the clinic's consultant neurologist Dr Edmund Forster. His examination had taken him only a few minutes, but the fact he knew the true reason for Hitler's blindness was sufficient to place his life in jeopardy once the Nazis came to power.

Edmund Meets Hitler
Even before he met Hitler for the first time, it is likely that his opinion had been unfavourably shaped by other

members of staff. The lance-corporal was, they told him, a restless and agitated troublemaker. Each evening a small group of patients would cluster around his bed as he voiced disgust for Austria, which he condemned as soft and rotten, while extolling the virtues of strong and virile Germany. He would ask rhetorically why Austria was so corrupt and effete. Then snarl out his answer: because *der Jude* had infected and poisoned the nation. Repeatedly, he returned to his theme that for the strong individual and the strong nation everything is possible and permissible, while one should never show even the slightest respect for a weak opponent. By what right, he once demanded, were crashed French pilots afforded the honour of a military funeral as if they had been German flyers? Far better, if their corpses were simply left to rot on the battlefield where they had fallen. While speaking to his superiors, however, Hitler's tone was completely different and his manner utterly subservient in a clear desire to remain on excellent terms with them.[13]

Edmund Forster, a man of democratic views with many Jewish friends, must have been in equal measure repelled by Hitler's opinions and intrigued by the psychiatric challenge his case represented. The lance-corporal, he concluded, refused to see because he could not bear to witness the defeat of Germany. Whichever treatment was finally devised would have to take this fact into account.

But how should this be approached? With Germany now poised on the verge of defeat, its armies being routed in the west and its civilian population rioting at home, there was no way in which Forster could persuade Hitler victory was still possible. All the doctor could do was change his patient's *perception* of the events now rapidly unfolding around them. He pondered on this interesting challenge until the first week in November, by which time a particular approach had crystallised in his mind. He would free Hitler of his hysterical blindness not with logical arguments but with a tremendous lie. He had come to the conclusion that, for Hitler, there was no absolute truth. Only the truth of his imagination, his striving, his urges, which suggested the best way of eliminating his symptoms was by using his 'desire to be like a God.'[14]

The success or failure of this approach, Edmund realised, would depend on whose will was the stronger, his own or Adolf Hitler's. If he failed, the lance-corporal would probably never see again. If he succeeded, the return of vision should be almost instantaneous.

Hypnotising Hitler

On the evening of November 6th, Edmund ordered Hitler to his consulting room and guided him into an upright chair before a table on which stood two lit candles. After examining his patient's eyes carefully, Forster replaced the instrument in its case and blew out the candles.

'Your eyes have been terribly damaged,' he told him regretfully, 'I should never have assumed that you, a pure Aryan, a good soldier, a knight of the Iron Cross, First Class, would lie or deceive... Everyone has to accept their lot. The individual is powerless where fate is concerned. Miracles do not happen anymore.' He paused before adding more optimistically, 'But that goes only for the average person, miracles still happen frequently to chosen people. There have to be miracles and great people before whom nature bows, don't you agree?'

'As you say, Doctor,' Hitler agreed meekly.

'I am no charlatan, no performer of miracles,' Edmund went on, 'I am a simple doctor but maybe you yourself have the rare power that only occurs once every millennium to perform a miracle. Jesus did this, Mohammed, the saints...I could show you the method with which you can see again, despite the fact your eyes have been damaged by mustard gas. With your symptoms, an ordinary person would be blind for life. But for a person with exceptional strength of will-power and spiritual energy there are no limits, scientific assumptions do not apply to that person, the spirit removes any such barrier - in your case the thick white layer in your cornea. But maybe you do not possess this power to perform miracles.'

'How can I tell?'

'Do you trust yourself to my will-power?' Forster demanded. Then, before Hitler could reply, ordered him to open his eyes wide, 'I will light my candle with a match. Did you see the sparks?'

'I don't know,' Hitler responded uncertainly, 'not a light but a kind of white, round shimmer.'

'You must have absolute faith in yourself then you will stop being blind,' Forster told him. 'You know that Germany now needs people who have energy and faith in themselves.'

'I know that.' Hitler stood up trembling and held on to the edge of the table.

'Listen. I have two candles here, one on the left and one on the right. You must see! Do you see them?'

'I am beginning to see,' he said, 'if only it was possible!'

'For you anything is possible! God will help you, if you help yourself! In every human being is a part of God. That is the will, the energy! Gather all your strength. More, more, more! Good! Now it is enough! What do you see now?'

There was a long pause before Hitler answered hesitantly, 'I see your face... your hand and the signet ring, your white coat, the newspaper on the table and the notes about me.'

'Sit down,' Forster told him, 'and take a rest. You have been cured. You have made yourself see. You behaved like a man. You managed to put light into your eyes because of your will-power.' Forster rose and walked around the room. Hitler followed him with his eyes just as a person with normal vision would. He looked at the table and tried to decipher the doctor's notes.

Instructing Hitler to lie on his examination table, he pushed back the locks of hair falling onto his forehead, stroked his damp, cold forehead and suggested to him, without a word, looking steadily in his eyes, that he closed his eyes and not open them again until the next morning.

Later he wrote, 'Everything happened as I wanted it to. I had played fate, played God and restored sight and sleep to a blind insomniac.'[15]

Edmund Forster felt professionally satisfied by the successful outcome of his unorthodox treatment. What he failed to appreciate was that in restoring Hitler's sight, he had implanted in his brain the conviction he had been chosen by destiny for some special mission. By failing to remove the hypnotic suggestion he had firmly planted in the lance-corporal's mind, Hitler would believe that every step he took from then on was dictated by supernatural power.

'Unless I have incorruptible conviction... I do nothing,' he once explained to his colleagues, 'I will not act; I will wait, no matter what happens. But if the voice speaks, then I know the time has come to act.'

The Eyewitness – Fact or Fiction?
The exchange between Hitler and Forster is taken from *The Eyewitness (Der Augenzeuge)* by Czech-born novelist Ernst Weiß. Written in 1938 but only published in the early sixties, the book was marketed as a work of fiction. There are,

however, good reasons for believing the hypnotic treatment described is taken from Hitler's medical notes. These were written up by Edmund Forster immediately after he had restored the lance-corporal's sight. In the absence of the original notes, which if they survived are most likely hidden away in some Swiss bank vault, we can only speculate on the similarity between them and the novel. Those parts of the book which can be compared to actual events, however, match perfectly.

Weiß's patient is described as 'a corporal of the Bavarian regiment, called A.H. He is being treated for hysterical blindness at a clinic named P.' An Austrian, whose father was a customs official, with a bitter hatred for the Jews. Before the War, he had been 'a poor student of art in Vienna' who was rejected by the Academy because they regarded him as 'an amateur who would be out of place in a painting class.' After failing to gain admittance, A.H. wandered the streets of the Austrian capital as a vagrant. 'Sometimes a good-hearted fellow vagabond gave him a few kreuzers or a fourth of a loaf of bread. There were many of these homeless vagrants who lived at night in deserted channels of the Vienna river under the earth.' After the war he would bring about 'massive changes and immeasurable suffering in Europe.'

The psychiatrist narrating the story is, in the words of historian Rudolph Binion, 'Pure Forster in everything germane to Forster's encounter with Hitler.' An innovator in brain surgery, he considers hysteria to be an all-out simulation that fools the simulator himself.[16] Of A.H. he remarks, 'In his lying he believed he was telling the truth. These hysterics talk of their love of country and their courage until they are carried away with themselves like the actor who, in playing Hamlet, takes himself for the Prince of

Denmark.'

Like Forster, Weiß's psychiatrist narrator was born in Munich, practises medicine on the Western Front, serves in a military hospital and earns the Iron Cross, First Class. The reader learns A.H. has been gassed by an English grenade causing his eyes to burn 'like glowing coals'. He is immediately sent for treatment, although 'not in one of the field hospitals with others who had been gassed, whose eyes had been seriously damaged by poison gas, mustard gas and chlorine gas, but he was among the emotionally disturbed.'

To determine the truth or falsity of the book's description of Hitler's treatment, we need to prove that:

(1) Hitler's blindness was due to hysteria rather than mustard gas.

(2) He was treated by Edmund Forster.

(3) Hypnosis was used to restore his sight.

What Gas Was Used?

As I explained in Chapter 8, while Hitler and his companions were undoubtedly victims of a gas attack on the morning of October 15th, the symptoms described by Ignaz Westenkirchner and the speed of their onset strongly suggest it was not mustard gas but White Star.

Comprising a mixture of phosgene and chlorine, the British Army dubbed it a 'workhorse gas' and used it in great quantities. Provided exposure was limited, any blindness it caused through swelling of the eyelids and profuse lachrymation would be only temporary and easily treated.

Yet, according to Westenkirchner's account, while the other soldiers went for treatment to a hospital outside Brussels, Hitler was transported hundreds of miles to the nerve clinic at Pasewalk. The doctors at Oudenaarde had no choice but to transfer him to a clinic specialising in nervous disorders once they had diagnosed his blindness was due to hysteria.

The second possibility is that while there was a gas attack that morning, we know this from the large number of other German casualties, Hitler was not directly affected. As I explained earlier, thousands of other soldiers became blind merely because they smelled gas or were told their units had been exposed to gas. Hitler may well have been among them.

Was Hitler Treated by Forster?

The identification of Edmund Forster as the neuropsychiatrist who treated Hitler at Pasewalk in 1918 became public knowledge with the declassification, in 1972, of a report prepared for US Naval Intelligence, in 1943, by Karl Kroner, the doctor who had first treated him at Pasewalk.

Entitled *Adolf Hitler's Blindness (A psychological Study)*, the full report states the following:

'When the first World War came to an end Private (*sic*) Adolf Hitler, as he then was, was not at the front. He was in a military hospital in the small town of Pasewalk in Pomerania.

According to the version given in the Nasi (*sic*) literature of the 1920's, he had gone blind as a result of gas-poisoning. We are not told however, how long he remained in hospital after the armistice. It cannot have been long, for soon after he turned up in Munich, where he was employed as a sort of spy of the military league, to report to them the activities of the working–class political movement. We are also not told what after effects, if any, on his eyesight were left behind by the blindness.

This is remarkable, for, as everybody knows, blindness is not normally cured without a trace. Nothing is known, however, of any permanent after-effects, in Hitler's case. In the numerous photographs which we have of him he always has the same studied, hypnotic stare, which is familiar to us from his prototype, Mussolini. There is no recorded example of gas-poisoning having had so favourable an outcome…Professor Forster, at that time Head Doctor at the Berlin University Nerve Clinic and consultant neurologist to the military hospital at Pasewalk, declared Adolf Hitler to be a psychopath with hysterical symptoms. This became known, in spite of all subsequent efforts to hush it up. It became apparent at an early period that Adolf Hitler comes into this category…His blindness was cured. But Germany became blind so blind that she chose him to be chancellor.

Then, in 1933, came the tragic ending to the story. Naturally it was important that it should not become known, what a pitiful part Private Adolf Hitler had played in the hospital at Pasewalk, and what the diagnosis of his illness had been. The story of this episode was hushed up by the well-known methods: already, from about the beginning of the 1930's, no further mention had been made of it. But this alone was not enough; the still surviving witnesses of the incident must be silenced. This was simplest in the case of Hitler's former company Sergeant-Major Amman. He was bought, being appointed by Hitler's business manager of the entire German press. Through this position Herr Amman had acquired a large fortune by highly disreputable methods. He is today a millionaire many times over.

Forster (sic) had, meanwhile, become head of the Faculty of Medicine of Greifswald University, and was not a man who could be bought. He had therefore to be silenced by other means. Shortly after Hitler came to power, Professor

Forster suddenly died. The cause of death was given as suicide. At the time doubts were felt, and these have grown to certainty, Professor Forster a man of excellent health. In the best years of his life, cheerful and successful in his career. Nothing, even the most trivial kind, was known which could have driven him to suicide. In short, there can be no doubt to the mind of anyone well acquainted with Nazi methods that Professor Forster was murdered and that the supposed suicide was a carefully arranged deception.'[17]

Did Forster Use Hypnosis?

Forster's preferred method of treatment was to exert his authority as an officer and forceful personality to bully patients out of their condition. The extent to which this succeeded cannot now be known, although the opinion of his colleagues – many of whom disapproved of his methods – was that the approach often succeeded. With Hitler, however, he was faced with a very different situation.

His observations of the patient would have confirmed that, far from being a malingerer, the lance-corporal was eager to return to the Front. Hitler's strength, as Forster would have seen it, was his fierce Nationalism. He would also have known from his years of treating hysterics they make especially good subjects for hypnosis, going into a trance quickly and following the hypnotist's instructions readily. They are especially susceptible to what is called 'waking hypnosis' in which the individual never closes their eyes and remains conscious of all that is happening but, at the same time, is unable to resist the hypnotist's suggestions.

In one of his colourful metaphorical analogies, the pioneering American hypnotherapist Milton Erickson described how as a teenager he came across a lost horse. Erickson clambered onto its back and returned it to the delighted owner, who was curious as to how he had known the address.

'I didn't know,' Erickson replied, 'but the horse did. All I had to do was keep his attention on the road.'[18]

The story illustrates the basis of what is called 'client-centred' therapy. The person undergoing treatment has the expertise and resources necessary to cure their condition. In Hitler's case, these were his readiness to follow orders, subservience to those in authority and intense Nationalism. Edmund's task was to use these to overcome of psychological trauma that had blinded him.

Dr Sandor Ferenczi, a Hungarian psychiatrist who worked with Sigmund Freud, distinguished between what he called 'mother' and 'father' hypnosis. The former involved gentle persuasion while in the latter, the hypnotist makes suggestions in a brisk and authoritative manner.[19] The script Weiß provides is very much in the 'father' mode and in keeping with everything we know about Edmund's domineering personality. It is also especially suitable when used with people, such as soldiers, trained to obey orders immediately and without question.

Some refuse to accept hypnosis was used because they mistakenly associate it with sleep, swinging pendulums and commands by the hypnotist to 'look into my eyes'. While this may still happen on the stage, it is far from the approach taken by research and medical hypnotists like myself. We see the key to hypnotism as based not on coercion but suggestion.

Firm authoritative statements and repetitions can be used to mould an individual's attitudes, beliefs and behaviour. Suggestions can also be used less indirectly, by insinuations, casual remarks, hints and verbal nudges. Finally, they can be implanted in the minds of others through associations with objects or situations. On occasions, all three may be used, especially when the intention is to hypnotised large groups of people. According to Weiß, Forster used his authority as a doctor and officer to impose his will on Hitler while also making use of medical items, his Ophthalmoscope and white coat to emphasise the clinical nature of his treatment.

Like many novelists, Weiß regularly wove factual events and real people into his narratives.[20] During a holiday in Lyons-la-Fôret in the summer of 1937, for example, he had met two Austrian women who told him a touching anecdote about a child. A few months later, when writing his novel *Verführer* (Seducer), Weiß recounted this story, word for word, as well as describing many other details and individuals from the holiday.

Individually, each piece of evidence might appear suggestive rather than persuasive. Taken together, however, they seem to establish beyond a reasonable doubt both that Hitler's blindness was psychological rather than physical in origin and that Edmund Forster treated him for a hysterical disorder. It is entirely consistent with all that is known about Forster's approach to the condition. In the words of Dr Jürg Zutt, a colleague at the Charité, he 'took hysteria to be mostly humbug and treated hysterics accordingly.'[21]

If Weiß's medical qualifications had been in psychiatry, it would be reasonable to assume that he was describing his own method of treating hysterical disorders. But he was a surgeon and although he had worked for a short while with Freud, would have had little experience of dealing with the mentally ill and none of hypnosis, a treatment the founder of psychoanalysis was never able to master.

Weiß's Narrator's Fate

When the war ends, the narrator becomes a doctor in private

practice, marries a Jewess named Victoria and has two children. Once the Nazis come to power, he finds himself in grave danger. One night his father, a fanatical Nazi, calls with an urgent warning, 'He wasted no words. He told me he knew from the best sources that shortly there would be a thorough search of my house ...'You are supposed to have papers about the Führer? I can't believe it. You are much too intelligent to keep something compromising, and it would be madness to take them along to Switzerland, for you know very well that our arm reaches far'.'

Trusting his father's promise that Victoria and their two children will soon be able to join him, he flees to exile in Switzerland, taking A.H.'s medical records with him. For safety, he deposits these in the vault of a Berne bank. After his wife is arrested by the S.S., he returns to try to secure her release.

Arrested, he is sent to Dachau and brutally beaten. 'They had turned the whips around so that they could use the gristly end... they no longer struck only the upper part of my body but also my legs and the soles of my feet. There must have been fifty to sixty blows. I did not count them.'

An S.S. guard whose child's life he once saved tells him the electrified fence and perimeter lights will be turned off for five minutes during the night while the generator is serviced. Using this knowledge, he escapes and is reunited with his family in Switzerland. After recovering from the injuries inflicted by his torturers, they move to France and settle in Paris.

The Eyewitness is a fast-moving and compelling story. But should we regard it as a work of fiction or, as many now believe, a largely factual account taken from Hitler's highly confidential Pasewalk medical notes? A file which, after the Nazis seized power in 1933, became a State secret and execution the likely punishment for anyone foolish enough to have knowledge of it.

Stories that Hitler had experienced some form of 'divine revelation' were circulating in Germany long before the Nazis assumed power. On January 9th, 1923, for example, the *Münchner Post* published an article which described how after the war 'he lay injured in a military hospital. It is said he was stricken by a kind of blindness. And he was freed from this blindness by an inner ecstasy, which showed him the way to free the pan-German [*Grossdeutsche*] people from the materialistic enslavement by Marxism and capitalism. He, Hitler, sees it as his duty to free his people. The whole will of this man is determined by the belief in his Messianic mission.'

Hitler's 'Crucible' Experience

Hitler, although couching his experiences at Pasewalk in mystical terms, certainly saw his time in the *Lazarette* as a turning point in his life. In their seminal books on leadership, Warren Bennis and Robert Thomas claim that every leader passes through at least one intense, transformational experience they call a 'crucible'. For Hitler, his 'crucible' was the treatment he received from Edmund Forster at the Pasewalk *Lazarette* in November 1918.

'Leaders create meaning out of events and relationships that devastate non-leaders.' comment Bennis and Thomas, 'Even when battered by experience, leaders do not see themselves as helpless or find themselves paralysed. They look at the same events that unstring those less capable and fortunate and see something useful, and often a plan of action as well.'[22]

CHAPTER 10
THE WAYS OF THE WOLF

*It was on a dreary night of November that I beheld the wretch –
the miserable monster I had created...I saw the dull yellow eye of
the creature open; it breathed hard, and a convulsive motion
agitated its limbs.* - Mary Wollstonecraft Shelley, *Frankenstein*[1]

At 10.59 on the morning of November 11th, 1918, American
soldiers were approaching a German roadblock in the
village of Chaumont-devant-Damvillers in Lorrains. Against
the orders of his sergeant, Henry Gunther, a 23-year-old
private, charged the barricade with his bayonet. Knowing
the Armistice would come into effect in less than a minute,
the Germans held their fire and tried to wave him away. But
Gunther kept coming and was killed instantly by a burst
from their machine guns. Almost as his body hit the ground
the ceasefire came into effect. He was the last soldier from
any of the belligerent nations to be killed in action.[2]

As Germany collapsed in defeat, the Navy mutinied and revolution broke out. In Berlin, the government resigned, the King of Bavaria fled in panic and newly created 'Soviets' of workers and soldiers carrying placards that read 'Brother do not fire!' marched through the streets. Few soldiers did shoot and many of them joined the revolutionaries.

When news of the uprising reached Pasewalk, Hitler was plunged into hopeless despair, '...suddenly and unexpectedly, the calamity descended. Sailors arrived in trucks and proclaimed the revolution: a few Jewish youths were the 'leaders' in this struggle for the freedom, duty, and dignity' of our national existence. None of them had been at the front. By way of a so-called 'gonorrhoea hospital', the three Orientals had been sent back home from the second line base. Now they raise the red flag in the homeland.'[3]

For the next few days, Hitler cherished the hope that it might be no more than a local uprising, but when he heard that Wilhelm II had left the country he abandoned all hope and bitterly reflected on the sacrifices which had been made on the fronts, 'Was it for this that these boys of seventeen sank into the earth of Flanders.... Did all this happen only so that a gang of wretched criminals could lay hands on the fatherland? There followed terrible days and even worse nights - I knew that all was lost. Only fools, liars and criminals could hope in the mercy of the enemy. In these nights hatred grew in me, hatred for those responsible for this deed.'[4]

On November 18th, Hitler left Pasewalk making his way first to Berlin and then Munich where, as Ernst Schmidt, a former Front-Line comrade of Hitler later explained, 'Snow lay deep in the streets. Soldiers were streaming back into Munich still, from all the battle-fronts, weary, battered, disorientated men. Coming home to a foundered country where neither food, nor peace, nor work was to be had. There were thirty thousand unemployed hanging around the streets. Food grew scarcer and scarcer. The people ate anything they could lay their hands upon that was remotely eatable. A fallen horse was a godsend. Such a carcass was immediately pounced upon by the starving populace, and in quicker time than it takes to tell every shred of flesh was stripped from the bones.'[5]

Hitler was one of the fortunate ones, able to eat adequately every day in one of the Stehrestauranst or emergency feeding rooms. While the room was always packed and the food poorly cooked, a meal and a hot drink could be purchased for just a few Pfennigs.

Hitler Gets Arrested

Many ex-soldiers were organised into Freikorps, private armies of tough, disillusioned men who had lost everything in the war except their hate. During training sessions, they practised techniques of street fighting with which they hoped to defeat the Jewish-Bolshevik menace. Hitler was stationed at the infantry's Maximilian II barracks in Munich-Oberwiesenfeld when Freikorps troops arrived. Shots were fired from the building which was immediately stormed and all those inside killed or taken prisoner. Hitler, together with a group of other soldiers, was marched at gunpoint through the streets to the cellars of the Max Gymnasium which had been turned into a make-shift prison. His situation was now even more desperate than it had been as a front line soldier since the Freikorps guards were eager for slaughter. On the first day of imprisonment, one in ten of his companions were lined up against the wall and shot. His own execution would certainly have followed except for a stroke of good fortune which Hitler later attributed to further evidence of divine intervention.

An officer who had known him at the front was visiting the Gymnasium and secured his immediate release. He also offered him the chance to work for a Commission which had been established to investigate revolutionary activity in the 2nd Infantry Regiment.

Hitler Becomes a Spy

Hitler's task was to 'eradicate the last traces of poison which had led to the setting up of 'Soldiers' Councils', and abortive revolutionary measures of that sort.'[6] According to Ernst Schmidt, 'Hitler was especially fitted for this job on account of his political acumen, and because he was considered to be a good judge of men.'[7]

On September 12th, 1919, he was instructed to attend a meeting of a small political party which had been formed in March 1918 by a disgruntled splinter group of the extreme right-wing Thule Society, called 'The German Socialist Workers' Party'. Hitler's brief was to prepare a report on their aims so the authorities could decide if they posed any threat. The meeting was held in the Sterneckerbräu, one of Munich's smallest and shabbiest beer halls, later to be transformed into a Nazi shrine as the cradle of Nationalist Socialism. Hitler arrived in the small, wood-panelled back room just before the meeting was due to start. Dressed in civilian clothes, he gave his job as that of a writer and took a seat at the rear where he could watch the audience as much as the platform.

The Birth of the Nazi Party

Dietrich Eckart was a large, jovial Bohemian; a poet, playwright and journalist who drank heavily, injected himself with morphine regularly and was an active member of the Thule Society. At one stage in his life, Eckart had been a tramp in Berlin and was later confined to a lunatic asylum where he staged his plays using fellow inmates as actors. After the war, he returned to Munich and took cheap lodgings in the Schwabing district, a quarter much favoured by artists. Through his increasing literary reputation, Eckart made friends and contacts in all stratums of Munich society.

At the meeting Hitler attended, an audience of some forty-five shabbily-dressed men listened with indifference to a lengthy and tedious speech by Gottfried Feder, an instructor on the political course he had attended. Hitler was soon convinced the party posed no threat but stayed on to listen to the discussion from the floor. He had no intention of speaking, until a Professor Baumann stood up and argued that Bavaria should break away from Germany and link up with Austria. Hitler, the fanatical proponent of Pan-German nationalism could not remain silent while such heresy was being advocated. He jumped to his feet the moment Baumann had finished and attacked the Professor's theory with such vigour and so much withering sarcasm that Baumann hurried from the hall.

The meeting was declared closed not long after this and Hitler made to leave with the rest. At the door, he was stopped by Anton Drexler, one of the Party's founders, who handed him a pamphlet he had written entitled My Political Awakening.

A few months before meeting Hitler, Anton Drexler had expressed the hope that 'someone would turn up with go and grit in him, who could make something out of us ...contrive a real driving force behind us. It would need to be an outstanding personality, anyhow, who could even attempt to do such a thing, a man of intense conviction, single-eyed, and absolutely fearless. A genius such as we needed – such as Germany needed – only turns up once in the century… It was only in the hope that our little group might at least offer a starting point – sooner or later – for greater and more efficient things.'[8]

Hitler thrust the pamphlet into his overcoat pocket and trudged back to the barracks where he went straight to bed. Around dawn, he was awoken by the sound of mice eager for the bread crumbs it was his habit to put down for them each night. Unable to return to sleep he decided to read Drexler's pamphlet in the hope it might provide a basis for the report he would have to prepare in a few hours' time. In sixteen short chapters, Drexler set out his political views and thoughts on the Jewish conspiracy. Although the pamphlet brought together, for the first time, the words National and Socialism, what is far more likely to have caught Hitler's attention was Drexler's prayer that a new leader would emerge in this, Germany's most desperate hour of need.

Hitler Joins the Nazis

On September 16th, 1919, Hitler received a postcard announcing that he had been accepted, without asking, as Committee Member number 7, Party member number 555. This might sound impressive but for the fact the numbering started at 501. After some reflection, Hitler decided to take up an invitation to attend a meeting of the executive committee to be held in a back room of the Altes Rosenbad, a shabby beer hall in the Herrenstrasse.

Four men sat at a paper-strewn table under the guttering light of a gas flame burning in a broken gas mantle. The German Workers' Party had 54 members, no offices, no employees, no printed letterheads and not even a rubber stamp to its name. Its entire property consisted of an old briefcase in which they kept correspondence and a battered cigar box containing the Party's funds of 7 marks.

But it was this very obscurity, as Hitler later acknowledged, that most attracted him. 'Only in a Party which, like himself, was beginning at the bottom that he had any prospect of playing a leading part and imposing his ideas,' points out historian Allan Bullock. 'In the established Parties, there was no room for him, he would be a nobody.'[9]

Given his interest in folk history, it is likely Hitler had heard the legend of a 15th-century German shepherd boy who possessed a remarkable gift for oratory. He became known as the Trommler (Drummer) because of the insistent and compelling drumbeat of his words. Instinctively, the Trommler knew how to exploit the bitterness of the downtrodden and impoverished. Everywhere he went, peasants and artisans flocked to hear him attack established authority and preach a fierce gospel of violent rebellion. He claimed to have been sent by God to guide, comfort and lead them out of the darkness and into the light. Before long, his fame was such that he provoked mass hysteria wherever he appeared and guards were needed to protect him from the enthusiasm of his own followers. His clothes became sacred relics and his hometown of Niklashausen, in the Tauber valley a place of pilgrimage for his supporters.

In 1476, determined to put an end to such a powerful and dangerous influence, the ruling princes sent their armies against him. Captured, an ecclesiastical court sentenced him to death on charges of sorcery and heresy. After being burned at the stake his ashes were scattered in the River Tauber to prevent his grave from becoming a shrine. Before he died, the Trommler prophesied that when his nation's despair was greatest, another such as he would emerge from the masses and lead his nation to glory by giving voice to the secret yearnings of the ordinary German people. It was a folk tale with powerful emotional appeal for a fervent nationalist such as Adolf Hitler.

Within a few weeks of attending his first meeting, he came to realise that this insignificant little party might become a 'drum' on which to pound out his political messages to the nation. But he also recognised that for this to happen he must first browbeat his cautious and unambitious fellow committee members into transforming and invigorating the moribund organisation. His first success came when after hours of heated negotiations, he persuaded them to spend money on three rubber stamps and agree that invitations to meetings should be hectographed (an early form of photocopying).

'Imagine that thundering voice, demanding three rubber stamps,' exclaims Konrad Heiden, 'And the speeches on behalf of hectographed invitations!'[10]

The Nazi Manifesto

Seated around the kitchen table in Drexler's poky apartment, Hitler, Anton Drexler, Gottfried Feder and Dietrich Eckart agreed the party's new manifesto should have twenty-five points. These included the confiscation of all war profits, the unification of Germany, rejection of the Treaty of Versailles, the expulsion of foreigners and the abolition of unearned income. Above all, their manifesto declared open war on 'those who work to the injury of the common welfare. Traitors, usurers, profiteers etc. are to be punished with death, regardless of race and creed.'[11] Later, when nervous industrialists and other potential financial backers referred to these demands, Hitler was able to reassure them that Germans need have no fears for their fortunes. His target was solely the capital of Germany's single greatest foe – international Jewry.

Hitler, whom the committee had placed in charge of propaganda, set about publicising the Party's meetings, expending some of their meagre funds on newspaper advertisements. Attendance started to rise and, in October 1920, Hitler addressed 111 people in the Hofbräuhaus Keller, his largest audience to date. It was an abject failure. Anxiety and his lack of public speaking experience left him floundering at the mercy of an increasingly hostile and restive audience. There was heckling from the crowd he seemed unable to deal with and his tongue-tied incompetence led even Party loyalists to the opinion that he had no talent for public speaking.

After such humiliation, anyone less assured of his destiny might well have retreated from the limelight and left the ordeal of addressing large crowds to others. Later, he received practical help and advice from Eric Hanussen, a 32-year-old showman, hypnotist, clairvoyant and self-styled Danish aristocrat. Hitler also learned his lesson about the need to control hecklers, if not by his powers of persuasion from the platform then by 'supporters' who would club down anyone who dared raise objections.

In July 1921, after being made leader of the renamed National Socialist German Worker's Party (NSDAP), Hitler reorganised these toughs who were more motivated by the hope of a good fight and free beer than by political considerations into a disciplined fighting group. Led by his former boss, Captain Karl Mayr, they were called the Party's 'Gymnastics and Sports Division'.

A recruiting pamphlet proclaimed their purpose was to 'embody and propagate the military idea of a free nation. It will instil a boundless desire for action in the hearts of our young members, hammer and burn into their brains that history does not make men, but men history.'[12]

In the early years of the movement, Hitler needed all the protection he could get, for his meetings usually degenerated into uproar and riot. The prospect of violence never deterred Hitler from speaking. In fact, he enjoyed the spectacle of flying beer-mugs, overturned tables and bloodied heads. When the battle was over and his men had finally ejected his political opponents into the night, he would cheerfully resume his speech amongst the litter of broken furniture and smashed tankards.

A regular member of his audience in those days was Frau Magdalena Schweyer, who ran a grocery store across the street from Hitler's new lodgings on the second floor of a modest house at 41 Thierschstrasse, where he had moved after leaving the army in March 1921.

Frau Schweyer retained vivid memories of a meeting on 4 November 1921, 'A real battle that was. If I hadn't kept my head low over the table that night and folded my arms above it, like all the rest of us women were told to do, sure as fate it would have been knocked clean off my shoulders. We womenfolk were told to get well up in front: it would be safest there far from the doors.... Hitler had been speaking for some time when the sign was given. Someone shouted Freiheit (the Marxist battle cry - Liberty) and a beer pot went crash! That was the signal for things to begin.

Three, four, five heavy pots flew by within an inch of the speaker's head, the next instant his young guards sprang forward shouting to us women to 'Duck down'. Pandemonium had broken out.

One heard nothing but yells, crashing beer mugs, stamping and struggling, the overturning of heavy oaken tables and the smashing of wooden chairs. Hitler stuck to his post. Never got off that table. He made no effort to shield himself at all. He was the target of it all: it's a sheer miracle how he never got hit .... The room was simply wrecked. There were over four hundred smashed beer mugs lying about everywhere and piles of broken chairs.'[13]

As his confidence grew, Hitler set about organising the Party's most ambitious meeting to date. This was to be held not in the confines of the Hofbräuhaus beer cellar but in its vast and echoing Festsaal (Festival Hall). On Tuesday February 24th, 1920, Hitler rose to face an audience of around two thousand people, a significant proportion of whom had come to make trouble.

'We ourselves were horrified at our boldness,' he recalled later. 'Would one of us be able to speak in this hall? Would he get stage-fright and start to stammer after the tenth sentence, and be shouted and whistled down?'[14]

The meeting started inauspiciously with a turgid address by Johannes Dingfelder, a homoeopathic physician. The crowd, who had expected something more radical and arousing, grew restless so by the time Hitler rose to speak their mood ranged from amused contempt to undisguised hostility. It was a challenge that would either confirm his divinely ordained mission or reveal it as hollow. Even before he started speaking, there were shouts of derision, whistles and yells. Within ten minutes, interruptions were coming from all sides of the vast hall. There was, he later alleged, so much intimidation that his supporters occasionally had to intervene in order to enable him to continue speaking. A few of them, he conceded, were armed – which is putting it mildly. The Munich District Army Command had sent along a troop of Reichswehr soldiers (according to some sources a company of mine-throwers) to drive opponents from the meeting using whatever means they chose, including cold steel.

Once the political opponents had been driven from the

Festsaal, Hitler yelled at the crowd, 'If anyone else dares, let him speak up against the programme!' No one did and the crowd, while undoubtedly terrorised by the violence used to eject the hecklers, was captivated by what was happening on the platform.

'Vehemence, passion and fanaticism,' Hitler wrote in 1923, 'the great magnetic forces which alone attract the great masses; for these masses always respond to the compelling force which emanates from absolute faith in the ideas put forward, combined with an indomitable zest to fight for and defend them.'[15]

At that meeting, the first mass gathering the Nazis had ever organised, the power and passion of Hitler's oratory were such that many of those present felt they were witnessing less the delivery of a familiar political message than the unleashing of some primordial force. It was akin to an elemental power capable of sweeping away rational arguments and intellectual objections with the same ruthless efficiency that the party's bully-boys employed when cleansing the hall of their opponents. Even educated Germans who before hearing him speak had dismissed Hitler as a slightly absurd and hysterical rabble-rouser often found themselves persuaded by the sheer force of his passionate self-belief.

After attending a meeting in 1922, Kurt Ludecke, gambler, businessman and adventurer, reported, 'When the man stepped forward on the platform, there was almost no applause. He stood silent for a moment. Then he began to speak quietly and ingratiatingly at first. Before long his voice had risen to a hoarse shriek that gave an extraordinary effect of an intensity of feeling. There were many high-pitched rasping notes... but despite its strident tone, his diction had a distinctly Austrian turn, softer and more pleasant than the

German. Critically I studied this slight, pale man, his dark brown hair parted on one side and falling again and again over his sweating brow. Threatening and beseeching, with small, pleading hands and flaming, steel-blue eyes, he had the look of the fanatic. Presently my critical faculty was swept away. Leaning from the tribune as if he were trying to impel his inner self into the consciousness of all these thousands, he was holding the masses, and me with them, under a hypnotic spell by the sheer force of his conviction.'[16]

Numerous reports of the rallies of this period corroborate Ludecke's testimony. Hitler's belief in himself and his divine purpose was absolute and his passionate oratory had the power to communicate that conviction to others. 'In the Volkischer Beobachter [the Nazi Party's newspaper] text these speeches stand before us in all their freshness,' says Konrad Heiden. At each meeting, a reporter would minute the speech before taking his copy to the 'print shop that very night, charged with all the power, the hatred, the self-reliance, the factual and grammatical mistakes of an agitated hour.'[17]

By the time Hitler had finished addressing that crowd in the Festsaal of the Hofbräuhaus, he had not only convinced the majority of those who had heard him of his unique abilities as an orator but had even impressed himself with his performance. 'When I finally closed the meeting,' he wrote later, 'we were not alone in feeling that a wolf had been born which was destined to break into the herd of swindlers and misleaders of the people.'[18]

The Growth of Nazi Power

By 1922, although few outside Germany had heard of it, the NSDAP had become a rising force in Bavarian politics. Hitler was proving himself a skilled propagandist who exerted his influence over every detail of the movement's development. When it was decided that the Party needed a flag he turned his artistic talents towards designing one, making scores of drawings before he was satisfied with the balance of colour on the banner. Against a blood-red field, a black swastika adopted from the emblem of the Thule Society stood boldly on a white circle. It was dramatic and eye-catching, full of energy and latent violence.

So too were the posters which Hitler designed to announce the Party meetings. Like the banner, they were calculated to stun the senses and arouse emotion rather than make any real appeal to common-sense. As propagandists, the Nazis are, perhaps, best known for Goebbels's remark that if you are going to tell a lie you must tell a big one. But, in reality, his techniques of persuasion were far more subtle and pervasive than this rather crude statement suggests. In 1931, he told a journalist, 'Propaganda is a matter of emotions, German emotions, and of unshakeable faith in a future for Germany.'

After some searching, the Nazis eventually found a room within their limited financial means. A drab, vaulted hall in a beer house on the Serneckergasse; a once lavishly-panelled room that had been used as a council chamber. When the NSDAP moved their few sticks of cheap furniture in, those elegant days were long gone. It was draughty, dirty and so dark that the gas light had to be kept burning even on summer days. Hitler had the room hung with Nazi banners but even these gaudy drapes trailing down the damp stonework could do little to relieve the gloom.

Their landlord allowed them to use two old sideboards for storing pamphlets. These, plus an ancient desk and a few chairs were the only furnishings. As funds came in, the office became better equipped and Hitler no longer had to scrounge a typewriter from the List barrack office. In November 1923, the Party moved again, this time to former shop premises in the working-class Corneliusstrasse. Here, they had window space for their posters and a large room where members could pay their dues and prospective members fill in the application forms, as well as two small rooms, one of which served as Hitler's office.

Although progress was slow, the Party was gathering momentum and expanding across Germany, with Hitler travelling as far north as Berlin to rally support. The swift expansion of the movement brought disunity within the ranks and there were many who grumbled at the way Hitler was leading them. But his hold on the Party was still secure for both they and he knew that without his oratorical ability, the NSDAP would be neither more nor less successful than a dozen other right-wing Bavarian political groups.

Every meeting was stage-managed as political show business. He would enter the hall only after the crowd had been marshalled into their seats and kept waiting just long enough for them to become expectant without growing impatient. Then he would stride down the centre of the hall, flanked by his bodyguards, looking neither to the left or the right. His speech concluded, he would immediately and abruptly depart; no period of discussion or questions from the floor. His message was not open to question. His statements were not to be discussed, merely accepted or rejected.

Hitler's Female Followers

Hitler was well aware of his power over women and their value to the Party. In 1923, he told his friend Ernst 'Putzi' Hanfstaengl, 'Do you know the audience at a circus is just like a woman? Someone who does not understand the intrinsically feminine character of the masses will never be an effective speaker. Ask yourself: what does a woman expect from a man? Clearness, decision, power and action. What we want is to get the masses to act. Like a woman the masses fluctuate between extremes. The crowd is not only like a woman, but women constitute the most important element in an audience. The women usually lead, then follow the children, and at last, when I have already won over the whole family, follow the fathers.'[19]

The brutal directness of Hitler's speeches proved of great attraction to women who made up a large proportion of Hitler's audiences. 'Women hung eagerly on every word of his speeches,' comments the German writer Hans Bleuel. 'It was sexual excitement which he knew how to kindle, especially among his female listeners, just as it was an erotic affinity with all the elements of passion and ecstasy which characterised his relationship with the masses – whom he in any case identified with womankind.'[20]

Emil Maurice, his chauffeur, recalled how teenage girls would try and hurl themselves under his Mercedes in the hope of being injured and attracting his attention. His fan mail, which came largely from women, included locks of hair, photographs, proposals of marriage and pleas that he should be the man to take their virginity. Often these letters were sent with gifts ranging from works of art to hand-embroidered cushions inscribed with such slogans as 'eternal devotion'. Doctors reported that female patients frequently invoked his name just before they were anaesthetised for an operation while others cried 'Heil Hitler' as they gave birth and insisted their newly born infants immediately be held up to a picture of the Führer.

Wealthy ladies contributed lavishly to the funds of the financially strapped Nazis. They not only persuaded their husbands to make direct payments to the party coffers, but gave Hitler jewellery and object d'arts worth millions of Marks as tokens of their affection. Among them was Frau Helene Bechstein, wife of the millionaire piano manufacturer. Not only were the Bechsteins early and generous financial contributors to the Party but they also helped the Nazi cause by introducing Hitler to potential patrons. Otto Strasser describes her relationship with Hitler as 'an ecstatic and faintly maternal devotion' and relates how 'when they were alone or occasionally in front of friends, he would sit at his hostess's feet, lay his head on her opulent bosom and close his eyes while her beautiful white hand caressed her big baby's head, ruffling the historic forelock on the future dictator's brow 'Wölfchen' ('wolf cub') she murmured tenderly 'mein Wölfchen.'[21]

Carl Bechstein's Mercedes was also used to transport illicit arms, ammunition and explosives for the S.A. – Hitler judging correctly that Munich police would never dare to stop and search such an opulent limousine. Not that such shipments were without their risks. Bechstein's chauffeur was an erratic driver and Hitler was terrified he would have an accident and blow them all to pieces. The piano millionaire explained they had to use him since the man was too stupid to ask questions or even understand what was going on, 'If he runs into another car it cannot be helped; up in the air we'll go.'

In public, Hitler could be foul-mouthed and abusive to those of either sex who opposed his political views, 'I dealt with the women from the Marxist camp who took part in the discussion by making them look ridiculous, by drawing attention either to the holes in their stockings or to the fact that their children were filthy. To convince women by reasoned argument is always impossible; to have them roughly handled by the ushers of the meeting would have aroused public indignation, so our best plan was to have recourse to ridicule, and this achieved excellent results.'[22]

Women who were granted a personal interview invariably came away enchanted. After meeting him for the first time, Madame Titayna, a journalist from Paris Soir told her readers breathlessly, 'The Führer comes to greet me with outstretched hand. I am surprised and astonished by the blue of his eyes... the face that brims with intelligence and energy and lights up when he speaks. At this moment, I comprehend the magical influence wielded by this leader of men and his power over the masses.'[23]

In 1932, Guida Dichl, founder of Neulandbund, a Nazi organisation for women, echoed the sentiments of many early female supporters of National Socialism when she announced, 'And so the Führer stands before us: upright, honest, thoroughgoing, God-fearing and heroic – a truly German man of the kind we women yearn for and demand in the Fatherland's hour of direst need.'[24]

The Munich Putsch

At 6.30am on November 8th, 1923, Hitler committed one of the gravest blunders of his career. He decided to seize power through a 'putsch' or armed uprising against the State. It was an ill-considered and ill-timed revolt which never had a chance of succeeding. But, at that moment, Hitler was confident he could emulate the astonishing success Mussolini had enjoyed when he marched on Rome at the head of his black-shirted army in October of the previous year and so intimidated the monarch he surrendered without a shot being fired.

What triggered his decision to strike was news that Gustav Ritter von Kahr, a monarchist who headed the

Bavarian government, had called a meeting for 3,000 officials of the government in the Bürgerbräukeller in the Rosenheimerstrasse. Hitler wrongly suspected that Kahr intended to announce the separation of Bavaria from the rest of Germany and the restoration of the monarchy. He determined to pre-empt this treachery by a revolution of his own. It was a revolt which began with the stark drama of a Hollywood movie, moving swiftly from the melodramatic to the farcical and ending in tragedy.

When Kahr rose to speak at 8.30pm, the beer hall was filled with dignified civil servants in tailcoats and top hats. But before the speaker could utter more than a few words, there was a commotion in the street outside. Hitler had roared up in a bright red Mercedes Benz tourer flanked by his bodyguards. Wearing a tailcoat and brandishing a revolver he stormed into the building surrounded by steel-helmeted Brownshirts, some of them carrying sub-machine guns. As his men spread out around the room, Hitler jumped onto the platform and fired two shots into the ceiling bringing down several chunks of plaster.

'The National Revolution has begun,' he screamed. 'The hall is surrounded by six hundred heavily armed men and no-one may leave. The Bavarian Government and the Reich Government have been deposed and a provisional Reich Government will be formed.' Kahr allowed himself to be hustled into a back room, where Hitler, putting the pistol to his own head, screamed, 'If I am not victorious by tomorrow afternoon, I shall be a dead man!'[25]

Returning to the main hall, he removed his trench coat to reveal a shoddy black tailcoat, which, one witness later observed, made him look like a bridegroom at a provincial wedding. 'I want now to fulfil the vow I made to myself five years ago when I was a blind cripple in a military hospital,' he told the bemused officials, 'to know neither rest nor peace until... there should have arisen once more a Germany of power and greatness.'[26]

Believing he was well on the way to victory, Hitler spent the remainder of the night racing around Munich in his Mercedes making speeches. Meanwhile, Röhm had taken over the war ministry and set up barricades.

The following day was bleak, with leaden skies and flurries of snow. Soon after 11am, Hitler, together with Göring, Hess and General Ludendorff began to march through the streets towards the war ministry with the intention of relieving Röhm. Their first obstacle was a line of armed police who had stationed themselves across the Ludwig bridge which spans the River Isar. They called on the marchers to halt but Hitler and Ludendorff ignored them. Apparently unnerved by the appearance of the General in their gun sights, the police lowered their weapons and allowed the procession of some three thousand, many armed, to pass. The route to the war ministry took them down a narrow street flanked by high, stone buildings leading to the Odeonsplatz and the Feldherrnhalle. Hitler was at the head of the marchers with two men carrying Nazi banners. In his right hand he clutched a pistol; if the Putsch failed he had sworn to kill himself.

Singing confidently, the procession funnelled into the street. Across its end was a line of one hundred policemen armed with sub-machine guns. For them, the situation was growing more dangerous with every moment that passed. Behind the front line of marchers, they could see cars carrying men with machine guns. Once the mass of humanity emerged from the confinement of the street, it would break like a flood tide into the vastness of the Odeonplatz.

If the procession was to be stopped, it had to be done before the first of the marchers emerged into the square. The police raised their weapons but the line came on unhesitatingly. Suddenly, a man broke from the lines and ran forward shouting, 'Do not shoot, his Excellency Ludendorff is coming.'

Hitler started calling, 'Surrender! Surrender!'

At that moment, Julius Streicher, the burly anti-Semitic rabble-rouser from Nuremberg, tried to snatch the carbine from a policeman. The next instant the narrow street became a charnel house. The police fired for about twenty seconds and the crowd returned fire. In that brief clash, sixteen of the marchers were killed together with three policemen. The policemen aimed low, intending to injure rather than kill, but their humane gesture had the opposite effect. Bullets tore into the granite cobbles and jagged pieces of stone ripped into the packed mob. The procession disintegrated in terror. Some people flung themselves through windows and into doorways to escape the flying lead and stones. Hitler had linked arms with the marcher on his left and now, either because this man was hit and fell or because his wartime instincts caused himself to fling himself down, he was hurled forward into the gutter with such force that he dislocated his shoulder. Göring was hit several times in the groin. In the confusion, Hitler managed to get free from the screaming people and drag himself to a side street where a yellow Fiat, driven by a Party doctor, was standing by with the engine running.

Hitler was taken to Hanfstaengl's house where his wife tended his injury. He was hysterical with fear and kept brandishing his revolver, threatening to blow his brains out if 'those swine' tried to take him. Frau Hanfstaengl hid him in the attic for three days. Then an informer, probably the

Hanfstaengl's gardener, tipped off the police who arrived in strength to take him away. By this time, Hitler had regained control of himself and instead of shooting it out he surrendered calmly.

His trial, and that of his fellow conspirators, began in the Infantry School on the Blütenburgstrasse on February 16th with the connivance of the Bavarian minister of justice, Dr Franz Gürnter, Hitler was allowed to make endless attacks on witnesses, air his political views and make a long speech in his defence from the dock. On March 29th, the judges handed down their verdicts. Ludendorff was freed immediately while Hitler received five years to be served in the fortress prison of Landsberg-am-Lech.

The German press responded angrily to the leniency of Hitler's sentence, with the Berliner Tageblatt of March 30th commenting under a headline declaring bankrupt justice, 'The verdict that was passed down today in the Infantry School in Munich and which exceeded the direst expectations of sceptical critics is tantamount to a declaration of bankruptcy of Bavarian justice. It is a verdict without example in a time when so many errors of justice are being committed daily in political trials... never before has a court more openly defied the foundation on which it rests, upon which every modern state is built.'

On April 2nd, the London Times commented if the trial had proved nothing else it had shown that plotting against the constitution of the Reich was not regarded as a serious offence in Bavaria. But the consensus among most foreign journalists was that the bungled Putsch had put an end to the brief and faintly comical career of a tiresome rabble-rouser.

Hitler in Landsberg Prison

For the first few weeks behind bars, Hitler appears to have shared this opinion. He refused to leave his cell and passed the time by reading and eating vast quantities of sweet cakes and cream pastries sent to the fortress by his female admirers. So many flowers, chocolates, books, wine and cakes were sent into the prison that a nearby cell had to be turned into a storeroom to house all his gifts. Within a few months, he had put on several pounds and the lean features of his post-war years were lost behind the plumper, more rounded profile that was to become familiar to millions.

Before long, Hitler regained his confidence and re-established himself as the Party leader. The National Socialists who had been imprisoned with him addressed him as the Führer. At meals, he sat at the head of the table and others stood to attention until he had taken his seat. During the day, he read or dictated his political biography Mein Kampf first to his chauffeur Emil Maurice and later to his second in command, Rudolf Hess.

Hitler and his fellow Nazis were initially viewed by the prison staff with nervous hostility who feared they would either attempt to escape or his followers would stage an armed assault to free him. Hitler used his charm to convert the wife of the fortress governor to Nazism and not long afterwards her husband became a Party member. After he came to power, Hitler rewarded the governor by putting him in charge of all of Germany's prisons. Many of the warders were also converted to National Socialism and would salute Hitler whenever they entered his cell.

While it had been a serious error of judgement, the Putsch meant that Hitler was no longer an obscure Bavarian politician. His name and face were known all over Germany and his future pronouncements and actions would be watched with interest by the press and public throughout

Europe.

After serving only nine months, Hitler was released on parole. Even in that short period, the Germany into which he emerged from the grey-stone fortress of Landsberg prison at ten o'clock on a drab and misty December morning five days before Christmas had become more prosperous and confident. It was increasingly a nation in which a majority of the population had lost interest in the extremes of both left and right politics and simply wanted to get on with their lives. Hitler was free, but in this less fevered political climate he knew it was going to be far harder to make the strident voice of National Socialism heard.

CHAPTER 11
BABYLON ON SPREE

In post-war Paris, a traveller could engage the services of a streetwalker for five or six dollars; but during the inflation in Berlin, five dollars could buy a months worth of carnal delights. -
Mel Gordon, Voluptuous Paris

In the early 1920's, Berlin was, for all but the very wealthy able to afford black market prices, a city of fakes. Men wore pink and blue dickies as substitutes for shirts; they smoked Havana-labelled cigars made from cabbage leaves steeped in nicotine; frostbitten potatoes passed for cakes; love too was faked – a commodity to be bartered simply in order to survive. More than 25,000 prostitutes, many preteen girls and high school boys, and approximately 10,000 pimps plied their trade in the city.[2] There were dozens of clubs, bars and cafes catering for any and every kind of sexual fantasy and desire. The majority, such as the Café Braun and the Heaven and Hell, were venues where men went to meet women of all ages, from sixteen to seventy. The Adonis-Lounge and the Cabaret of the Spider were exclusively for homosexuals; the Café Domino and the Mali and Ingel served the interests of lesbians; the Free Sunland and the Territory Adolf Koch were for nudists and the Eldorado and the Monocle for transvestites.

The desperate poverty and grinding misery under which most Germans struggled to live after 1918 was a direct consequence of the 1921 Reparations Act. Angered by the slowness with which the German's were fulfilling their obligations under the 1919 Versailles Treaty, British and French politicians stepped up their demands for compensation. Germany, they declared, must pay more than six billion marks in raw materials and industrial products. The result was economic catastrophe. In January 1921, a dollar was worth 7 marks. By August, the rate was 550 marks to the dollar; by May 1923, 54,300 per dollar. Six months later, one dollar was worth a staggering 4.2 billion marks. Pensioners and anyone on fixed incomes became destitute, those in work were seized by a desperate madness as they raced to exchange their vast, worthless wages for anything that might be bartered for something else. Millions of marks would be paid for shoes that didn't fit, unwanted clothes and trashy trinkets which only months earlier would have cost no more than loose change.

After giving a concert, the pianist Artur Schnabel had to ask a fellow musician to help him carry his fee home. Passing a delicatessen, he lightened their load by using half his earnings to purchase two sausages. By the following morning, he was unable to buy a single sausage with the other half.

The inevitable consequences were growing desperation,

rising inequality, widespread poverty and increasing starvation. A visitor shown around the children's ward of a Berlin hospital was told by the doctor, 'You think this is a kindergarten for the little ones. No, these are children of seven and eight years. Tiny faces, with large dull eyes, overshadowed by huge, puffed, rickety foreheads, their small arms just skin and bones, and above the crooked legs with their dislocated joints the swollen, pointed stomachs of the hunger oedema...this child consumed an incredible amount of bread, and yet he did not get any stronger. I found out that he hid all the bread he received under his straw mattress. The fear of hunger was so deeply rooted in the child that he collected the stores instead of eating the food: a misguided animal instinct made the dread of hunger worse than the actual pangs.'

Many middle-class families were compelled to take extreme and degrading steps simply to survive. Ilya Ehrenburg, a Russian writer visiting Berlin, was accosted one evening by a man offering to take him to an interesting night spot. 'We travelled by underground,' he recalled, 'and finally found ourselves in a respectable flat. On the walls hung portraits of members of the family in officer's uniform and a painting of a sunset. We were given champagne - lemonade laced with spirits. Then the host's two daughters appeared - naked - and began to dance. One of them talked . . . [about] Dostoevsky's novels. The mother hopefully eyed the foreign guests: perhaps they would be tempted by her daughters and would pay: in dollars, of course.'[3]

Journalist Michael Davidson describes how a senior official in a prominent international organisation kept an apartment in Berlin to pick up underaged boys. One morning the official was awoken by a ring of his front doorbell and found a neatly dressed man wearing a

Homburg hat and carrying a briefcase standing on his mat. 'I believe you're a friend of a boy named ---?' the man enquired before adding reassuringly. 'It's all right. I just came to call – I always like to know what sort of man my son is going with.'[4]

'Berlin found its outlet in the wildest dissipation imaginable,' wrote Netley Lucas in her 1927 book Ladies of the Underworld. 'The German is gross in his immorality, he likes his Halb-Welt or underworld pleasures to be devoid of any Kultur or refinement, he enjoys obscenity in a form which even the Parisian would not tolerate. The post-war young generation...spend their evenings in the many haunts of the Berlin Halb-Welt where they are able to satisfy their jaded appetites in whatever sensual debauchery or extravagance they wish for. Here are drugs, women, obscene films, cruel sports at which animals are sacrificed wilfully, and the inevitable cafés and Bierkellers where one may see any night hosts of Berliners young and old, consuming large bocks and tankards of lager beer.'[5]

During this period, the fledgling Nazi Party was still too insignificant to exploit the social and financial chaos to the extent they would following the Wall Street crash of October 1929. The best they could do was ferment and participate in street fights, riots and strikes.

The violence, excitement, sleaze, danger, intrigue and financial opportunities offered by the city known throughout Europe as 'Babylon on the Spree' was the perfect milieu in which risk-taking entrepreneurs thrived and clairvoyants, astrologers and confidence tricksters flourished.

In 1930, one such person arrived to take advantage of all the city was able to offer. His name was Erik Jan Hanussen who claimed to be a clairvoyant Danish aristocrat. He was also an astrologer, hypnotist, newspaper tycoon, businessman and blackmailer. Within a few months of arriving in the capital, this Jewish psychic was helping to fund the Nazis and had become an adviser to Adolf Hitler.

CHAPTER 12
HITLER'S JEWISH PSYCHIC

The illusion of the supernatural must surround (the artist) in the eyes of his audience, which will be a thousand times more manageable when it has become a group of believers. With success comes self-confidence, and with self-confidence the power of persuasion itself. - Erik Hanussen, *A Primer for Telepathy*

Erik Jan Hanussen, who claimed to be a clairvoyant Danish aristocrat, was born Herschmann-Chaim Steinschneider in a Viennese jail cell on June 2nd, 1889. The same year as Hitler.

His mother, Julie, was the only daughter of Sami Cohen, a wealthy fur importer. His father, Siegfried, was a performer at the Theater am Wien who also doubled as a travelling salesman. Outraged that Julie had allowed herself to become pregnant by a lowly Schmierekomödiant, (grease-paint monkey), Sami had her arrested on trumped-up charges. Released and brought home by her penitent father, Julie and her baby spent only a few nights at the family house before she was lured away by Siegfried's charms. This time the break was final, Sami never spoke to or mentioned either his daughter or grandson again.

Details of Hanussen's early life remain obscure; the sole and generally unreliable source being his 1930 autobiography Meine Lebenslinie (My Lifeline).

'To call it self-aggrandising is an understatement,' comments author Richard Spence. 'If he is to be believed, his psychic powers first manifested in the womb, when he willed his unwed parents to marry.'[1]

Some parts do have the ring of truth, however, such as when he described the lawless nature of his neighbourhood. 'The Ottakring is in the northernmost north of Vienna and anyone who went there at night was advised to bring a machine gun! It contained the scum of Viennese criminals, such as the notorious 'Beer Hall gang', thugs who would attack anyone. Local innkeepers fearful of the violence they could inflict and the damage they would do, paid them protection money to stay away.'[2]

Even as a young child, Steinschneider claimed to have experienced premonitions. In his unreliable autobiography he describes how, aged three, he had run to the house of their landlord, a pharmacist, whose daughter, Erna, he often played with. 'As if directed by an invisible hand' he dragged her from bed and pulled her down behind a tombstone in the nearby cemetery. Moments later, the pharmacist's house exploded in flames.

At the age of fourteen, he ran away from home, allegedly with a forty-five-year-old actress from the Theater am Wien, to embark on a frequently precarious stage career. He travelled throughout Central Europe finding work in vaudeville and circuses as a glass eater, fire breather, sword swallower, lion tamer and acrobat. He performed with magicians, hypnotists, fortune-tellers and faith-healers, learning their secrets, inventing a few of his own and putting together a stage act based on mind reading and hypnotism. [3]

One of his more spectacular tricks involved a volunteer concealing some small item such as a needle or thimble anywhere in the theatre or even in a city. Lightly grasping the man's arm, or holding one end of a handkerchief while the man held the other, a blindfolded Hanussen would then instruct the volunteer which direction to take and, with little difficulty, discover the hidden article. For many in his audience, this was Hanussen's most astounding trick and the highlight of the show.

So how did he do it?

Lessons from Clever Hans

To understand the basis of this trick, which has subsequently been performed by scores of magicians and illusionists, we have to go back to the early-19th century and a horse called Clever Hans. Owned by Herr von Osten, the animal became famous for his amazing counting ability. Given a problem, for example, multiplying seven by five, Hans would provide the answer by tapping with his hoof until he reached the right answer, in this case 35, at which point he would stop. After carefully investigating horse and owner, scientists concluded no trickery was involved. Hans really could perform simple arithmetic. It took German biologist and psychologist Oskar Pfungst to solve the mystery.[3]

Careful observation revealed that van Osten's head and shoulders dropped slightly forward towards the horses counting foot when asking a question. As Clever Hans reached the correct number of taps, his master raised his head and shoulders by a minute amount. He was unconsciously signalling the horse when to start and stop tapping. Once he had identified the body language involved, Pfungst found he could make the animal give any answer he chose, no matter how absurd, merely by keeping his head down until Hans got to the selected number. The psychologist also showed that most of us produce these involuntary movements, although they can be very slight; no more than a millimetre in some cases. In one study, Pfungst asked twenty-five people of both sexes and all ages, including children aged only five, to think of a number between one and ten or one and a hundred. Taking the role of the horse, he would start tapping with his right hand, looking intently at the subject as he did so to spot the expected head jerk. [4]

'He found some sort of consistent head movement in all the subjects except two,' report psychologists David Marks and Richard Kammann. Both these were 'scientific men whose mode of thought was always the most abstract.'[5]

In another study, he asked his subjects to focus their attention on one of five pieces of paper fanned out before them. By observing the movements of their heads and eyes, Pfungst was able to identify the correct sheet on 82% of occasions.

Performing this trick requires a great deal of practice, preferably starting at an early age. In Hanussen's case, he probably started training his perceptual ability while still in his teens. As an adult performer, he was able to use changes in the body language of both the volunteer and the audience – who knew where the item was hidden – to guide him to the location. 'Our muscles speak a language that we don't even know we are capable of speaking,' comments author Arthur Magida. 'Often we know ourselves so poorly that others can figure out our intentions before they reach our own consciousness. For this reason, we are more at the mercy of people attuned to the subtleties of the human body then we would like.'[6]

Hanussen the Blackmailer

The man who would become a newspaper tycoon also tried his hand as a journalist when he took a job with Der Blitz, a Viennese scandal sheet. The tabloid earned a large proportion of its considerable income by uncovering the misdemeanours of prominent people and then blackmailing them into paying large sums of money not to have the stories published.[7]

During the First War, he was conscripted into the Austro-Hungarian Army and rose to the rank of sergeant. He used his 'mind reading' and clairvoyance skills to secure himself a comfortable billet safely behind the lines. During his act, he would 'reveal' intimate personal details about his fellow soldiers which convinced them he possessed psychic powers. The secret was rather more mundane – he had bribed the army censor to delay issuing letters from home until he had read them himself.[8]

In 1918, Hanussen returned to Vienna where he gradually gained fame from his demonstrations of clairvoyance and hypnotism. After playing a clairvoyant detective in Hypnose (Hypnosis), a low budget film, he augmented his income from show business by becoming a 'psychic' detective in real life.

Hanussen the Psychic Detective

Engaged by the Austrian State Bank to investigate the theft of newly printed banknotes, he used his 'clairvoyance' to deduce it must have been an inside job. Within a short while, he had identified the thieves and recovered most of the money.[9] While this coup brought valuable publicity, it did not endear him to the authorities who suspected him of having a hand in the theft.

Among the crimes he claimed to have solved, the most notorious was that of serial killer Peter Kurten. Between 1929 and 1930, this handsome, charming and dapper young man dubbed the Vampire of Düsseldorf by the press, brutally murdered sixty-eight girls and young women. One of his most horrendous killings occurred on August 23rd, 1920, when he approached two sisters as they were leaving the county fair. He asked one, 14-year-old Louise Lensen to get him some cigarettes while he 'looked after' her 5-year-old sister. As soon as the older girl was out of sight, Kurten strangled the little girl before slitting her throat with his pocket knife. When the older sister came back with his cigarettes, she too was strangled and then almost decapitated. Clearly a dangerous and highly deranged individual,[10] Kurten was finally captured in the summer of 1930 and although Erik claimed credit for tracking him down, the vampire's capture seems to have been mainly a matter of luck.

Hanussen the Arms Dealer

Growing weary of his antics, the Viennese authorities banned stage performances involving hypnotism and Hanussen was obliged to look elsewhere for his income. In the early 1920's, he teamed up with Hans Hauser, an Austrian tobacco tycoon to sell surplus military equipment to the Greeks for use in their war with Turkey. His role was to employ his powers of hypnosis to assist their negotiations and ensure they got the best possible deal. The British backed the Greeks and, as Richard Spence points out, 'It may be significant, that in the Balkan tobacco trade, Hauser almost certainly dealt with the Tobacco Company Ltd, a British firm which also happened to provide cover in Europe for S.I.S [MI6] agents and ex-employees of the secret service.'[11]

While Erik's time in the Levant and North Africa greatly increased his knowledge of Eastern mysticism, it also gave him further opportunities for solving crime. He claimed to have aided Egyptian police in combating a ring of hashish smugglers, although the suspicion remains that he may have been organizing the smuggling himself.

During his youth, Erik worked under a number of aliases including Siegfried Krakauer and Saul Absolom Herschwitter, none of which made any attempt to conceal his Jewish heritage. It was not until the age of thirty that he finally settled for Hanussen, also claiming to be a Danish aristocrat who had become a performer and psychic detective as a result of his clairvoyance and mind reading abilities.[12]

In 1924, he sailed for America and spent a few months performing but he found the audiences harder to impress with his 'psychic' abilities than those in Europe. Returning home, he added palmistry, graphology and astrology to his mind reading and clairvoyant performances and was soon topping the bills at major theatres.

In his act, the self-styled 'Wizard of the Ages' would ask members of the audience to pass handwritten questions to an assistant. Then, without looking at them, the 'Wizard' would describe their problems and offer answers. While he claimed this was due to his telepathic abilities, the truth was he used coded messages and stooges to baffle and amaze. One technique was to have his assistant palm a small sponge soaked in alcohol with which he or she would covertly wipe the back of the envelope containing the enquiry. This momentarily renders the paper transparent and enables the assistant to read the question which was then passed to Hanussen by means of a code.

Hanussen's increasing fame brought with it attention from the authorities who, disbelieving the existence of 'occult' powers accused him of being no more than a confidence trickster. In 1929, the prosecutor for the Czechoslovak town of Leitmeritz charged him with fraud and larceny. During the lengthy trial, several people came forward to say that Hanussen had charged them significant amounts of money for giving them advice so poor it ended up costing them more money. One witness, Leo Reidel, told the court he had asked the seer to find his father who'd been missing for over six years. He was told his father had been murdered and was buried in a nearby forest. Hanussen had offered to take him there for 3,000 kronen. Another prosecution witness, Emile Steberl, said she had asked him to find her husband's murderer and was told he worked for a local factory. The psychic offered to confront him for a fee of 10,000 kroner.

Other witnesses, however, spoke in his favour. Dr Heller told the court that while they were having dinner together, Hanussen suddenly cried out 'I see a man dying of a heart attack.' Later that night, Dr Heller learned his brother had died of a heart attack.[13]

In the end, Judge Schalek decided the best way to decide whether or not the defendant was a fraudster or a genuine clairvoyant was to put him to the test. Hanussen agreed, knowing that under the gaze of public and press, his success or failure would not only either ensure his liberty or condemn him to imprisonment but also make or break his career. It was a gamble but one the risk-taking showman was perfectly willing to take.

Within minutes of the courtroom opening, it was packed with people eager to witness the seer's triumph or humiliation. The first test involved something Hanussen had been performing for years – finding a hidden object. Taking the hand of the man who had concealed it, the seer easily and successfully completed the task. The judge next handed Hanussen samples of handwriting and ask him to reveal details about the writers. Once again, his analyses were correct. One, he said, had been produced by a man who 'pretends to be what he is not'. This turned out to have been written by a confidence trickster who had impersonated an American Archbishop.[14]

Given a set of dates he then correctly identified the birthday of a relative of a court employee and the date of a serious road accident. But the answer that truly amazed all those present in court came from the last question: 'What happened on February 26th, 1927, at the Karolinum (university) in Prague?'

'I see a room...glass...laboratory... an explosion,' Hanussen answered. 'But the year is wrong it happened in 1926 not 1927.'

Watching from the public gallery, hypnotist Franz Polgar later wrote, 'The court was amazed. Unbelievable. This man must be in league with the devil. Even today I can't explain it myself, because I was convinced, as was the Court, that this test he could not fake.'[15]

'There is no question that Hanussen solved the experiments and there is no way he could have faked the results,' Judge Schalek said when acquitting the seer. 'His metaphysical abilities are beyond doubt.'[16]

He was found not guilty and released to the cheers of his many supporters.

While there are a number of ways such a practiced

deceiver could have tricked the court, the most likely explanation is that someone connected with the prosecution was bribed to leak the information to him. Remember how, during the First War, he convinced fellow soldiers of his clairvoyant abilities by making entirely accurate statements about personal and family matters. This, as I explained, was only possible because he was in league with a censorship clerk.

Hanussen Moves to Berlin

In 1930, the clairvoyant secured top billing at the prestigious La Scala, Germany's best-known vaudeville theatre[17] where he played to packed houses. Among the many celebrities who flocked to his performances were Marlene Dietrich, Peter Lorre, Fritz Lang, Sigmund Freud and Hermann Goering. The fact that he achieved such acclaim was all the more remarkable given the sheer number of clairvoyants, hypnotists, mystics, faith healers and seers seeking to earn a living in the city.[18]

In 1931, Hanussen started editing and publishing several newspapers and magazines including Die Andere Welt (The Other World); Illustrated Weekly, Hanussen Magazin and a tabloid, Berlin Wochenschau, (Berlin Weekly). These quickly gained a large readership by printing a compelling mixture of gossip, scandal and superstitious nonsense. Hanussen knew his readers were far more interested in learning about magic formulas, astrological predictions, magnetic healing or how to achieve luck with women through hypnotic suggestion than hard news. The Other World carried first-hand accounts of the paranormal; 'A ghostly experience from my time as an Artist' and features such as 'Séance of the Month'. Such news as the Bunte Wochenschau reported was either scandalous or sensational. There were illustrated features on a ten-year-old prostitute, the kidnapping of Charles Lindbergh's baby and the life of Tog, a telepathic dog. He also wrote and published practical guides to popular occult techniques such as palmistry – 'You Could Read Hands In Five Minutes' – astrology, graphology and mindreading. One of his most popular was 'How to Hypnotise Your Lover into Ecstasy'.

Hanussen Makes Powerful Friends – and Enemies

Ambitious for wealth and success, as well as being aware of the precariousness of being a Jew living in Berlin under forged papers, Hanussen spent much of his rapidly accumulating fortune on cultivating friendships with anyone with influence in high places. One was Hanns Heinz Ewers[19] a writer of horror stories, occultist and fervent Nazi with direct links to Hitler. He had endeared himself to National Socialists by writing a biography of Horst Wessel, a young S.A. troop leader who had written the words to a marching song (The Horst Wessel Lied) which rapidly became the Nazis' anthem. In 1930, following his murder by Communists, allegedly over a debt, the Party transformed him into a National hero and martyr to the cause.[20]

The two first met after Ewers had expressed an interest in writing a book about a clairvoyant who meets a tragic end. This prophetic work was never completed but the two men became friends and, through Ewers, the clairvoyant was able to meet other high-ranking members of the S.A. The most important of these was Count Wolf Heinrich Graf von Helldorf, chief of the Berlin Stormtroopers and the black sheep of a wealthy and aristocratic Prussian family. He was a tall, blonde-haired, blue-eyed sadist, habitual gambler and connoisseur of the occult. Among the many money-making scams perpetrated by a man German author Konrad Heiden described as 'a gangster...from the dregs of the upper classes,'[21] were the use of his S.A. thugs in various kinds of protection rackets. As the Nazi terror caused wealthy Jews to flee Germany, he developed the practice of confiscating passports from the wealthy and then selling the same essential documents back to them for hundreds of thousands of marks.

Helldorf, a former Free Corps officer, had joined the National Socialists in 1925 and within six years been promoted to a senior officer in the S.A. and later to Police President of Berlin. After watching him perform at La Scala,

Helldorf became a fervent admirer, friend and regular guest at the lavish parties Hanussen hosted on his luxurious motor-yacht, the Ursel IV.

Parties on the Spree

Even in the depraved moral climate of 'sin city', the parties hosted aboard the vessel nicknamed 'The Seven Deadly Sins' were notorious for their hedonism and depravity. While cruising on the River Spree, Hanussen's guests were able to indulge their every wish and satisfy any sexual desire. They could drink unlimited quantities of champagne, take exotic drugs and enjoy the company of willing young girls, many of them aspiring actresses, or handsome boys. What the partygoers did not know, until it was too late, was that these sexual pleasures came at a price.

In a repeat of the blackmail scams he had learned when working for Der Blitz, Hanussen had installed hidden cameras and concealed microphones aboard the sixty-foot yacht. The politicians, aristocrats, movie stars and industrialists caught on film in compromising situations were offered the choice of paying handsomely to keep their indiscretions secret or see them splashed all over Hanussen Magazin or Hanussen Zeitung. [22]

The Flogging of Kabir

One incident, if no other, must have brought home to the 'Magister Ludi of Sex' (Master of the Sex Game) the type of people with whom he was mixing and the risks he was running by doing so.

Among the Ursel's crew was a 14-year-old Indian boy named Kabir, whose job it was to help with the musical entertainment and hand out towels to the bathers as they swam back to the yacht. On one occasion a female guest, who had swum naked as many of Hanussen's guests chose to do, complained the teenager had stared too closely at her breasts while handing her the towel. Erik dragged Kabir to a cabin where he ordered him stripped and tied to a table. Watched in shocked silence by other guests, Helldorf pulled a riding crop from his boot and started to beat the boy. So ferociously did he apply the crop that the screaming Kabir passed out from pain. As other quests pleaded for the punishment to stop, and perhaps sensing that he had gone too far, Helldorf flung down his crop and yelled at them, 'I'm a sadist! I admit it. We're all sadists! In the S.A., my friends, one must learn to be desensitised to petty human compassion.'[23]

The depravity of this cruel action is compounded by the probability that Hanussen deliberately stage-managed it to please his influential friend by pandering to his twin perversions of paedophilia and sadism.

Hanussen - Money Lender to the Brownshirts

Following the enormous expense of the April 1932 elections, the National Socialists were on the verge of bankruptcy. Wages for the S.A. had been reduced to such penurious levels they were often obliged to attend Communist-run soup kitchens. Even the once wealthy Helldorf was in deep financial trouble having run up more than 300,000 Marks in gambling debts. To ingratiate himself with those closest to Hitler, Hanussen became a member of the Party and loaned senior officers increasingly large sums of money. He not only paid off all Helldorf's heavy gambling debts but even let him drive his brand new Bugatti to the bank to settle his overdraft in style. In making these loans and becoming a paid-up member of the NSDAP, Hanussen was demonstrating not so much his political leanings or generosity but a shrewd business strategy that would bind him closer to power.

Hanussen the British Spy?

As I explained above, during the twenties Hanussen had been involved with the British-owned Tobacco Company Ltd, a front for MI6. Whether he remained in contact with British intelligence or made contact with another European agency is not known. But it may be significant that Aleister Crowley, a leading British practitioner of the 'black arts' dubbed the 'wickedest man in Britain' and the Beast 666[24] by the tabloid press was working in Berlin during that period. Through his friendship with Hanns Ewers, who was also a close friend of Aleister Crowley, Hanussen and 'The Beast' met on a number of occasions. It has been claimed that Crowley, whose links with British Intelligence went back to before the First World War, was tasked by MI6 with infiltrating the Nazis and reporting on high-ranking individuals. According to some writers, Crowley was instructed to recruit the clairvoyant to MI6 so he could provide first-hand reports on Hitler and his senior Nazi contacts. In 1972, writing under the name Werner Gerson, French author Pierre Mariel, who had ties to French intelligence, claimed Hanussen spied for Britain.[25]

'Whatever his occult abilities,' comments Richard Spence, 'Hanussen was a clever, unscrupulous and venal character who insinuated himself into the confidence of important people in Germany, and elsewhere. He clearly had a talent, one way or another, for obtaining secret information. His currency as an informant only increased when he gained access to Hitler. All this made the phony Dane an asset that any intelligence agency would have been anxious to exploit.'[26]

The Prophet of the Weimar

On May 15th, 1932, after a sell-out performance at La Scala, Hanussen hosted a dinner party to which he invited Princess Lobkowicz, an old friend and mother of a rising young racing driver Prince Leo Lobkowicz. She declined, explaining that her son, who was to take part in a forthcoming Avus Automobile race, had been taken ill and she had to stay home to look after him. On the day before the race while drinking at the Roxy Bar, Hanussen was challenged to predict the winner. After some persuasion, he wrote two names on a piece of paper, folded it into an envelope and handed to the barman, with instructions that it was not to be opened until after the race. 'One of us at this table will win tomorrow,' Hanussen informed the drivers, 'another will die. The two names are in this envelope.'[27]

Berlin journalists, most of whom considered Hanussen a charlatan, dismissed the prophecy. The following day, Prince Lobkowicz, who had been hotly tipped to win, died just four minutes into the race when his Bugatti spun out of control and rolled down a steep bank. When the envelope was opened it was found that Hanussen had correctly predicted the names of both the victim and the winner. A few days after the race, it was reported that the 'psychic' had tried, without success, to persuade Prince Lobkowicz not to take part in the race. From then on, the press and the dumbfounded public hung on his every word and believed his every prediction.

Hanussen and Hitler

Exactly when and how Hanussen met Hitler is uncertain. Quincy Howe, an American journalist, states their first encounter was in 1930,[28] however a more likely date is May

1932 after he had correctly foretold the death of Prince Lobkowicz. Following the story's publication, Hitler sent him a note asking if they could meet up. It was the start of a professional relationship between the two men during which the master of stagecraft would impart decades of experience in winning over an audience to the soon to be dictator. He also used his skill as a hypnotist both to build Hitler's self-confidence when speaking to mass audiences and to show him how to use hypnosis himself to literally entrance spectators.

After a successful first meeting, Hitler asked the psychic to help him improve his stagecraft when speaking to tens of thousands at his ever more popular and well-attended rallies. 'Hanussen instructed Hitler in autosuggestion, acting, and stage presence,' says author Joseph Howard Tyson, 'to captivate audiences Hanussen suggested that speeches be delivered at night, when listeners psychological resistance ebbed low. He paid special attention to gestures, inflection, days, timing, and 'extrasensory attunement.' Sets also played a role in mass hypnosis; colourful banners, music, processions, and lighting all heightened dramatic spectacles.' [29]

Eric Hanussen stands just behind Hitler and to his right

While there is no surviving written record of these lessons, based on contemporary accounts of techniques being taught by voice coaches, it is likely they included demonstrations of how different hand movements can be used to communicate emotions. This is supported by the fact that Hitler instructed his personal photographer, Heinrich Hoffmann, to take pictures showing him rehearsing these gestures. He spent hours studying them to assess their visual impact and learn how best to present himself before the cameras.

Body Language for the Führer

Hanussen explained the importance of different hand movements when communicating a wide range of emotions. High-plane gestures, which end with the hand raised above the shoulders, express emotional, physical or mental elevation while what he termed low-plane gestures, terminating below the waist, convey the opposite meaning. These he contrasted with front-plane gestures used to communicate unity, advancement, strong agreement and direct, personal involvement. The secret of success, the psychic told him, was to make every single member of even the largest audience believe he was speaking directly and personally to them alone.

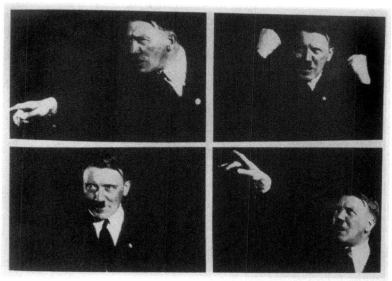

Hitler practises his gestures before Hofmann's camera

The most powerful gesture and one Hitler increasingly used during his speeches, was the raised clenched fist in which the fingers are locked with the thumb on the outside. This, Hanussen told him, conveys determination, defiance, forcefulness and extreme intensity. 'Owing to the close analogy between physical force and mental or emotional power, the clenched hand is also a telling figurative gesture for suggesting any forceful attitude,' comments Joseph Mosher, an American-based contemporary of Hanussen, 'the scope of this hand form may be stated as follows. Striking, threatening, defying, challenging, anger, all of these with more intensity than is expressed by the supine or the index; also seizing, gripping, crushing, literally or figuratively.'[30]

Hanussen also emphasised the importance of using both hands when making gestures since by doing so he could increase the intensity of what he was saying. Hitler practised these gestures until they became a natural part of his repertoire.

Among the hypnotic techniques Hanussen taught were ways to mesmerise his audiences through the power of facial expression, eye contact and voice tone. He showed him ways of using content, voice tone, expression and eye movements to increase his already considerable attraction to female followers. He explained the importance of the prone hand, in which the palm is turned downwards with the fingers straightened out indicating submission. When meeting women, Hanussen encouraged Hitler to ensure they presented their hand to him in this way. It would, he assured the Führer, make them even more willing to submit to his will.

In addition, Hanussen used hypnosis to further strengthen Hitler's already powerful belief in his own divine destiny, teaching him self-hypnosis techniques so he could quickly and easily place himself into a trance. Finally, he pandered to Hitler's superstitious streak by supplying him, through the pages of his newspapers and magazines, with positive astrological predictions.

Although never part of the Führer's intimate circle in the way his personal photographer Heinrich Hoffman was, Hanussen was sufficiently valued by Hitler to appear in the same photograph as the great man, albeit standing in the background.

The Wall Street Crash

The Wall Street Crash of October 1929 and the Great Depression that followed provided the breakthrough for which Hitler and the Nazis had been waiting and praying. Germany, which was more dependent on foreign loans than any other Western nation, was worst affected by the downturn. Factories closed and the unemployment figures again soared. Banks collapsed and inflation wiped out the savings and income of the middle-classes. In 1929, with 1,320,000 people out of work, the National Socialists had 176,426 members and were attracting 800,000 voters. By 1932, after unemployment had risen to six million, Nazi Party membership was over a million and six million voters supported them at the ballot box. Greater financial support from the major industrialists began to show itself in ever-larger rallies and increasingly opulent offices.

On March 23rd, 1932, the Berliner Wochenschau gave front page prominence to Hanussen's prophecy that Adolf Hitler would be appointed Reich Chancellor in exactly one year's time. He explained how, while in a trance, he had 'seen' that those who placed him in power would be Hitler's former enemies, Field Marshall Paul von Hindenburg and the Nationalists. Once again, the 'man who is never wrong' was right.

Palace of the Occult

On February 26th, as the Weimar Republic entered its final days and Hitler was on the verge of seizing absolute power in Germany, Hanussen held an opening night gala at his newly created Palace of the Occult (Palast des Okkultismus). It had taken two months of round the clock work by craftsmen to convert an apartment at 17 Lietzenburger Strasse into what one writer later described as a 'supernatural appendage to Versailles ... an exquisite pagan temple supplemented with the latest 1930s technologies.'[31]

Hanussen's VIP guest list for the important night included almost everyone of social and political importance in Berlin: Louis Ferdinand, the Prince of Prussia[32], Prinz Heinrich von Reuss [33] and a White Russian lady who claimed to be Grand Duchess Anastasia Nikolaevna Romanoff of Russia.[34] There were writers such as Curt Riess[35] and Hanns Heinz Ewers together with leading journalists and editors from the main Berlin newspapers. There were ambassadors, artists and stars of stage and screen as well as high-ranking S.A. officers in uniform. Among them were Count von Helldorf, Karl Ernst and Wilhelm Ohst. A few weeks after the gala, Ohst would be one of the three men who abducted, tortured and murdered the clairvoyant.

Hanussen and the Hall of Silence

On entering the candle-lit foyer, guests were greeted by blue-eyed, blonde-haired 'priestesses' scantily dressed in thin white and pale green tunics. Indian prayer stools lined the walls of an entrance hall dominated by a giant bronze statue of Hanussen dressed in the toga of a Caesar with the left arm raised in a Nazi gesture of victory, which stood in the centre of the exquisitely tiled floor. Male guests were handed white rubber slippers to place over their shoes and all were told to remain absolutely quiet on entering the aptly named Hall of Silence. The high-domed ceiling was decorated with stars and mystical Egyptian and Babylonian astrological signs. Spotlights lit up walls painted grey and purple and four large Buddhas stood in each corner. At precisely 10 o'clock, a green mist filled the crowded room and an organ began playing the thunderous music of

Wagner.

'The lights dimmed and went out, leaving only a brilliant spotlight slashing down on the centre of the floor,' recalls Joe Labéro, one of the guests. 'Hanussen was not in sight. Slowly, the floor moved, a chasm appeared in it. Two panels moved back and a throne rose majestically to tower fifteen feet in the air. On an ebony-black throne was Hanussen clothed in a scarlet robe. He was holding a large crystal, with coloured lights flickering through it, and there was a half-dazed expression on his face. He began to speak, his rich voice seeming to come from the walls. He predicted the blood purge that was to come later and the war with England, Russia and America.'[36]

Following his dramatic entry, Hanussen and ten of his most important guests including Count Helldorf retired to the 'Room of Glass'. In this inner sanctum reserved for private psychic readings, people were seated around a circular table and placed both hands, palms downwards, fingers splayed, against its frosted-glass surface. Beneath it was a wheel, decorated with occult symbols, which slowly revolved. Hanussen, seated on a swivel chair in the centre of the table waited until the wheel stopped and then foretold each guest's future based on the mystical signs beneath their hands.

Hanussen tells the fortune of his guests in the Room of Glass

The readings completed, he asked for a volunteer to help with mindreading. When no one came forward, he selected Maria Paudler, a popular young actress, who had just arrived from the theatre where she was performing. 'I didn't want to be a spoilsport,' she recalled in her autobiography *Laughing Has Also to Be Learned*.[37]

Hanussen escorted her to a chair facing the other guests and offered her a glass of champagne. 'Then,' she recalled, 'the small man… waved his hands around my head, trying to pierce me with his eyes.' When this failed to send her into a trance he started to stroke her face, something she initially found extremely unpleasant. After closing her eyes, she felt herself start to float away. From what seemed like a great distance she heard Hanussen asking in a soft and persuasive voice whether she could see red circles. When she agreed that she could, he asked if they were actually flames 'coming out of a big house'.

The more he persisted with these images, the more she began to feel that 'this whole scene was getting beyond a normal parlour game and I was being used as more than an object of entertainment by this gentleman. I really did not want to be used in this manner... what does a lady do at a moment like that? She faints! After all, why shouldn't I take advantage of my womanly prerogative.'[38]

The following day, this prediction appeared in Die Hanussen-Zeitung, with the article warning readers that some 'great provocation' would shortly occur. Three days later, Germany's parliament building, the Reichstag, was set ablaze.

The Reichstag in Flames

Around 9.03pm on the night of February 27th, 1933, a young theology student named Hans Flöter was passing the south-western corner of the darkened and deserted Reichstag.[39] Hearing the sound of breaking glass, he turned to see a man with a burning object in his hand. He hurried off to find a police officer, Sergeant Karl Buwert, who returned with him to the building.

Shortly after 9.30pm, Detective Inspector Helmut Heisig of Division 1A of the Berlin Police Department received a phone call reporting that the 19th-century Reichstag parliament building was ablaze.[40] The officer making the call also announced they had arrested Marinus van der Lubbe, a 24-year-old Dutchman and communist. According to Gestapo head, Rudolf Diels, when interrogated, Marinus Van der Lubbe was 'naked from the waist upwards, smeared with dirt and sweating...breathing heavily. He panted as if he had completed a tremendous task. There was a wild triumphant gleam in the burning eyes of his pale, haggard young face.'[41]

Who Was Van der Lubbe?

Marinus, who was born into extreme poverty, left school early and worked as a bricklayer until an accident seriously damaged his sight. He was in hospital for several months and on discharge was too handicapped to ever work again. Forced to exist on a small invalidity pension and with plenty of time on his hands, he became increasingly interested in left-wing politics. As chairman of the Leyden Communist Youth League, in 1928, he wrote leaflets and pamphlets attacking capitalism. His presence at every strike, heckling and public speaking soon made him a familiar figure, especially among the unemployed.

Believing Germany to be on the verge of revolution, he walked to Berlin over a period of fifteen days. His intention was to take matters into his own hands by setting a number of public buildings on fire. After buying matches and four packets of firelighters on February 25th, he attempted to set fire to a public toilet, the town hall and the Imperial Palace. In each case, the fire was discovered soon afterwards and no real damage was done. Three days later, he entered the Reichstag with the intention of setting it ablaze.

'He was a solitary individual', comments historian Ian Kershaw, 'unconnected with any political groups, but possessed of a strong sense of injustice at the misery of the working class at the hands of the capitalist system. In particular, he was determined to make a lone and spectacular act of defiant protest at the Government... in order to galvanize the working class into struggle against their repression.'[42]

In a statement made on March 3rd, the young Dutchman confessed, 'I myself am a Leftist, and was a member of the Communist Party until 1929. I had heard that a Communist demonstration was disbanded by the leaders on the approach of the police. In my opinion, something absolutely had to be done in protest against this system. Since the workers would do nothing, I had to do something myself. I considered arson a suitable method. I did not wish to harm private people but something belonging to the system itself. I decided on the Reichstag. As to the question of whether I acted alone, I declare emphatically that this was the case.'

He also admitted using firelighters and his own clothing to carry out the arson attack. 'The first fire went out,' he told his interrogators. 'I lit my shirt on fire and carried it further. I went through five rooms.'[43]

Van der Lubbe – Arsonist, Scapegoat or Both?

Apart from his confession, there was no direct evidence against Marinus. Helmut Poeschel, the police officer who had arrested and searched him found only a 'pocket knife, a wallet, and a passport'. The only fire setting material found was a petrol can and a box of matches.

As an expert testified at the trial, it is almost certain that van der Lubbe had help when starting the fires, in at least two places, which gutted the building. The Nazis accused well-known Communists, Ernst Torgler, Georgi Dimitrov, Blagoi Popov and Vassili Tanev of being implicated in the plot but all four were exonerated by the court. Although there was no link to Hitler, many commentators suggested a likely role of senior Nazis.

Before long, those suspicions extended to Erik Hanussen. Pointing to his prediction of a 'great building' on fire, more and more people wondered how such uncanny foresight could be explained? While some attributed it to genuine clairvoyance and others dismissed it as a 'lucky guess', many claimed it pointed to sinister inside knowledge. Had Hanussen been tipped off about the arson attack by Count von Helldorf or S.A. Major Wilhelm Ohst both of whom were implicated in the plot?

Some alleged the clairvoyant might have an even deeper

responsibility for it. Contributing to this belief was the fact that, throughout his trial, the young Dutchman's behaviour and manner were anything but those of a skilled and dedicated arsonist. He came across as lethargic, rambling, empty-headed and almost robotic. His voice was so low as to be barely audible, his answers mono-syllabic, his explanations banal and his posture one of abject resignation. For the majority of the time in court, he remained slumped forward in his seat. The sole exception was a moment when, obeying Count Helldorf's command to stand straight, he jerked to his feet with a puppet-like motion. Some Berliners wondered whether Hanussen had hypnotised van der Lubbe and directed him to both start the fires and respond to Helldorf as he did at the trial.

These suspicions received support in 1934 from a report by Walter Korodi.[44] This former S.S. officer who had been close to the plot later defected and fled to Switzerland. He claimed that Helldorf had brought van der Lubbe, a vagrant caught sleeping on the street, to see Hanussen. The master hypnotist had put him into a trance, explained how to break into the rear of the building (located a few blocks from his apartment), provided a plan of the building and showed how best to start the fires. He then used post-hypnotic suggestion to enable Helldorf to return van der Lubbe to his hypnotic trance whenever it became necessary. Hanussen remained in court throughout the trial, keeping a careful eye on van der Lubbe's behaviour, ready to intervene should he start to deviate from the script. Three decades later, this claim was supported by Doris Hertwig-Bünger, widow of trial judge Wilhelm Bünger. She confirmed that while Hanussen's name had cropped up frequently in pre-trial statements, all mention of it was expunged from the trial documents. Further confirmation came from Dr Gerda

Walther, a para-psychologist who during World War II had worked on top secret projects for German Naval Intelligence.[45]

That van der Lubbe came to Berlin with the aim of setting fire to public buildings seems certain, as does his presence within the Reichstag. But whether he alone was responsible or by himself even capable of such a professional piece of fire raising is far more questionable. The most likely scenario is that Nazis, who had become aware of his amateurish plans, used him to further their own scheme for destabilising the Republic.

It has been suggested that the reason why he refused to defend, or at least justify, himself in court was his homosexuality. Deep shame about his sexuality and the fact it was illegal may help explain why, even when the likely outcome was a death sentence, van der Lubbe preferred to remain silent.

Many believe the Dutchman was as much a scapegoat as an arsonist. They claim the true fire-setters were a group of S.A. men led by Karl Ernst. Entering the parliament building by means of an underground tunnel leading from the Palace of the President of the Reichstag, they sprayed carpets, curtains and upholstery with a chemical that spontaneously ignites after a suitable delay.

The Terror Starts

The following day, Hitler, who had only been appointed Reich Chancellor on January 30th, enacted a decree 'for the Protection of the People and the State'. At the scene of the blaze, his face was purple with agitation and he shouted uncontrollably, 'There will be no mercy now. Anyone who stands in our way will be cut down. The German people will not tolerate leniency. Every communist official will be shot where he is found. Everybody in league with the Communists must be arrested. There will also no longer be leniency for social democrats.'

Although in the elections that followed the National Socialists failed to secure an outright majority, on Monday March 23rd they used the 'outrage' to pressure President Hindenburg and the Nationalists Party to pass, by a vote of 444 to 94, an Enabling Act whereby all of parliament's legislative powers were transferred to the Reich Cabinet. At the stroke of a pen, he did away with all constitutional protection of political, personal, and property rights.

Hitler's dictatorship had begun.

The Noose Tightens
Freed from parliamentary control and scrutiny, Goering's police could arrest and imprison anyone they perceived as an enemy of their regime. Initially applied with special ferocity to members of the Communist Party, it rapidly extended to all those whom the Nazis believed might threaten or undermine their power. Press freedoms were suspended, private property confiscated, all personal freedoms abolished and attacks on Jews legalised.

Given the precariousness of his situation, Hanussen was becoming increasingly reckless in his behaviour and his boasts. Believing in his friendships with high ranking S.A. officers, his association with Hitler and his very public position as the 'Prophet of the Third Reich', he was outspoken in his views. Telling friends, for example, that the Führer, 'looked more like an unemployed hairdresser than a Caesar.'[46]

Less than a month after he had ridden the wave of public acclaim and professional success with his lavish opening gala at the Palace of the Occult, the 'Prophet of the Third

Reich' was dead. Ironically, the man who claimed to see the future of others failed to forecast his own brutal end at the hands of the same S.A. men he trusted.

CHAPTER 13
BETRAYAL

Whatsoever I shall see or hear in the course of my profession, as well as outside my profession in my intercourse with men, if it be what should not be published abroad, I will never divulge, holding such things to be holy secrets. ⁻ Hippocratic Oath.[1]

In the decade following the First War, it seems unlikely Edmund Forster gave any thought to his former patient's political ambitions. He had his own career and personal life to concentrate on and during the twenties both were running very much to plan. As soon as he was freed from military duties and obligations, Edmund devoted all his time and attention to research and clinical activities at the Charité. He continued with investigations begun before the war on the pathology of brain tumours and the effects of syphilis spirochete on the nervous system.

As the senior neurological consultant who often acted as

locum for the Director Karl Bonhöffer, his clinical duties kept him busy around the clock. His department, staffed by some thirty-six doctors, had two hundred and forty psychiatric and neurological beds and was always full. Although he did not publish widely in the academic field, he did contribute chapters to two major textbooks and more importantly, as far as professional advancement was concerned, spent much time lecturing and conducting demonstrations at gatherings of the Berlin Neurological Society, a highly influential organisation described as the 'meeting place for outstanding experts'.[2]

Edmund Forster in the 1920's

Before the war, Edmund had become friendly with Marie Pauline Bretschneider, known to family and friends as Mila. A slender woman with reddish-brown hair, she was seven years his junior. Both her parents died when she was young and as the eldest daughter, she had the responsibility of bringing up her siblings. The fact that her family was poor and her childhood full of privations always rankled with Mila and after Edmund's death, her relationship with the rest of his family was characterised by disputes over money.

The couple married on Thursday September 12th, 1918. Edmund moved out of the hospital accommodation, his home since he started working at the Charité, and rented an apartment on the third floor of 8 Boznerstrasse (literally high-status street) in Berlin's affluent Schönberg district.

Edmund's first apartment in Boznerstrasse as it is today

On February 20th, 1920, their first son Balduin Konrad was born and just over a year later, on August 6th, their second, whom they christened Ruprecht. With his secure and well-paid job at the Charité and private consultancy work, Edmund was able to keep his family well-fed and comfortably housed throughout the grim, immediate post-war years.

Mila with Balduin and Ruprecht

On February 12th, 1921, there was another family wedding in Berlin when Edmund's brother, Dirk, married Lilly Bredow, a beautiful and accomplished woman, whom he had met at a wartime ball. Her Jewish grandmother who belonged to the wealthy Nivea cream family had been a friend of Brahms with whom she made music; Lilly inherited these artistic talents. A gifted musician and painter who had studied under the eminent German artist Lovis Corinth[3], Lilly counted many eminent musicians, artists and writers among her close friends.

It was rumoured she had an affair with the celebrated conductor Wilhelm Furtwängler and urged him to promote the career of another of her friends, a gifted Austrian conductor named Herbert von Karajan. 'Dirk and Edmund had always fought over girls,' his granddaughter Marie Rose told me, 'and in the family, it was often said that Lilly was Dirk's revenge on his brother.'[4]

Edmund's Daily Life
In 1926, Edmund was appointed Director of the University

Clinic for Neurology at the University of Greifswald, a town some 133 miles north of Berlin in the state of Mecklenburg-West Pomerania.

The nerve clinic at Greifswald

In the clinic, Edmund cultivated a relaxed atmosphere of mutual trust and co-operation among his medical staff at all levels. Although welcomed by most, this aroused the antagonism of some of the older and more hidebound traditionalists who favoured a formal and hierarchical command structure. What Edmund regarded as a friendly attitude towards junior doctors and nurses, they sometimes considered over-familiarity. This fostered an undercurrent of disapproval towards him at the university.

At Greifswald, as at the Charité, Forster was involved in a wide range of research projects. One of his studies was on the effects of syphilis on the central nervous system, especially in relation to the progressive paralyses that occur during the final stages of the disease. While at the Charité, he had succeeded in demonstrating the existence of the syphilitic pathogen within the brain by using a syringe to extract cells from the brains of living but paralysed patients.

He continued this research with the aim of growing the pathogen in a culture, this time mostly using animals in his experiments. Although his findings were not of any great scientific interest, of lasting significance was his development of a simple method for preparing cells from the spinal fluid for microscopic examination. His success here represented a significant technical breakthrough that provided a valuable new diagnostic tool.

With his medical colleagues Konrad Zucker and Julius Zádor, he also researched the effects of mescaline (3,4,5-trimethoxyphenethylamine) and its possible use in the treatment of mental illness. By taking the powerful hallucinogenic themselves, Forster and his colleagues demonstrated that its effects were due to an individual's inability to distinguish between events in the real world with what was going on in their heads. Their pioneering work was not to be replicated for over a decade. It was on April 19th, 1943, that research chemist Albert Hoffmann gave himself a dose of a substance he had derived from the ergot fungus. That molecule was LSD and Hoffmann is often cited as the first scientist in history to embark on an acid trip under controlled conditions; an honour which should, by rights, go to Forster and his team.[5]

Even more controversial and ultimately damaging to his reputation was the encouragement Forster gave to Zádor in what became known as the Kipptischversuche or 'tilting-table' experiments. These involved placing volunteers (in many cases brain-injured patients) on a specially designed platform that could be tilted in any direction. The subjects – naked if male and wearing only pants and a bra if female – were placed in a starting position, for example, seated, lying on their stomach or back, or on all fours and then filmed as the platform wobbled backwards, forwards and from side to side. Their responses were then compared with those suffering from a variety of neurological disorders. They were filmed while on the table and these images would later lead to accusations of tormenting vulnerable patients.

In a paper presented to the Paris Neurological Conference in May 1933, Zádor explained, 'If you put a normal person on the table and then tilt it first left and then right it is possible to observe certain consistent reactions through which he or she strives to maintain their balance and original position.' But when it came to patients suffering from various diseases of the central nervous system, 'the balance reactions when they were tilted to the left were absent whereas when they were tilted to the right the reactions, even when slightly inhibited, were clearly present. This indicates severe damage to the balance mechanisms on the left side of the body.'[6]

Julius Zador (extreme left) and family

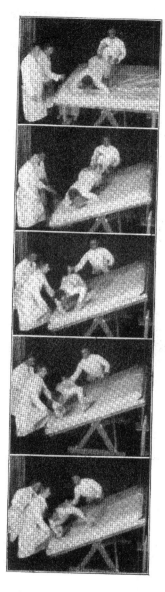

Tilting table studies, pictures from 16mm research film

At the time, many were shocked by these experiments but in the days before CAT and MRI scans could be used to pinpoint the location of brain injuries, Zádor 's research was of potential value as a diagnostic aid.

Forster chose his friends not from among his colleagues but in artistic, writing and show business circles. As a result, he became increasingly isolated within the clinic, where he appears to have had only one close friend; ironically, this man was a former Nazi Party member.

Thirty-eight-year-old Rudolf Degkwitz, married with four children, was a paediatrician who joined the university in the same year as Forster. In 1918, he had belonged to the extreme right-wing Freikorps Oberland. Later, he joined the Nazis and in 1923, even marched alongside Hitler during the November 9th Munich Putsch. For reasons now not known, he fell out with his former friends and was dismissed from the party. Perhaps out of resentment for this treatment, he abruptly switched from being one of Hitler's most fanatical supporters to a sworn enemy of the Nazis. He was the only member of staff who supported Forster when the university decided to rid itself of his assistants, Julius Zádor and Konrad Zucker, purely because they were Jews.

In January 1933, Forster tried, without success, to save Zádor's job. His involvement may even have been counterproductive; such was the antagonism towards him from certain sectors of the Medical Faculty. Forster, however, refused to accept the university's decision and after Zádor's dismissal, allowed him to continue with his research until May 1933, when they left together for the Paris conference at which Zádor gave his presentation on his tilting-table experiments. Forster's defence of Konrad Zucker may well have been more ambivalent because, during 1926, they had both had affairs with the same woman. Fraulein Rietzkow was employed as a laboratory assistant and Forster, who always had something of a roving eye, appears to have been infatuated with her, at least for a short time.

What he did not realise was that this tall, dark-haired Jewess was also involved with Zucker, visiting him in his rooms at the clinic while Forster was lecturing. Inevitably, given the narrow and claustrophobic atmosphere within the clinic, the clandestine triangle soon became common knowledge. When Mila found out what had happened she was hurt and angry, but would not countenance a divorce.

After visiting his brother in December 1926, Dirk wrote to Lilly, 'I was not happy about Edmund, as I am afraid he is no longer happy at home. I can only hope things will work themselves out.'[7] This hope was partly realised and domestic peace was restored, although it seems likely Mila never entirely forgave Edmund's infidelity.

Mila with Ruprecht and Balduin

By the end of the 1920's, Edmund's life had settled into a routine. He spent much of his time away from home attending conferences, presenting papers or taking leaves of absence, sometimes with his family but often alone. He loved driving and criss-crossed Europe in his little Opel car which he had named 'Opel-Popel', thinking nothing of motoring the hundreds of miles between Greifswald and Munich on trips to see his mother. He was either unaware of or unconcerned about having made more enemies than friends at the clinic. Nor did it seem to trouble him that the university authorities were becoming increasingly scandalised by his noisy parties and bohemian friends.

Edmund behind the wheel of Opel-Popel with Balduin as passenger

Hitler's Rise to Power

After Hitler had been appointed Chancellor in January 1933, Jewish doctors and nurses at Greifswald were driven from their posts and Edmund's Jewish friends experienced increasing persecution. Every day, he saw first-hand the violence and destruction being wrought by groups of brown-shirted Nazis.

In Berlin, writer Michael Davidson described how 'overnight the streets seemed to have turned Nazi; overnight the air, which before had been soft and warm and human, had become harsh and malignant. Strutting police officers wearing swords flaunted their Hakenkreuz (Swastika) armbands...The streets were brown with clumping S.A. free now to bully and chivvy and show their power – soon they were picketing the doorways of Jewish shops like Wertheim...he loudspeakers blared at every street corner – the interminable Die Strasse frei of the 'Horst Wessel Lied', sickeningly beautiful as a deadly snake. Each day one awoke to the same terrible chorus of brutality, cynicism and hypocrisy: designed to bring under the Nazi power by bludgeoning or romantic blandishments the young men and boys and groom them for death.'[8]

The Kurfürstendamm, one of the city's most famous avenues, was plastered with scrawls and cartoons. ''Jew' was smeared all over the doors, windows, and walls in waterproof colours,' reported Bella Fromm, diplomatic columnist with the Vossische Zeitung ('Aunty Voss to Berliners). 'It grew worse as we came to the part of town where poor little Jewish retail shops were to be found. The S.A. had created havoc. Everywhere were revolting and bloodthirsty pictures of Jews beheaded, hanged, tortured, and maimed, accompanied by obscene inscriptions. Windows were smashed, and loot from the miserable little shops was strewed over the sidewalk and floating in the gutter.'[9]

She was about to enter a small Jewish-owned jewellery shop when it was stormed by Hitler Youth brandishing knives and screaming, 'To hell with the Jewish rabble! Room for the Sudenten-Germans!'

'The smallest boy of the mob climbed inside the window and started his work of destruction by flinging everything he could grab right into the streets,' noted Bella Fromm. 'Inside, the other boys broke glass shelves and counters, hurling alarm clocks, cheap silverware, and trifles to their accomplices outside. A tiny shrimp of a boy crouched in a corner of the window, putting dozens of rings on his fingers and stuffing his pockets with wristwatches and bracelets. His uniform bulging with loot, he turned around, spats squarely into the shopkeeper's face, and dashed off.'[10]

In her book Blood and Banquets she provides endless examples of Nazi attacks on all aspects of Jewish life. One of the most ludicrous new laws being the ban imposed on cows owned by Jews from being impregnated by bulls owned by Germans. 'There was not much more I could say,' she comments, 'I was too overcome to discover that there is such a thing as a non-Aryan cow.' [11]

The Rise of the 'Brown Terror'

From 1933 onwards, domestic espionage – what became known as the 'Brown Terror' – became ever more sophisticated and pervasive. As the Gestapo's ability to monitor conversations improved, most German's grew increasingly wary of voicing their opinions to anyone but close friends or family. Postal workers, a majority of whom were strongly pro-Nazi, routinely tapped telephone calls, searched letters and opened packages. In the words of émigré writer Ernst Weiß, they 'were not ashamed to be betrayers and hangmen of people who had taken professional integrity for granted.'[12]

The dangers of the situation are illustrated by a joke that circulated in Germany during the early 1930s: Two men are fishing from a bridge. One is catching fish after fish while the second fails to catch any.

'How is it you get all the luck?' he asks his companion.

'It's the badge you're wearing,' comes the reply. 'The fish are not fools. When they come up and see that swastika they know better than to open their mouths.'

Even foreigners learned to be cautious about what they said and to whom they said it. Berlin-based British historian John Wheeler-Bennett recalled how the 'fear of being spied upon never really left him'.

'I am still, even after 40 years, very careful on the telephone; I have a phobia against talking in a room with the door open, and a marked preference for sitting with my back to the wall in a restaurant.'[13] By the mid-thirties, the atmosphere had become so oppressive that he began to spend less and less time in Nazi Germany, 'I felt myself to be in a kind of waking nightmare from which one only became free on crossing the frontier back into the Western world, where one literally and physically took great gulps of free air.'[14]

Despite the manifest dangers, Edmund, who was never one to keep his opinions to himself, made no attempt to conceal the contempt in which he held Hitler and the Nazis. Because he expressed his criticisms with irony and earnestness, less sophisticated colleagues sometimes failed to realise the point he was making. Those who did were so appalled at his recklessness started to avoid any conversation with him for fear of being damned by association. One day, while speeding through Greifswald in Opel-Popel Edmund was stopped by a policeman, 'Anyone who drives as fast as you do has to be crazy!' the officer told him.

'I decide who is crazy around here!' Forster snapped

back.[15]

The flippant riposte may have struck him as a good joke at the time but like the Frankenstein monster he had inadvertently created in Pasewalk, it would all too soon come back to destroy him.

Edmund Breaks his Oath

The extent to which Forster felt responsible for the monster he had inadvertently created can never be known. What we do know is that by May, he had made up his mind to break his oath as a doctor and as a former German Naval officer, loyalty to his Commander in Chief. Both must have weighed heavily on his conscience. The importance of safeguarding patient confidentiality had been drilled into him from early in his medical training and as an officer, loyalty to superiors was no less fundamental.

On graduating, he had sworn the Hippocratic Oath which included the promise that he would never discuss anything he saw or heard in the course of giving treatment. The same applied to his oath as a decorated Naval office; he had been awarded the Iron Cross, First and Second Class, to display unquestioned loyalty to superior officers. The importance of serving officers of this code of conduct is clear from a comment made by Field Marshal Keitel, 'I was brought up in the Prussian officer's tradition to obey orders with honour and loyalty,' the former Chief of Staff of the Wehrmacht High Command told G. M. Gilbert, the prison psychologist at Nürnberg where he was on trial for his life. 'God knows how honourable and immaculate and incorruptible the Prussian Officers Code was! A code of honour that was the pride of the nation ever since Bismarck, and had a fine tradition going back to Frederick the Great! Why, if an officer didn't pay a debt of 25 marks he was arrested and disgraced. It never occurred to me that Hitler had any other code.'[16]

Medical ethics and military loyalty aside, Forster would have known the disclosures he was about to make would place himself and his family in the gravest possible danger. In a conversation with Jewish émigré writers during the three days he spent with them in Paris, he remarked in resigned tones that 'his turn' would come and if they learned that he had committed suicide they should not believe a word of it.[17]

At the end of May 1933, Forster left Greifswald accompanied by his colleague and friend Julius Zádor, to attend a neurological conference in Paris at which Zádor was to present a paper. At the conference, Forster met Dr Alfred Döblin, a fellow neurologist who had found literary fame with his bestselling novel, Berlin Alexanderplatz. Nazi persecution had forced him into exile and the conference was an opportunity to meet old colleagues and gather information about work prospects in France. Forster, who enjoyed the company of writers, had undoubtedly heard of Döblin and probably went out of his way to arrange a meeting. The neurologists talked shop, gossiped and exchanged notes on interesting medical cases.

During their conversation, Forster, perhaps encouraged by Zádor, began to disclose some details of Hitler's hysterical blindness and the method he had adopted to treat it. Döblin, always a fierce opponent of fascism, had particular reasons for feeling especially bitter at that moment. Two weeks before the conference, he had learned that a group of Nazis had ransacked his former home in Germany and burned all his books. He was therefore especially intrigued by Forster's account and realising the enormous political damage it would cause Hitler (still only a few months into his Chancellorship at this point), pleaded with him to reveal all he knew to a wider public.

Such entreaties would have gained a sympathetic hearing from Forster who never made any secret of his contempt for Hitler and his Party. He may also have felt some responsibility for the monster his treatment had inadvertently helped to create and whose destruction he would dearly like to engineer. He would have been well aware of the damage his revelations could do to a leader who was constantly emphasising his 'exceptional strength of will'. At the same time, he cannot have been under any illusions as to the risks he was running by leaking details from Hitler's medical file.

Only a few months earlier, a fellow academic, Professor Karl Wilmanns of Heidelberg, had been accused of likening the Führer to the founder of some crazy religious sect. He, too, asserted Hitler had suffered from hysterical blindness and that Göring was a morphine addict. According to his daughter, Ruth Lidz, then a 23-year-old medical student,[18] sixty-year-old Wilmanns was suspended from the University and sent to Dachau concentration camp.

Edmund knew his own case would be treated far more seriously and dealt with much more brutally. He, after all, intended not merely to voice such opinions but hand over proof their leader had suffered a mental breakdown.

Where the German public was concerned, hysteria indicated a 'weakness of the will' caused either by an 'inferior nervous system' or a 'degenerate brain'.[19] So contemptuous were the Nazis of hysterics that their infamous laboratory for 'race biology' would later extol the bombing of congested cities on the grounds that 'the person whose nervous system is deficient will not be able to survive the shock. In this way, bombing will help us discover the hysterics in our community and remove them from social life.' [20]

Following his meeting with Döblin, Forster believed he had found a way of resolving his ethical dilemma and safeguarding himself. There was, he probably concluded, nothing unethical in handing over a copy of Hitler's medical file to a fellow doctor. What this colleague then chose to do with the information would be a matter for his own conscience. Furthermore, if the truth about Hitler's blindness was published by a neurologist, his own involvement might never be suspected. In retrospect, this may seem like a naive conclusion, but to Forster, it must have appeared the only way to resolve his ethical crisis.

On returning to Greifswald, he prepared three copies of Hitler's medical notes. The first he intended to place in a Swiss safety-deposit box, another one he would hand over to Döblin in Paris towards the middle of July. The third he would make available to a group of émigré writers, to whom he also intended disclosing medical information about Hermann Göring and Bernhard Rust, now Prussian Minister of Education. Göring he had treated for morphine addiction, while he had seen Rust while preparing a report on his mental health at the request of the criminal court. Because both of these stories had already received mentions in the foreign press, Forster believed this would not involve a significant breach of patient confidentiality. As a cover for this meeting, he would arrange to travel home via Paris after attending his mother's eightieth birthday party.

Edmund Meets the Émigrés

When the conference finished, Forster drove Zádor to Budapest and from there, on June 9th, wrote to his brother Dirk[21] suggesting the celebrations for their mother's birthday on July 16th should be held in the small town of Lindau, on Lake Constance, rather than at her home in Deisenhofen. Although Wilhelmina seems to have liked the house she had built in the 1920s, the rest of the family considered it badly designed, shoddily constructed and located near an uninteresting and impoverished village. From Edmund's point of view, though, the main advantage of Lindau was its proximity to Basle in Switzerland where he intended to conceal Hitler's medical file. The family agreed to his suggestion and only a few weeks after his return to Greifswald, Forster applied to the Rector for a month-long leave of absence, commencing on Wednesday July 12th, in order to attend his mother's birthday party.[22]

It seems likely that he asked Dirk's wife Lilly to contact some suitable Jewish writers who would be interested in meeting him since she had a wide range of friends among emigre writers, artists and musicians. Nor was this talented and self-possessed woman likely to have been deterred by any risks involved in setting up the meeting.

Early on the morning of July 12th, Edmund and Mila loaded 'Opel-Popel,' with luggage and set off with their sons on the four-week holiday. They arrived at Lake Constance three days later for what proved to be a large and exuberant party, with all the extended Forster clan gathering to toast Wilhelmina's health. When Edmund and his family finally departed it was with the promise to pay another visit before the end of summer. Wilhelmina would never see her son again.

Their first overnight stop was in Basle, where Edmund deposited a copy of Hitler's Krankenblatt in a bank vault[24] before the family continued their drive to Paris. They arrived at Dirk and Lilly's comfortable apartment, not far from the German Embassy at 78 Rue de Lille, late on a Friday afternoon. The following morning, Edmund strolled to the Royal Café[25] in the Place du Théâtre Français where the meeting was to take place. It was a cool Saturday afternoon[26] and the wood-paved, tree-lined Boulevards de la Madeleine and des Capucines were busy with horse-drawn carts and carriages, buses crammed with sightseers and taxis, many driven by recently arrived Russian immigrants. On the asphalt pavements, shoppers walked among the 'blaze of azaleas, carnations, lilies, lilac, and chrysanthemums of the Madeleine flower market'.[27]

Edmund and Dirk with their wives in Paris 1933

A new weekly, German-language magazine, Das neue Tage-Buch (The New Diary) had appeared in the newspaper kiosks a few days earlier. While at a cost of 3 Francs – the thirty-page journal was considerably more expensive than any of its rivals[28] – its high price was justified by the number of exclusive articles by notable journalists, politicians and thinkers in the first issue.[29]

In the magazine's foreword, Im Strom der nationalen Revolution (In the Power of the National Revolution)[30] its editor, Leopold Schwarzschild, wrote about the 'exceptional circumstances' under which the German periodical was being published in a foreign country.

'Jewish and leftist intellectuals had begun to leave not long after Hitler's appointment as Chancellor on January 30th, 1933,' comments Timothy Nunan of Princeton University.[31] While those with a valid German passport could reach France, Austria, the Netherlands, or Czechoslovakia, it had been forbidden since 1932 for German citizens to take more than 200 marks out of the country and a 25 percent tax was levied on those who wished to transfer their assets.[32]

The first mass exodus of refugees began immediately following the Reichstag Fire. Nine hours after the blaze started, S.A. men broke into the apartment of author Theodore Plievier at 6am to arrest him. As Plievier had stayed out that evening, the storm troopers beat up his roommate, and, upon learning of their mistake, 'smashed the apartment amid yells that they will yet avenge themselves on that swine Plievier.'[33]

Gustav Regler, a Communist writer, watched the Reichstag burn and knew he would be wanted by the police but, still, he wandered the streets of Berlin for several hours that evening. Only after a friend told him that his apartment had been searched, and after a sympathetic prostitute offered him the key to her squat, did he realize his predicament. 'Berlin contained hundreds of thousands of workers who only yesterday had been my comrades. Now the time had come that there were only two equally threatened writers, and a street-girl, to offer me help against being struck down.'[34]

Out of the all too real threat of similar attacks or being sent to a concentration camp, an unprecedented number of intellectuals emigrated from Germany. This flight to safety occurred unabated despite greater emigration controls. Train officers questioned passengers carrying much luggage on trains within Germany and one émigré recalled a friend who had both his French visa and German passport confiscated as he tried to cross the border at Aachen.

Leopold Schwarzschild, a recent refugee from Munich, ended his foreword with a bold reflection on the émigré's position in exile, 'Emigration, separation from one's topsoil, can have two effects. It can set a splinter in one's eye but can also focus one's vision. It can spark hate and bitterness to such a degree that it makes one mad. And yet emigration, like any kind of distance from things and events, can bestow greater prescience, more thoughtful objectivity, and a penetrating insight. The history of emigration furnishes examples of both cases. We hope to be counted among the second group. And so we turn to our work. Das neue Tage-Buch is a unique case in the history of 20th century journalism and antifascism.'[35]

Consistently anti-Nazi, it featured more than 3,500 articles from contributors such as Winston Churchill and Ilya Ehrenberg and was read by German exiles around the world. The journal was also subscribed to by chancelleries and general staffs of Europe as well as being debated in the House of Commons, the Parliament of the Third Republic, and in the Dutch States General. In other words, whatever it printed was taken very seriously by people controlling many of the levers of power not only in Europe but the US and Britain. It was undoubtedly in the expectation that by publishing Hitler's private and confidential medical notes and revealing his hysterical personality to the world he would be able to bring the Führer's career to an abrupt halt before it could ever get going.

At the Café de Paris

Shortly before 10.30am on that morning, Edmund Forster pushed open the café's stylish glass doors to greet a group of German Jewish writers. Seated around a large table were Alfred Döblin, the poet Walter Mehring, novelist and playwright Leopold Schwarzschild and surgeon-turned-novelist Ernst Weiß, a German-speaking Czech.

Although Forster's original plan had been to provide details about Hitler's treatment only to Döblin, his medical colleague and fellow neurologist, having overcome his reluctance to speak he talked openly to all present. In 1951, Walter Mehring referred to that 'creepy Parisian exile episode' when Forster 'treasonably revealed the ominous Pasewalk hospital documents to the collaborators of Das neue Tage-Buch: Leopold Schwarzschild, Ernst Weiß and myself'.[36] Mehring later confirmed that during the three days he had spent with them, Forster handed over two copies of the Krankenblatt for safekeeping. Further confirmation of the medical file's existence came in 2010 when historian Thomas Weber of Aberdeen University discovered letters written by two prominent American neurologists, Victor Gonda and Foster Kennedy, in 1943. In these they describe their conversation with the notable German neurosurgeon Otfrid Förster, who had read the file in 1932 and was able to confirm that Hitler had been treated for hysterical blindness at Pasewalk.[37]

This evidence notwithstanding, some historians still question whether Hitler's medical notes would have still existed in the 1930's, over a decade after the Pasewalk Lazarette closed. Others argue that if such documents had survived, they would have been filed away in some official repository rather than remaining in the hands of Edmund Forster. Both objections miss the point that as a part-time consultant, Forster would have kept copies of all his patient files at the Charité Hospital in order to refer to the relevant notes prior to each visit.

A distinction must also be made between official records entered on hospital forms and the personal notes a psychiatrist would keep not only for subsequent treatment sessions but to provide material for reports, lectures and academic publications. Hysteria, as we know, was of great professional interest to Forster. He had published one paper on the topic in 1917 and in 1922 included details in a chapter for a textbook on neurology.[38] As he considered Hitler's case unusual and his treatment unique, it seems perfectly reasonable to suppose he would have retained the notes on file.

Forster's hope that his revelations would bring an end to Hitler's political ambitions were dashed when the weeks passed with nothing appearing in Das neue Tage-Buch. Although a courageous and independent-minded journalist, considered by many to be one of Nazism's most eloquent opponents, Leopold Schwarzschild knew that to publish Hitler's medical history would be tantamount to suicide. Even though there was little love lost between the French and German governments, such a powerful and well-substantiated attack on the Reich's leader was bound to result in tremendous political pressure for retribution. Schwarzschild may reasonably have feared that publication would lead to the magazine being shut down by the authorities, and equally likely his deportation back to

Germany where execution awaited. Instead of publishing the documents, he passed the file to Ernst Weiß for safe keeping. Given the political pressure on the émigré writers not to step out of line, it seems unlikely that any details of Hitler's medical notes would have become public knowledge but for Ernst Weiß's desperate need for money.

Weiß Enters a Competition

In the summer of 1936, following the death of his mother in Prague, Weiß moved to Paris where a mutual friend introduced him to a young German-Jewish couple, Mona and Fred Wollheim. Fred, a lawyer, worked at the Institut de Droit Comparé while Mona, a philologist who had studied at the Sorbonne, supplemented their income by giving private lessons in German, French and English. A few months after their meeting, Weiß wrote to ask Mona if she would be willing to type the manuscript of a new novella. She agreed and, as a result, Weiß and Mona started seeing far more of each other. He was in his fifties, she thirty years his junior.

Ernst Weiß

Although not conventionally handsome (Mona once described him as 'stocky with a bony face'), he captivated Mona with his intellect, humour and casual talk of such literary friends as Franz Kafka, Thomas Mann and Stefan Zweig. Before long, she began writing him poetry and soon after that they became lovers. Their affair lasted until 1938, when Mona rejected Weiß's ultimatum that she must leave her husband. Despite this abrupt parting, Mona remained friendly with him, and when later that year he pleaded poverty and begged her to type one final manuscript free of charge, she agreed. Had she refused, it seems unlikely that The Eyewitness would ever have seen the light of day.

By early 1938, Weiß, like many exiled Jewish writers, had fallen on hard times. France's policy of appeasement meant it was all but impossible to find a publisher willing to take the risk of bringing out their novels. Even if they did, few readers showed any interest in them. 'They had left behind their readers, their publishers, the magazines and newspapers that had published their works,' says Klaus-Peter Hinze, 'and thus they lost their source of income.' [39]

Weiß was living alone in a back bedroom on the fifth floor of the Hôtel Trianon at 3 rue de Vaugirard, close to the Place de la Sorbonne on the left bank of the Seine. His financial situation, although precarious, would have been even more desperate but for the kindness of Thomas Mann and Stefan Zweig, who had arranged for the New York-based American Guild for German Cultural Freedom to make him a stipend of thirty dollars a month. In the summer of 1938, he read an article in the German emigrant newspaper Pariser Tageszeitung that appeared to offer an escape from his increasingly precarious existence in Paris. The same guild that paid him a stipend was offering a literary award for the best German novel by an exiled writer. The American firm

Little, Brown and Co. was to give the award as an advance payment for the American edition of the prizewinning novel. The judges would include Thomas Mann, Rudolf Olden and Bruno Frank. Entries had to be written under a pseudonym and the competition was solely for works of fiction. When writing Hitler's medical notes as a work of fiction, he was simply complying with this stipulation.

Despite the October 1st deadline being less than a couple of months away, Weiß decided to attempt to submit an entry, not only in the hope of winning the cash prize but to improve his chances of gaining a U.S. visa. While hunting for a plot, he recalled his meeting five years earlier with Edmund Forster and decided to use the Krankenblatt as the basis for his novel, written under the pen-name Gottfried von Kaiser. He began writing immediately, barely sleeping or eating until the manuscript was completed and Mona finished typing the clean copy.[40]

With the typing complete, Mona helped parcel up the Der Augenzeuge and mail it to the United States. There, the manuscript was added to a pile of 239 other competition entries from hopeful authors. Weiß failed to win. The prize went instead to thirty-six-year-old Arnold Siegfried Bender, a minor novelist who wrote under the pseudonym Mark Philippi.

By sending his manuscript out of France, however, he had saved it from certain destruction. In June 1940, German troops raided Mona's apartment and carted away all her books and papers. 'Among the documents taken away were Weiß' diaries,' she recalled years later, 'as well as novels by Thomas Mann and Stefan Zweig, containing handwritten dedications to Weiß by the authors.'[41] Mona managed to escape from France and start a new life for herself in New York, but her husband Fred was arrested and later perished in a French internment camp.[42]

Weiß's manuscript lay gathering dust in a New York filing cabinet for over twenty years. In the early 1960s, it was discovered by publisher Paul Gordon who offered it, unsuccessfully, to a number of West German newspapers and publishing houses. In 1963, a young publisher named Hermann Kreisselmeier agreed to its publication but insisted that the book should be judged purely as a literary work drawn from the author's imagination and inspiration, without any reference being made to its factual origin. It was a decision that was to doom any chances of commercial success and, of the five thousand copies printed in 1964, less than half had been sold a decade later.

On returning home, Forster settled into his clinical and research work and, for a few weeks, everything seemed to have returned to normal. Then, just when he felt that his betrayal had gone unnoticed, a train of events was set in motion that threatened his academic reputation and ended in his violent death.

It all started with a letter.

CHAPTER 14
THE TRIAL OF EDMUND FORSTER

There will be no mercy now. Anyone who stands in our way will be cut down. The German people will not tolerate leniency. - Adolf Hitler, February 1933[1]

On Tuesday 28th August, 1933, a hand-written letter arrived by second class post to the desk of fifty-year-old Bernard Rust, recently appointed by Hitler as Prussian Minister for Science, Art and Education. Written by Berlin student and fanatical Nazi, Eugen Oklitz, it denounced Edmund Forster as amoral, corrupt, traitorous and the worst crime of all in Oklitz's eye, a Jew lover. Full of malicious tittle-tattle and unsubstantiated accusations, it rambled on in a disjointed fashion for seven pages. Any sane minister would have immediately thrown it into the wastepaper basket. Rust took it very seriously indeed.

The Rise of Bernard Rust?

Rust was a former secondary school teacher who 'preached the Nazi gospel with the zeal of a Goebbels and the fuzziness of a Rosenberg'.[2] After studying philosophy at Berlin and Munich, he had fought as a lieutenant during the First World War receiving the Iron Cross, First and Second Class for gallantry. Invalided out with a serious head wound, he returned to teaching. In 1922, he joined the Nazis.

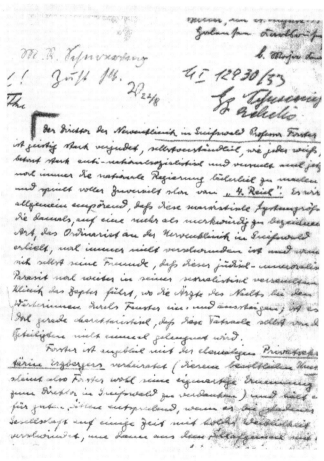

First page of Oklitz's denunciation letter

In 1930, he was dismissed from teaching after indecently assaulting one of his young, female pupils. Asked by the court to prepare a report on Rust's mental state, Edmund, perhaps out of sympathy for a decorated former soldier, claimed his actions were due to war injuries to his head. As a result, no further action was taken against him. The diagnosis proved no obstacle to Rust's political career and he was elected to the Reichstag later that same year.

The Rise of Herman Göring

The year 1933 also saw another and even more dangerous of Edmund's former patients gain high office in Germany, Hermann Göring. 'Göring is the personification of direct force and, if need be, insensate brutality,' commented Professor Stephen Roberts. 'He is never subtle or aloof. He has none of the hysteria of a Hitler or the deliberate calculation of a Goebbels. He has no fixed principles. He is an opportunist, ready to embark on any course of action that will make Germany strong. Eighteen stone of geniality or brutality as the occasion may warrant'.[3]

During the First War, he trained as a pilot and by 1917, had shot down twenty enemy planes and received Germany's highest Imperial award for valour, the Pour le Mérite. Demobilised with the rank of Captain, he travelled to Sweden where he earned his living as a commercial pilot, mechanic and a shopkeeper before meeting his future wife, the wealthy and well-connected Karin von Kantzow. Persuaded by her to return to Germany, Göring met Hitler in Munich and fell under his spell. He offered to reorganise and, thanks to his wife's money, help finance the Party while also bringing Hitler to the attention of his wealthy and military friends.

Seriously injured during the failed November Putsch, he

escaped arrest only by fleeing to Switzerland where he spent six weeks in an Innsbruck hospital. The overuse of morphine by his doctors caused him to become an addict and in 1925 he was committed by the courts to Langboro Sanatorium. When Hitler was released and a general amnesty declared in 1926, he returned to Munich and five years later became a member of the Reichstag and Hitler's deputy. The death of his wife in October 1931 may have been the trigger for a resumption of his addiction for which he sought treatment from Edmund Forster.

As part of his internal political battle with S.S. Chief Heinrich Himmler, Göring established a new and independent force in the form of Abteiling IA of the Prussian Political Police. On April 26th, he officially named this new force the Geheimes Staatspolizeiamt or Secret State Police. Not long afterwards, an anonymous postal official, given the task of designing a franking stamp for the new department, abbreviated it to Gestapo, a word which soon became one of the most sinister in the German language.

Göring housed his new department in a disused Arts and Crafts School in Prinz-Albrecht Strasse, not far from his own office in the Leipzigerstrasse. He appointed 33-year-old Dr Rudolf Diels,[4] a civil servant in the political police branch of the Prussian Ministry of the Interior, to become his personal combination of spy, blackmailer and watchdog. Diels, who had been a member of the extreme right-wing Students' Corps in the Weimar Republic, was clever, subtle, humourless, cynical and highly educated. Although never a card-carrying Nazi, he promised to create for his master an instrument of power the likes of which had never previously been seen in the history of Prussia. He was to prove as good as his word.

Under Göring, the number of officers employed by the

Gestapo increased rapidly from around sixty to almost three hundred. Göring exempted his new authority from the restrictions imposed by Paragraph 14 of the Prussian Administrative Police Law which stated that the police could only carry out their duties 'within the framework of current laws'. In other words, they had a licence to act outside the law and entirely ignore any notion of human rights. One of Göring's first orders was, 'Shoot first and inquire afterwards. If you make mistakes, I'll look after you.' Later in Dortmund, he added, 'Any mistakes my officials make are my mistakes. The bullets they fire are my bullets.' While in Essen he boasted, 'I make a habit of shooting from time to time. If I sometimes make mistakes, at any rate I have shot.'[5]

After the Reichstag Fire, he reintroduced execution by axe, claiming that 'decapitation is an honest old German punishment,' and hung a giant executioner's sword in his study against a wall of flaming red and gold. 'I am not concerned with meting out justice,' he announced. 'My task is to destroy, to exterminate.'[6]

Around the time Edmund was revealing the truth about Hitler's blindness to the émigré German writers in Paris, a Nazi show trial was taking place in Cologne where seventeen Communists faced trumped-up charges of murdering two S.A. men and wounding a third during a gun battle. On July 24th in anticipation of death sentences being passed, the Nazi Westdeutscher Beobachter ran a leader claiming, 'The iron desire for order of the National Socialist movement lies heavily and powerfully upon our people. There are to be no more half way measures of sentimentality. Every act of opposition will be nipped in the bud.'[7]

Six of the accused were, as expected, given the death

sentence and executed in Klingelpütz prison a short time later. Following Göring's orders, they were beheaded by axe. It was a gruesome and bloody business which more than fulfilled the Westdeutscher Beobachter prediction that their end would offer a 'frightful warning to the entire German people.' Here was a man prepared to destroy anyone who stood in his way or appeared to pose even the slightest threat to himself, his Party or, above all, his beloved Führer.

Given Forster's professional connections with the two most powerful and murderous men in Germany, it would have been remarkable if news of his meeting with the anti-Nazi émigrés in Paris had not been brought to their attention. He was clearly a potential danger to the Party and Führer which had to be removed. Since Edmund was an eminent and widely respected academic, they knew it would be politically risky to have him arrested or murdered. Too many questions were likely to be asked both within Germany and abroad. Some preparatory work needed to be done first to strip him of his academic credentials, then brand him as amoral and dishonest before, most ironic of all, having him dismissed as crazy.

The Purging of Education

In the Reichstag, on March 23rd, Hitler announced that as part of his programme to purify public life, his government would set about morally purging the educational system. 'Simultaneously with this purification of our public life,' he proclaimed, 'the government of the Reich will undertake a thorough moral purging of the body corporate of the nation. The entire educational system, the theatre, the cinema, literature, the Press and the wireless – all these will be used as a means to this end and valued accordingly. They must all serve for the maintenance of the eternal values present in the essential character of our people...the expression and the reflection of the longings and the realities of an era...Blood and race will once more become the source of artistic intuition.'[8]

Bernhard Rust was to be the instrument of this 'purification,' enthusiastically purging the Prussian education system of any teachers or lecturers who were not wholeheartedly committed to Nazi ideals. Those who had voiced doubts about National Socialism were immediately dismissed, as were all Jews and anyone holding left-wing views. In the space of a few months, more than a thousand teachers and lecturers had been sacked, arrested, imprisoned or forced into exile. Among them were physicists Albert Einstein and James Franck, and chemists Fritz Haber, Otto Warburg and Richard Willstätter.

A Letter from Eugen Oklitz

The machinery of Edmund Forster's disgrace and elimination was set in motion on Tuesday 22nd August when a letter arrived by second class post to the desk of Bernhard Rust. This confused, rambling and deeply unpleasant document, a mixture of clinic gossip and malevolent imagination is reprinted, in full, below.[9] (Underlining in original document).

'The director of the Greifswald neurological clinic, Professor Forster is a Jew lover, and, of course, as everyone knows, makes no secret of his anti-National Socialistic views. (He) continues to try and ridicule the national government and even now talks confidently of the '4th Reich'. 'It seems outrageous that this prominent Marxist who obtained his position at the neurological clinic in Greifswald by devious means, is still around and even his friends are surprised that this Jewish amoral parasite is still in charge of his sexually perverted and contaminated clinic where, at night, doctors climb in and out of the nurses' windows, it is absolutely typical of the place that those involved do not even bother to deny what is happening ...he appears to regard it as good manners, when in company, if he disappears upstairs with some lovely lady, and to emerge from a bedroom with the woman clad only in pyjamas. His female employees are victims of his alcoholic excesses and thanks to his powerful position he forces his attentions on them in the way I have just mentioned, as an example one can mention the farewell party for the Jew doctor Zader (sic).

'Because of this it is hardly surprising, that the matron is not permitted to discipline her nurses or her employees/co-workers as all these ladies are having affairs with the doctors. The perverted conversations which can be heard in the clinic are enough to make every decent person blush with shame. A particularly amoral type is the Czech Dr Woider, a very close friend of the Hungarian Jew Dr Zadow (sic) who will be mentioned later in this letter.

'This Czech sends a daily, detailed, report to Dr Zadow in Paris, which proves Woider is guilty of sabotage and spreading negative news about Germany (Horror news!). This Czech is despite the general unemployment and against the lawful regulations still in work, receives free board and even a salary! Furthermore, this cheeky foreigner and hater of Germans boasts about his filthy 'goings on' and believes it is permissible, when surrounded by people with opposing views, to read his foreign newspaper in a provocative manner and speak in negative terms about the national government!

'It is also interesting that Dr Forster has delayed, for as long as possible, the lawful dismissal of this previously mentioned Jew Dr Zadow in order to purchase with tax payer's money a photographic table, which is just a joke against the German government since this table costs 6000 RM. Zadow gains a personal financial advantage in this purchase since Zadow receives 15% for each one supplied. Furthermore, several thousand metres of film have been wasted by this foreign Jew, we estimate it is about 30,000 metres. All this happened after the January 30th and particularly after April 1st, 1933.

'The scientific loot from these films Zadow with the help of his boss Professor Forster took in Forster's private car, with Forster to Paris where Forster's brother, Embassy Counsellor Forster, did everything for his friend, the parasite Dr Zadow, who now very cynically says he hopes to return here very soon.

'This trip to Paris is said to have been done on expenses and like everything else which has been claimed as business trips seems very suspicious indeed. These 'business trips' were a fairly regular event in Forster's clinic. On one of these business trips in his own car to his brother in Paris, Forster took with him an assistant Miss R. (now dismissed), she returned with <u>three ball gowns</u>! Miss R. was later dismissed at the same time as Dr Z. when it became known that she was betraying Forster and had enjoyed a relationship with this Dr Z, liaisons which had taken place while Forster was lecturing. After this female assistant had been dismissed, negatives and prints of Miss R. and director Professor Forster were found, which showed they had been <u>photographed in the 'nude'</u>!

'Furthermore, Forster only listens to Paris on the radio and claims it is the only way to hear the truth and that the <u>speeches of Hitler were only for lunatics and the mentally insane</u>.

'When Forster at the beginning of April (or May) was in

Berlin, and was asked by a colleague, how he had liked the speech of our people's chancellor and this colleague had spoken enthusiastically about our Führer, all Forster could do was to speak negatively about Hitler's speech.

'It is also a fact that the neurological clinic has been embellished with particularly charming pictures (beautiful women's breasts etc), which are the works of a painter who at the time was employed out of friendship and an enthusiasm for this kind of Kitsch 'art': approximately four of these repulsive paintings had to be removed because they were causing a public outrage! <u>This is how institute monies were wasted!</u>

'It wasn't enough that one X-ray department was constructed at a cost 85,000 RM, plus a further 35,000 RM to equip it. One asks oneself who obviously lined his pockets there!!! It should therefore be strongly recommended that a commission with powers to carry out a detailed check of the account books is set-up, especially as in the past such checks have uncovered wasteful practices by the clinic: although without discovering the person responsible for these dishonesties! It is an indisputable fact that certain amounts were spent without justification! To mention just one other small detail. Very recently, allegedly for a business trip to his hometown the foreign Jew Dr Zadow was paid 55 RM, as can be seen in the account!

'For this foreign Jew, large amounts of money are available, for an unemployed party member however there wasn't even any lunch!

'Professor Forster is supposed to have packed his suitcases just in case anything is discovered so that he can disappear across the border to Paris 'on a business trip'.'

The letter was signed simply 'Oklitz'.

Who Was Eugene Oklitz?

The eighteen-year-old was not, and never had been, one of Forster's students or, indeed, worked at the University. He did, however, have family links to Greifswald. His father had been the bursar since 1925 and his sister, Luise, had worked as a laboratory assistant in the neurological clinic. Klara Korth, a typist, and Johanna Rätz, Forster's secretary, later claimed that in an attempt to gain promotion, Luise had twice attempted to blackmail Edmund. This happened on two occasions, the first in the summer of 1931 and the second in July 1933.[10] Both attempts failed and Edmund had her sacked.

This suggests that revenge for his sister's treatment might have motivated the letter. It is, however, equally likely that the order to Oklitz came from high up in the German hierarchy, if not from Göring then from Rust.[11] In any event, they wasted no time in acting on his disjointed and unsubstantiated accusations. Rust and his officials examined the document with almost forensic care, which is clear from the numerous margin notes and comments.

The Trial of Edmund Forster

The 'trial', in which the University Senate would be the judge and jury, was designed with one purpose in mind – to destroy the reputation and career of a man whose outspoken anti-Nazi opinions and dangerous knowledge meant he had to be disgraced, dismissed and disposed of. That same afternoon, a senior Ministry official named G.M.R Schnoering, telephoned Dr Sommer, Greifswald's Kurator[*] and another ardent Nazi, ordering him to launch an internal

---

[*] *A Kurator was the government's officer in charge of University administration, whereas the Rector was in charge of academic matters.*

investigation into Oklitz's allegations.

The following afternoon, an official from the Ministry, G.M.R Schnoering, telephoned Sommer instructing him to launch an internal investigation. In his official diary Sommer noted, 'Sister Braun will hand me a list of the witnesses I should question, and I am then to hand over the matter to the police who will decide whether or not to proceed. Regardless of what action the police take however, my instructions are to suspend Professor Forster with immediate effect.'[12]

On the afternoon of the August 29th, when he telephoned to report the outcome of the first two witness interrogations, Schnoering asked for copies of the transcript in order to hand them to the police. He also ordered that the clinic's accounts and the films made by Zador of the 'tipping table' experiments were to be impounded adding, 'I request that the investigations into Professor Dr Forster now proceed at high speed...I would ask you to start by concentrating strongly on the political aspects of the accusations made against him and to inform me about this promptly and if possible no later than the 20th September.'[13]

The charges against Edmund were identical to those alleged by Eugen Oklitz. He was accused of making derogatory remarks about Hitler and high-ranking Nazis, of denigrating National Socialism as a political ideology and of expressing doubts about the causes of the Reichstag Fire. He was additionally accused of immoral and indecent behaviour that had undermined his authority as Director and brought the University into disrepute. Finally, it was alleged he had been involved in financial irregularities ranging from fiddling his travelling expenses to spending government money on expensive items of equipment on which he had received a pay-off.

Dr Sommer telephoned Edmund, at home, only to be told by his wife that he had just left to drive to Berlin to seek an urgent meeting with senior officials at the Ministry. Sommer then informed Mila that her husband was forbidden to enter the clinic or any other department of the University and must, until further notice, remain confined to the Director's house. Not long after this call, Schnoering again telephoned and instructed Sommer to impound the Clinic's account books and 16mm films of Zádor's 'tipping table' experiments.

On Monday September 3rd, another letter arrived from the Ministry requesting that 'Investigations into Professor Dr Forster now proceed at high speed. Enclosed please find for background information, the summary of a report by a reliable person (i.e. Oklitz) who is well informed about the circumstances at the clinic. I would ask you to start by concentrating strongly on the political aspects of the accusations made against him and to inform me about this promptly and if possible no later than the 20th September.'[14]

The Evidence of Matron Braun

The first to give evidence was Sister Edith Braun, the Clinic's middle-aged Matron. Her lengthy testimony (it ran to seven pages of closely typed text) illustrates the extent to which these hysterical denunciations reflect the flimsy nature of the charges he faced, 'Where politics are concerned I can confirm that Professor Forster often makes outspoken and ill-considered remarks. I have been told that shortly after the Reichstag Fire he said, in the hearing of nurse Thürk, junior doctor Goralewski and sister Elfriede, that only lunatics would believe it to be a case of arson and that in reality the fire had been started by the national government for propaganda purposes...Professor Forster made these remarks without being prompted to do so by anybody else. I myself did not hear Professor Forster say, in the spring of this year with reference to the speeches of the Reichskanzler (Hitler) that these were likely to appeal only to lunatics and the mentally insane. He has however made similar remarks in the presence of Sister Martha, with whom I have spoken in the last few days about this. He also commented that the speeches were directed at 'provincials' in other words the ill-educated and lunatics. This statement was made in the presence of Frau Stohwasser, a female patient who is perfectly sane and a National Socialist. After the national government came to power Professor Forster remarked to other doctors, in the hearing of patients and in the presence of Sister Martha, that the present minister for education and cultural affairs, the minister named Rust, was an unsuitable choice since to avoid military service he had deliberately shot himself.'

Braun then discussed another of Oklitz's charges, the support and encouragement that Edmund had given to doctors from outside Germany, 'Professor Forster favoured Jewish junior doctors and did not hold Christian doctors in the same esteem. Until recently the Hungarian Jew Zádor was the head junior doctor at the clinic. This spring he was sent on leave in compliance with the law on the purification of the Professional Civil Servants and resigned from his job around the 1ˢᵗ July.'

She then dealt with Edmund's alleged dishonesty and mistreatment of patients, 'In the spring the purchase of another expensive tilting table was negotiated by Dr Zádor, for which he received a licence fee of 500 RM...While Dr Zádor was on leave, a great many experiments were carried out using this table. Mentally ill people, as well as former patients, were being tilted around on this table, that is moving about while either lying down or standing up, and their responses were filmed. In my opinion those conducting the experiments, especially Dr Zádor failed to treat these mentally ill patients with sufficient care and I often regarded what was being done as a form of torture. However, whenever I voiced my objections I was told that there was no place in such research for sentiment. Many thousand metres of film were used. It is possible that Zádor took some of them with him to Paris. I witnessed one female patient being jolted around on this tilting table for such a long time that she became utterly exhausted and had to be given an injection of Camphor. This costly table is now standing idle. In June Dr Forster and Dr Zádor went to Budapest with these films. As far as I know this journey was paid for out of clinic funds (500 RM).'

Finally, and from reading the transcript with considerable relish, Matron Braun turned her attention to what she considered the Professor's lewd conduct and his encouragement of similar immoral behaviour in others, 'Standards of morality and decency within the clinic left much to be desired. Dances and dinners were held in the doctors' refectory at which female laboratory workers were present. I have witnessed how, early in the evening, laboratory assistant Frau Rietzkow from Greifswald and Fräulein Wilder came to the refectory in ball gowns and partied there with the junior doctors Zádor, Weiß and Dr Zucker. Later the same night everyone, including Professor Forster, would drive off in a small car obviously in high spirits, with a great deal of screaming despite the late hour. They would then return in the early hours and all sleep in to about eleven or twelve o'clock, so that the work of the clinic suffered tremendously as a result.

Dr Goralewski, who left recently, and Dr Wayda together

with some student doctors...held a farewell party in Dr Goralewski's room with a great many female nurses from what is called the 'disturbed' ward. Naturally this placed patient in considerable danger. Also, the celebrations went on until about six o'clock in the morning. A few years ago, Professor Forster had an affair with Fräulein Rietzkow. At the same time Dr Zucker, who was employed at the clinic, also started an affair with Fräulein Rietzkow...When Professor Forster found out that Fräulein Rietzkow had started an affair with Dr Zucker, there was an argument the upshot being that both left the clinic. Laboratory assistant Fräulein Wilder said that after parties they would drive to the beach and bathe in the nude.

As Professor Forster attended all these parties I assume he also took part in the nude bathing. Fräulein Wilder...once she showed me and Sister Elfriede who is still in the clinic, a photo depicting Professor Forster and junior doctor Marienfeld with my predecessor Lotte Kaiser sitting on Professor Forster's lap while Dr Mariemfeld had Frau Professor Forster seated on his lap. I have been told by the doctors that Dr Zádor had a relationship with the wife of Professor Forster's brother, who is an ambassador councillor in Paris...and Dr Zádor then spent a lot of time in Professor Forster's home. Zádor had said that he would return to Greifswald once again at the end of August, and until then the nurse Thürk should prepare a large number of copies of the films for him.

Frau Professor Forster used to be the private secretary of Erzberger. Her reputation where decency and morality are concerned is very bad. She is said to fool around with every student...nurse Thürk can provide you with information about orgies that have taken place in Professor Forster's house.

Dr Zádor had a very close relationship with a student doctor called Wayda who is still at the clinic. During the last fortnight, he has started to call himself von Wayda and recently also obtained the flag of the Hungarian National Socialist party.

While guests were drinking coffee at one of the numerous farewell parties at which Dr Zádor and Frau Professor Forster were present, Dr Wayda indecently assaulted a nurse called Schulz. I have heard that Professor Forster then made an indecent proposal to Fräulein Oklitz, a laboratory assistant. It is not surprising that under these circumstances Professor Forster lacked the respect of his staff. One afternoon, with my own eyes, I saw Frau Forster, the wife of ambassador councillor Forster leaving Dr Zádor's room at the clinic. I did not tell any of the other doctors about this, but the former junior doctor Weiss, Goralewski and Dr Facilides all told me, independently, that Dr Zádor had had an affair with ambassador councillor Forster's wife. Whenever the wife of councillor Forster was in Greifswald staying with her brother-in-law Professor Forster, Dr Zádor would hardly been seen around the clinic since he spent all the time in their home.'[15]

Far from dismissing her wild and unsupported allegation as the farrago of innuendo and tittle-tattle they undoubtedly were, both the University and Ministry took Edith Braun's accusations extremely seriously with Kurator Sommer emphasising her honesty and truthfulness. On August 30th, an official in Bernhard Rust's Ministry named Achelis, wrote to the Curator: 'Based on the law of the reestablishment of professional civil servants of the 7th April 1933 (RGBL.S.175ff.) I deem it necessary to remove the orderly Professor at the medical faculty of the university Dr Edmund Forster from office until a final decision has been made, this is with immediate effect. This suspension also applies to those activities which Dr Forster carries out in connection with his position at university. His salary should until further notice be paid in the usual way. I request that Prof Dr Forster is informed of this immediately. Signed pp Achelis'[16]

The Case Against Edmund Collapses

Up to that point, the charges against Forster which from the Ministry's point of view had started so well, began to unravel. Edith Braun's testimony was undermined when the two colleagues, Max Thürk and Martha Bolz, whom she had claimed would confirm her allegation, refused to do so. From that point on, not one of the witnesses was prepared to support Oklitz's wild claims.

Professor Krisch, while conceding that Edmund had described a speech by the Führer as 'lacking in any distinction whatever' also insisted his remarks were not prompted by antagonism towards the Nazis, 'Professor Forster, as far as I can see, has no comprehension and no understanding of the National Socialist Movement and its ideals...I never heard anything which could be considered as ridiculing or blackening the name of the Führer, of his leading officials or the National Socialist Movement. For example, I never heard Professor Forster talk about a 'fourth Reich' and I would never class him as a particularly vehement anti-National Socialist. He really isn't enough of a politician for that to apply. I am also certain that Professor Forster has no Jewish blood in his veins.

Alone and accompanied by my wife I was a frequent visitor in the Forster household, where the atmosphere was never formal but always very casual and relaxed. Neither in my own or my wife's presence did anything happen that would have infringed on normal manners and decencies.

It is absolutely impossible that in my presence Forster ever disappeared upstairs with a lady and returned in his pyjamas, totally impossible. Yesterday, for the first time, I heard from the Kurator and saw in the files the allegation that Professor Forster was supposed to have had sexual intercourse with female clinic employees. I only know that the laboratory assistant Fräulein Rietzkow is alleged to have had a relationship with Dr Zucker and that during this affair Dr Zucker was supposedly visiting this woman in one of the rooms at the clinic.

I also attended, with my wife, social events held in the clinic's refectory where the atmosphere was always very relaxed and friendly. There was dancing. In my presence, there were never any occasions where there was indecent behaviour or anything bordering on the indecent. I am extremely surprised to hear what Matron Braun says about Professor Forster's relationship with Fräulein Rietzkow.

I have never heard about or seen any photographs depicting Professor Forster in the nude with one or two others. Nor have I seen the picture in which sister Kaiser is allegedly sitting on the Professor's lap and Mrs Forster was supposed to be sitting on the lap of a junior doctor.

I am not sure whether Dr Zádor derived any personal financial advantage from the neurological department acquiring the so-called tilting table. This table Dr Zádor used for quite a number of scientific research experiments and was hoping that if his tilting table examination methods were adopted as standard clinical practice, he would receive some patent fees for distributing this table. I also consider the tilting table experiments conducted by Dr Zádor to be both important and scientifically valid... I never had any reservations about these experiments.

I heard for the first time today that Professor Forster is alleged to have taken the former laboratory assistant Fräulein Reitzkow with him in his car and is alleged to have allowed himself to be photographed in the nude with Fräulein Reitzkow. I know Professor Forster brought back presents for Fräulein Reitzkow and his secretary from Paris... I never saw anything wrong with these gifts, because I knew how much time, outside normal working hours, both his secretary and the laboratory assistant had spent on preparing Professor Forster's speeches for the congresses.'[17]

Other witnesses, even those professing themselves Nazis, also contradicted the Matron's allegations that Forster had attacked Hitler or the National Socialist movement. Kroll, a junior doctor, told the investigation, 'Without being a member of the party, I have been a National Socialist for a considerable period of time and...in my presence Professor Forster never made a political remark slandering the Führer Adolf Hitler or ridiculing him or his officials or indeed the whole National Socialist movement and its activities...I do not at all regard Professor Forster as someone who actively is against National Socialism or acts as a serious opponent of it.'[18]

With insufficient evidence to provide ground for dismissal under the new Civil Service rules of defaming Adolf Hitler or the Nazi Party, Kurator Sommer's next move was to undermine Edmund's position at the University while offering him substantial financial incentive for taking voluntary retirement. On September 5th, he wrote to the Ministry, 'Today I discussed the suspension of Professor Forster with all six of his colleagues who unanimously agreed he could no longer remain at Greifswald. They requested me to approach Professor Forster and ask him to resign voluntarily on the understanding that I would secure him a pension amounting to three-quarters of his present salary. The Professors believed that this would be the best solution both for the University, to avoid a scandal, as well as for Professor Forster himself. He is said to be a psychopath, at times easily excitable, and other times very prone to depression. Not a single one of his six colleagues with whom I discussed Forster's personality in detail, was in favour of allowing him to retain his job at Greifswald.'[19]

That afternoon, he asked Edmund to call at his office, noting afterwards, 'Dr Kroll had previously told me that he was suffering from severe depression and asked me to treat him gently. I therefore carefully explained all the accusations made against him. He considered the comments of the matron and nurse Türk to be utterly fantastic and described Sister Belz as mentally retarded. He denies ever having made any derogatory remarks about the minister Rust but does admit to the possibility, that he might have made remarks about the Reichstag fire although not quite in the way that has been alleged. He also denies ever having made any statements or offered any opinions about the speeches of the Reich chancellor Adolf Hitler. He believes that his political activities in no way give cause for the Ministry to dismiss him from service. He frankly admitted that where the accusations of immorality were concerned his position at Greifswald was compromised, unless one also considered the fact that the relationship had occurred several years ago and that he himself had brought it to an end.

After receiving your telephone instructions, I once again made it clear to him in order to grant him a pension the Ministry would have no option but to dismiss him from service on the grounds of his political activities. He replied that he understood this, requesting only that if at all possible, news of his dismissal from the service on the basis of paragraph 4 of the Professional Civil Servant law would not be made public. He said that if he could receive a pension to the value of about three quarters (of his old salary) he would regard this as acceptable. He also asked me to talk to his brother who happened to be in Greifswald at the time. I happily agreed to this, since it enabled me to shift responsibility for advising Professor Forster who was very unwell. Forster then said goodbye to me in a calm and completely composed manner. I talked to the ministerial councillor Schnoering by telephone about the possibility of setting aside the accusations of immorality and indecency against Forster, which was what five of the University's clinical directors and the University council had proposed. Forster would then resign voluntarily, so avoiding disciplinary proceedings and the consequent damage to his own and the Faculty's reputation this would involve. Ministry councillor Schnoering said he was in favour of my suggestions and asked me to put them in writing.'[20]

Half an hour later, Dirk called to see Sommer, who noted in his diary, 'I read out to him the complete contents of the file and together we drew up a letter of resignation for Professor Forster and an accompanying letter, which was intended to secure the three quarters pension. Ambassador Councillor Forster took both these with him, and said that he wanted to think the matter over further before advising his brother whether or not to accept. He too considered the offer of a three-quarter pension would be the best outcome. Ambassador Councillor Forster also asked for the accusations regarding his own wife to be clarified and for him to be informed of this immediately.'[21]

A short while after that meeting, Sommer noted, 'Schnoering has just telephoned to say that he and Achelis have agreed in principle to my proposal, although this should not be regarded as a formal decision by the Ministry. I knew, however, that if he and Achelis were in agreement, I could accede to Forster's pension request. At my request Schnoering assured me that it would be in order to inform Forster of their consent and this I immediately did.'[22]

Edmund then sent the Kurator this brief note of resignation addressed to the Minister: 'I would ask to be released or dismissed from the Prussian State Service.' With it he wrote a note to Sommer explaining the reasons for his resignation and the conditions under which he was prepared to leave quietly. 'After you informed me today that, following your telephone conversation with Ministerial Councillor Schnoering that the Ministry is prepared to award me a pension amounting to three quarters of the legal pension and to grant me this as soon as I have handed in my request for dismissal, I enclose this request. I ask that you only forward my request to the Ministry once their offer of the three-quarter pension has definitely been secured for me.'[23]

Mila, however, was against her husband's request to resign, believing correctly it had been made under duress. She appealed for assistance from a leading Greifswald Nazi, Dr Herrmann Brüske, who immediately contacted the University's Rektor, Wilhelm Meisner.

'Dr Brüske informed me today, that Frau Professor Forster had asked him to intervene,' Meisner noted. 'She alleged that the Kurator had pressured her husband into agreeing to a voluntary resignation. I gave Dr Brüske all the files and suggested he advise Frau Forster after reviewing the documents. When Dr Brüske returned the files to me it was with the comment that even if three quarters of the allegations were false and only one quarter of them were true then Forster could no longer be tolerated at

Greifswald.'[24]

After reflecting on his best course of action for the rest of the week, on Friday September 8th, Edmund sent a telegram to the Ministry withdrawing his resignation. Ninety minutes later he telephoned Sommer and said he had now decided to accept voluntary resignation. When the Kurator asked what he should do next, Schnoering replied that he was 'not in a position to offer any advice and that Professor Forster should think things over for perhaps a week or so before deciding and meanwhile he would leave the letter of resignation locked up in his desk.'[25]

Despite Forster's agreement, the authorities continued interviewing his medical colleagues in the hope of unearthing any evidence that would justify dismissing him under paragraph 4 of Berufsbeamtengesetz, (Professional Civil Servant Law). In this quest, they were unsuccessful with many of those interviewed, from assistants to senior physicians coming out strongly in his support. Faced by the collapse of their strategy, the Ministry officials instructed Sommer to try and discover any financial irregularities attributable to Forster in the Clinic's finances.

That the whole sorry story from Oklitz's letter of denunciation to the witch hunt that followed was deliberately contrived to discredit and destroy Edmund seems beyond doubt. But what truth, if any, was there in the allegations? Forster was a man of liberal views who, perhaps, in part, because of his education outside Prussia, was far more of an internationalist than most of his contemporaries. He alone at Greifswald encouraged the employment of doctors from other countries and took no part in the Faculty's anti-Semitic or racially-motivated actions. He was also a staunch patriot who, shortly before his death, told his eldest son Balduin that he would certainly fight for his country in the event of war.[26]

So far as alleged financial irregularities were concerned, a detailed examination of the clinic's accounts produced not a shred of evidence to substantiate the charges of fraud. The equipment for the new X-ray building had been purchased from a highly reputable supplier, Reiniger, Gebbert and Jeifa and a Ministry accountant who examined the books considered it 'an impossibility that they would have paid any monies to either Professor Forster or any other medical, civil servants or other staff,' in return for the contract. He also confirmed that 'only the normal payments had been made to the doctors involved as well as to a technical assistant for the X-ray apparatus films etc. that had already been there and purchases were only made once the quotations had been checked out carefully.'[27]

The auditor's only grounds for concern were in the payment of approximately 600RM to purchase Aquarelles (a technique of painting in watercolours), sculptures and furnishings from Lattner. As to the charges of immorality and indecency, apart from his brief affair with Rietzkow, which he ended himself, the remainder of the allegations seem to have been either unfounded gossip or the result of a conflict of lifestyles between the cosmopolitan liberalism of Berlin and the small-minded provincialism of this bleak little town on the Prussian plains.

Conduct, which would have passed if not unnoticed then certainly unremarked at the Charité, became topics of intense and prurient outrage among the less-sophisticated Greifswald staff.

Two years before Edmund arrived at Greifswald, there had been an eerie forerunner of his own disciplinary hearing in charges levelled against another member of the medical faculty, Dr Ernst Friedberger, who from 1915 had been

Professor of Hygiene. This inquiry had been ordered by the Prussian Minister for Science, Art and National Education on May 30th, 1923 after an anonymous letter had charged Friedberger with a range of villainies eerily similar to those being alleged against Edmund. In addition to poor standards in his lecturing, research and academic publications, he was charged with promoting the employment of foreigners over German doctors, expecting employees to work outside office-hours; using funds for purposes other than those agreed upon by the University and treating employees in a 'rough and tactless manner'.

The internal investigation, initiated on the basis of Oklitz's bizarre accusations, proved to be the last act in Edmund Forster's turbulent life. September had always been a significant month in the life of Edmund Forster; he was born on the 3rd and married on the 12th. The enquiry had begun to hear witnesses on the September 3rd and, exactly one week later at 8am, Mila found him dead in the bathroom. He had been shot through the head.

CHAPTER 15
THE STRANGE SUICIDE OF EDMUND FORSTER

Red of the morning, red of the morning, thou lightest us to early death. Yesterday mounted on a proud steed, today a bullet through the breast. - From the Diary of Viktor Lutz S.A. Commander Hanover[1]

Over the days of the disciplinary hearing, Edmund had become increasingly depressed and unbalanced. Between Thursday August 31st and Monday September 4th, he had, according to Mila, twice attempted suicide – the first time by hanging and the second by swallowing nicotine. On each occasion, she claimed, it was only her prompt intervention that prevented him from succeeding.

After brooding over his fate all weekend, he awoke early on Monday morning having decided, at some time during the long and sleepless night, that he would attempt to take his own life for the third time. On this occasion, he would use his only Naval service pistol to put a bullet into his brain.

After dressing in his second-floor bedroom, he went down to the basement kitchen where his two sons, thirteen-year-old Balduin and twelve-year-old Ruprecht, were finishing breakfast in preparation for school. It was just after 7am. Lessons at the Friedrich-Ludwig-Jahn Gymnasium began at 7.45am and the walk between their home on Ellernholzstrasse and school took around fifteen minutes. The boys, both diligent scholars, were never late. Once they had left, Edmund retired to his study where he spent the next forty minutes contemplating his fate. Dismissed from his job, and with any future employment dependent on the good will of Bernhard Rust, he knew his academic career was at an end. Even worse, he feared that by handing over Hitler's medical file to 'enemies of the State', he had put his whole family at grave risk. Ahead he could see not only professional and personal disgrace but arrest, interrogation by the Gestapo, imprisonment and, quite possibly, execution.

A few months earlier, the Nazis had opened their first concentration camp on the site of a former gunpowder factory at Dachau, a picturesque little town ten miles north of Munich. The alleged purpose of this and the scores of other *Konzentrationslager* they established was to provide, as the Gestapo phrased it, 'A term of education...to get acquainted with the doctrine of the Third Reich.' Edmund knew this education was administered through starvation, slave labour and unparalleled brutality.

Suicide – A Rational Choice?

Faced with this situation, Edmund concluded his only option was to take his own life. Earlier that year, in an academic paper, he had commented that suicide need not always be considered pathological if it was the only rational way out of an impossible situation.[4] Now the time had come for him to act in the same rational manner himself. By making an honourable end to himself, Mila and his sons would be left in peace, while his life insurance[5] together with his University pension would guarantee their financial security.

Taking his 9mm Browning service pistol from a desk drawer and loading it, he went upstairs to the second-floor bathroom,[6] placed the muzzle of the pistol against his right temple and pulled the trigger. Considerate to the end, he had killed himself in the one room in the house with tiled walls, enabling blood spatter to be washed away most easily. Around 8.30am Mila, who had come upstairs to find out whether he wanted breakfast, discovered his body. Dr Kroll, summonsed from the clinic by telephone, came over and pronounced him dead.

Forster family home. The window of the bathroom where Edmund was shot can be seen on second floor left

Was Mila Lying?

Mila's claim that prior to shooting himself Edmund had

made two unsuccessful attempts to take his own life, the first by hanging and the second by taking nicotine, would appear to support the case for an ultimately successful suicide. This was the view of Dr Kroll and many of Edmund's medical colleagues who believed he had shot himself while depressed. In fact, her allegations point in a far more sinister direction.

Everything we know of Edmund's character and his sense of honour as a German officer suggests that both hanging (the fate of the felon) and poison (the choice of the coward), were the least likely methods he would have chosen to end his life. Especially since he apparently possessed a pistol and ammunition. His alleged ownership of such a weapon, illegal under Prussian law, raises a further question over Mila's version of events; no one seems to have known of the existence of this weapon before Mila found it beside his body. And if Edmund was not the owner of the gun, murder becomes far more likely than suicide.

Mila's other assertion was that at his second attempt, Edmund had attempted to poison himself using nicotine. This colourless alkaloid, three times as poisonous as arsenic, can be fatal at a dose of just 500mg. If he had swallowed this amount or more, only prompt medical attention could have prevented death from heart failure. Forster would probably have needed his stomach washed out and a drug such as atropine administered. Since she lacked both the training and resources to accomplish this, Mila would have had to summon help from medical staff at the clinic and so made his suicide attempt public knowledge. Yet, according to Kurator Sommer, the first he heard about this supposed earlier attempt was when he was informed of it by Dr Kroll.

This raises the possibility Mila invented the two alleged attempts to lend greater credence to the notion his death was self-inflicted.

Why Not Flee?

It is hard to believe that a man with the foresight to leave a copy of the damning Pasewalk Krankenblatt in a Swiss bank vault, to meet with the German émigrés in Paris and to provide them with a copy of the medical dossier would not also at least have given some thought to his escape from Germany. He was not under house arrest or even surveillance. Apart from the ban on entering the clinic, no restrictions had been placed on his movements. Perhaps, as Oklitz had claimed in his letter, he really did have his suitcases packed in readiness for immediate flight. If so, why did he stay?

In Opel-Popel, he could have been in Poland within a few hours or France within a day. Had he decided to travel further afield, Greifswald was a harbour town and the Baltic only twenty miles away. Although as events transpired he would have faced increasing dangers had he moved anywhere in Europe as the years passed, he had no reason to know that in 1933.

As to worries over their financial situation, Forster had negotiated a settlement of three-quarters pension from the Ministry of Education. This meant that although it was impossible for him to work in Germany as long as the Nazis remained in power he could either have enjoyed a comfortable retirement or found work in another country. Given his fluency in Dutch, English and French together with his qualifications, experience and international reputation, he would have had no difficulty in landing a job almost anywhere in Europe or the United States. By moving abroad, he would not only have found well-paid employment but also safeguarded himself and his family against Nazi reprisals.

When asked by Rudolf Binion why he believed his father had killed himself rather than flee abroad, Balduin replied, after a characteristically long pause for thought, 'Papi had told Mutti it was pointless, the Gestapo would pursue him abroad just the same.'[7] In making this statement, he spoke with deep earnestness and with a scrupulous sense of the importance of each and every word he uttered. As Binion recalled, 'As if he were before a high tribunal in permanent session.'[8]

Balduin accepted his mother's explanation. But, as I shall show, this cannot be taken at face value.

Was Forster Mentally Ill?

When, in 1973, American historian Rudolph Binion carried out his research at what had become the Ernst-Moritz-Arndt University,[9] he met two archivists who had been there during Edmund's time and chuckled at the mention of his name. 'He was crazy', one said while the other nodded in agreement.[10]

The consensus among the university staff was that a mind already unbalanced had been driven to suicide by the stress of disciplinary hearings and the disgrace of having his immorality made public knowledge. After the funeral, Kurator Sommer – who had described Edmund as a 'psychopath' – sent a letter to Mila that combined hypocrisy and humbug in equal measures. 'Dear Lady', he wrote. 'Please allow me to express my sincerest sympathy following the death of your husband...It was with great regret that I recently learned of the serious difficulties that your husband was faced with and, on the 4th of this month, from Dr Kroll about *his severe depression and the overwrought emotional state.* I was very grateful to Dr Kroll for letting me know because, one hour later, your husband visited me for the last time in his life and I was able, by a show of great friendliness and tact to make our very difficult conversation less embarrassing for him. When he left me, I was very happy to see that, as a result, he had calmed down completely...I hoped that the matter had been resolved in his own and his family's best interests. I am, therefore, especially deeply saddened that yesterday *your husband came to a different conclusion and decided on a different course of action*. By this final act all criticisms against him have been expunged...When I, as a Kurator of the University, laid a wreath on his coffin, dear lady, it was with cordial sympathy towards you and your children, who have suffered such a tragic fate.'[11] (my italics).

But what evidence is there that Edmund was 'crazy' and, if so, what form did his mental illness take?

In other correspondence, Kurator Sommer spoke of mood swings and claimed Edmund was, on some occasions, over excitable and at others prone to deep depression. This suggests bi-polar affective disorder (manic-depression), an illness in which emotions see-saw between extreme elation and profound despair. While there is some evidence that this condition has greater prevalence among the highly intelligent, there is nothing else in Edmund's history or behaviour to support Sommer's opinion. Balduin said he had enjoyed an excellent relationship with his father and claims he was 'never depressed, did not possess an uncontrollable temper and was always thoughtful.'[12] He denied that he seemed especially depressed or suicidal during the final days of his life. Professor Nissen, who had met Edmund in Basel in July noted he was 'as before a very sociable and talkative colleague.'[13]

While, unsurprisingly, distressed by the trumped-up

disciplinary hearings and concerned about his family's financial future, Edmund gave no indication of being suicidal or even especially depressed. As soon as he learned of the allegations against him, he drove to Berlin to consult colleagues at The Charité and seek clarification from the Ministry. He telephoned Dirk in Paris and asked him to come to Greifswald. During his interview with Sommer, he seems to have argued his case cogently and successfully negotiated an outcome that guaranteed financial security and a comfortable retirement. There is also evidence he carried on with mundane domestic tasks such as paying domestic bills. All of which strongly suggests that Edmund was coping energetically and rationally with his predicament. It is certainly not the behaviour of someone so depressed as to be suicidal.

With Edmund dead, what Mila wanted above all else was to ensure financial and political security for herself and her children. This view is supported by a postcard Lilly wrote home from Greifswald a few days after the funeral. 'Mila does not say a word about his death,' she told her husband. 'All she talks about is money!'[14]

As for her claim that Edmund was terrified the Gestapo would track him down no matter where he went, in 1933 this was pure speculation. Several years would pass before the power and reach of the SS and Gestapo posed any real threat to those living outside Germany.

Suicide or Murder?

The official version of Edmund Forster's death I have outlined above is a plausible account of the tragic death of a man described by Ludwig Zürn, one of his colleagues, as 'an excellent scholar, an outstanding teacher, and the saviour of the sick.'[15]

One might reasonably argue that, even if a Nazi did not shoot him, Edmund's death was the moral equivalent of murder since the actions they initiated drove him to take his own life. But can any more direct involvement be shown? Did Edmund choose to end his life on the day before his 15th wedding anniversary or was that choice made for him? Was he murdered on the orders of Hermann Göring to safeguard Hitler's reputation and political future?

Edmund certainly believed he might be silenced by the Nazis. During his meeting with the émigré writers in Paris he had announced it would soon be his turn and none of them should be surprised if, one day, they heard that he had committed suicide. 'They should interpret it in the same way as news about someone hanging himself in a cell or accidentally falling out of a window.'

All the relatives I talked to – grandson Arne, Pam, the wife of Dirk's son Vincent and Marie-Rose, Dirk's granddaughter – claimed Edmund was murdered. Balduin added that while he had no reason to doubt his mother's assertion he had taken his own life, she refused to discuss her husband's suicide with any of her family. A silence which may, in itself, be suggestive.

Flaws in the Official Version
The starting point in a quest for the truth about these events has to be Eugen Oklitz's letter of denunciation whose timing, only a few weeks after Edmund's return from Paris, appears suspiciously coincidental. The idea that the letter of denunciation was written at the instigation of a vengeful young woman was one Rust's Ministry was eager to foster.

But how much sense does this charge make? Luise is said to have first attempted blackmail in 1931 and again in July 1933. But why, since her attempt failed once did she try again eighteen months later? If Edmund took her action at all seriously, why didn't he have her dismissed after the first attempt? What could she have attempted to blackmail him about? If Luise was alleging, as Matron Braun had suggested, that Professor Forster 'made an indecent proposal,' this was common gossip around the clinic. Did the supposed indecency occur only prior to the 1931 blackmail attempt or did Edmund, for no apparent reason, repeat his sexual harassment in July 1933?

While most of Oklitz's allegations appear nothing more than gossip and innuendo, some of his specific charges, such as the cost of the new X-Ray department at '85,000 RM, plus a further 35,000 RM to equip it;' the commission of '55RM' paid to Zádor for his licence to the Tilted Table and '30,000 metres' of 16mm film used in the experiments seem likely to have been provided by a better-informed source than his sister. Here the finger of suspicion points to Oklitz's father, who had been appointed as Bursar the same year that Edmund was made Director. But what motive could he have had for wanting a fellow academic dismissed and disgraced? Although Edmund had, over the years, been embroiled in bitter rows with his medical and surgical colleagues there is no evidence at all of his falling out with the Bursar.

All of this gives rise to the suspicion that, far from being the solitary act of a vengeful young Nazi, the denunciation was part of a much wider and deeper strategy of character assassination. A suspicion which gains further credence from the fact that Rust and his bureaucrats treated it so seriously.

The Murder of Edmund Forster?

There is an alternative version of Edmund Forster's violent death. While in the absence of any records that would shed clearer light on what happened the following account is, inevitably, speculative. However, it fits all the known facts and explains a number of otherwise inexplicable aspects of the case.

Confronted with Edmund's refusal to accept voluntary dismissal, the Nazis decided to have him killed and to pass off his murder as suicide. Sometime over the weekend preceding his murder, Mila was invited to the Kurator's office on the pretext of discussing her objections to the plans for her husband's dismissal. It is doubtful that Sommer himself would have dealt with her and more likely she met someone who presented himself as an official from the Ministry of Education. After swearing her to secrecy, he informed her that the real reason for her husband's dismissal was his disclosure of highly confidential medical details about the Führer. By betraying his professional oath and his country in this way he had committed an act of treason for which he could be arrested and imprisoned. We know that Mila was aware Hitler had suffered from hysterical blindness since, many years later, she confided this fact to Balduin.

The official presented Mila with a stark choice. She must either drop objections to her husband's dismissal or face extremely grave consequences. These would include his arrest together with the loss of all pension rights. She and her two sons would have to survive as best they could under the stigma of a husband and father imprisoned for treason. Not only would Balduin and Ruprecht grow up in poverty but their educational and employment opportunities would be severely jeopardised. Mila, whose own parents had been poor would have been determined to spare her sons the same fate.

Having painted the bleakest picture of what would

happen if Edmund refused to go quietly, the official now sought to reassure the despairing Mila. There was, he told her, only one way to safeguard their future. Early on Monday morning an official from the Ministry of Education would visit her husband at home in a final effort to persuade him to accept the University's generous offer of dismissal. If he agreed, despite the extreme seriousness of his conduct, no further action would be taken. He and his family would be left alone by the authorities to enjoy a peaceful retirement. The official went on to suggest that her husband would find it easier to discuss matters frankly if he was alone in the house. For this reason, Mila must stay away from home between 7.30 and 8.30 that morning. He concluded with a grim, dire warning that if she ever mentioned their conversation to anyone, including her sons, she would face immediate arrest and lengthy imprisonment. Whether Mila would have understood the implications of his instruction to be out of the house first thing on Monday it is impossible to know. Perhaps she took the official at his word and believed that something could be salvaged from the mess Edmund had created.

Once breakfast was over, Mila told her sons she would walk with them to school. After the three left the house around 7.15, a waiting Nazi killer mounted the stone steps to the front door and rang the bell. Edmund, whom Mila had told to expect a visitor from the Ministry of Education, let him in. As soon as the door had closed behind them, the man produced a 9mm pistol and ordered Edmund into the bathroom where he shot him once through the head at point blank range. Dropping the gun beside the lifeless body, he walked out of the house and returned immediately to Berlin where he reported that his mission had been successfully accomplished. A fact confirmed the following day in a letter from Dr K. Deibner, the University's Director, to Bernhard Rust, 'This is to most obediently inform you that Professor Doctor Forster at present on leave took his own life on the 11th of this month.'[17]

The Nazi Murder Machine

That the Nazis were sufficiently ruthless to have carried out such an assassination is not open to doubt. Between Hitler's accession to power and Forster's death, more than five hundred individuals met violent ends at the hands of the Nazis. Some were gunned down, kicked or beaten to death, others were said to have been 'shot while trying to escape from custody'. But a significant number of senior academics and political leaders were, like Forster, alleged to have 'committed suicide'. Among the victims was Gustav von Kahr, the official who eleven years before had failed to support Hitler's Putsch. Now aged seventy-three and living in quiet retirement, Kahr was dragged from his home by S.A. thugs. A few days later his body was discovered in a swamp close to Dachau concentration camp. He had been hacked to death with pick-axes.

Innocence offered no protection. Willy Schmidt, a music critic, was the victim of mistaken identity when his SS killers confused him with another man of the same name. When his fiancé contacted the police to ask them to find out what had happened, she was asked contemptuously, 'Do you really think he is still alive?' A few days later, his remains were returned to his relatives in a coffin marked with a warning that it was not to be opened.

The Nazis' readiness to slaughter anyone against whom they harboured the vaguest suspicion cannot be doubted. Nor can the ease with which they could have found someone, within the Gestapo or S.A., willing to kill without ever asking, or even wondering, why. As Heinz Höhne points out, 'They did not think; they simply obeyed. They did not grumble; they simply acted. Without a word, they carried out the duty assigned to them...All they wanted to know were the names of their victims.'[18]

Murder by Suicide

The Nazi killers were never averse to dressing their killings to seem like suicide. When S.S. Hauptsturmführer (Captain) Kurt Gildisch was ordered by Reinhard Heydrich to assassinate Erich Klausener, Director of the Reich Ministry of Transport and a former head of the Police Section of the Prussian Ministry of the Interior, he never asked what the man might have done to deserve being executed without charge or trial. He merely obeyed his orders.

'Klausener was just coming out of his office to wash his hands when he saw the steel-helmeted S.S. man in front of him,' says Heinz Höhne. 'When the latter told him he was under arrest, Klausener turned and went to a cupboard to get his jacket. Gildisch thereupon drew his automatic and shot Klausener through the head; he fell to the floor dead. Gildisch seized the desk telephone and dialled Heydrich's number. The unnaturally high-pitched voice from the Prinz-Albrecht Strasse ordered him to fake a suicide, so he placed the Mauser near Klausener's limp right hand and put a double guard on the door. As far as the Third Reich was concerned, the Klausener Case was settled.'[19]

In 1934, after describing the Nazis as *Mordbuben* (murder-yobs) and *Kriegshetzer* (warmongers), the Communist novelist and pacifist Erich Mühsam was arrested and shipped off to Oranienburg concentration camp. A fellow prisoner later described the results of the beatings he received on a daily basis, 'His glasses were smashed and his teeth knocked...He developed a cauliflower-ear, with a large blister appearing out of his ear-hole. He was left for eight days in this condition without medical attention. On another occasion, he was forced to dig his own grave. He was stood against a wall, making him believe he would be shot. They then ordered him to sing the Nazi Horst Wessel song. Instead, Mühsam sang the Internationale, the Communists' song. His torturers dragged him back into the hut, and when he commenced writing to his wife, one of them bent his thumb back, dislocating it, saying, 'Now write to your wife!''[20]

After July 6th, 1934, the camp was taken over by the S.S.[21] and Mühsam's ill-treatment became even worse. Aware they intended him to die as a result of beatings, overwork and starvation, he, like Forster, warned his companions they should not believe any claim by the authorities that he had committed suicide. In the afternoon of the 10th July 1934, Mühsam was ordered to report to the guardroom, where S.S.-Sturmführer Ehrat handed him a rope and said, 'You have until early morning to hang yourself. You understand clearly what I mean, that is to hang yourself by the neck? If you don't carry out this order, we'll do it ourselves!' Mühsam returned to the barrack where he informed the other inmates that, having survived months of suffering, he was in no way prepared to take his own life. At 8.15pm, he was escorted to the administration building and never returned.

'The following morning, he was found hanging by a cord in latrine number four. His feet were dangling in the hole of the latrine-seat. The knot was skilfully tied in a manner which the half-blind Mühsam could not possibly have accomplished.'[22]

'That Old Nazi in the Fur Coat'

While never a paid-up member of the Party, Edmund's relatives believe that Mila, like many women, worshipped Hitler and supported his policies. When later owners of her house were redecorating in the nineties, they uncovered Swastikas drawn and scratched on wallpaper and skirting boards dating from the thirties. Whether these were produced by Mila or her children it is impossible to establish. However, when trying to sort out Edmund's affairs, she had appealed to her only friend at the University, the Nazi Brüske.

Dirk's wife Lilly, while remaining on good terms with Balduin and Ruprecht, refused to ever speak with her again, describing Mila in a letter to her husband, as 'that old Nazi in a fur coat.'[23]

Did Mila know that Edmund had been murdered or did she convince herself that he had, indeed, taken his own life if a fit of depression? Dirk and Lilly seem to have suspected that she might have colluded in his murder, if only by remaining silent about what she knew. But even if they had their suspicions, given the circumstances of the time, there was absolutely nothing they could have done about it. Dirk would never have dared to challenge the authority of the State, especially since to do so would have placed Lilly, with her Jewish background, in the gravest possible danger. Dirk's feelings about Edmund's strange suicide may, perhaps, be judged from his refusal to attend the funeral, sending Lilly in his place.

Reactions to Edmund's death varied widely. Karl Bonhöffer attributed it to a depressive crisis while other colleagues expressed no surprise at his suicide given his temperament and the conditions in Greifswald. Curiously, the University Rektor, Wilhelm Meisner, blamed both Mila and a senior physician for the professor's 'failure'. 'If Forster had had a different wife and a different consultant, he remarked, 'he would not have come to such a sad end but would have been able to cope with events.'[24]

The Funeral

After Dr Kroll had pronounced Edmund dead, his body was covered in a blanket and transferred immediately to the hospital mortuary. The Greifswald and Stetin police were informed but no post-mortem appears to have been carried out and, if there was any investigation, all documents relating to it have vanished.

An announcement of Edmund's death appeared in the local press and brief obituaries in a number of foreign newspapers. The following day, under the title, 'Reich Educator a Suicide' the *New York Times* noted, 'Professor Edmund Forster, head of the University Clinic for Nervous Diseases, shot himself dead at his home here today. He had been put 'on leave' by the Nazi Minister of Education pending an investigation into 'offences' charged against him. No hint was ever published by the authorities as to what these alleged offences might be.'

On the 13th, *Le Temps* wrote, 'The Jewish (sic) professor Forster, a specialist in nervous disorders, suspended from his position at the University of Greifswald, has committed suicide.'

Three days later, under a headline 'Suicide of Dismissed Official', the London *Times* 'own Correspondent' reported, 'Professor Edmund Forster, who was recently retired from his post as director of the clinic for nervous disorders at Greifswald University has committed suicide.'

Edmund was buried at 3.30pm on Thursday September 14th in the chapel of the Neurological Clinic.[25] Pastor

Schwedendick, a Protestant Priest from nearby St Jacob's, conducted the funeral that was attended by senior members of the faculty. Colleagues who only days earlier had been determined to disgrace him now read eulogies and professed their regrets. Professor Bonhöffer and several of his former colleagues from the Charité made the journey from Berlin.

Lilly, attended in the place of Dirk, who, for reasons that remain unclear, refused to be present. That night she wrote to him, 'You asked about the funeral. It is hard to describe, and I shall have to tell you about it when we meet. A great many people were present. The Priest was very bad and mother told him so in no uncertain terms. Bonhöffer's speech was half-hearted, but went down well mainly because he had bothered to attend. The Rector was very moving. A great many flowers and sincere expressions of grief from the (clinic) staff. salutes fired by the Marine-Association. You should have been here to say something nice. That was what was missing the most.'[26]

Edmund's body was interred in Greifswald's *Neuer Friedhof* cemetery and, once his wife and children had left the area, forgotten. Today his long-neglected grave is hard to find among the thick undergrowth.

Edmund Forster's grave today

A simple headstone bearing his name and dates of birth and death is all that remains of a doctor whose life was cut short by Nazi terror and whose unconventional treatment of a hysterical lance-corporal was to change the world forever. His final resting place, like the man himself, is rapidly becoming lost to history.

CHAPTER 16
DEATH OF A PSYCHIC

I wasn't as shrewd as I thought, nor as stupid as you believed.
But stupid enough... - Erik Jan Hanussen

On Friday April 7th, 1933, a farm worker named Mathias Hummel stumbled across a shoe attached to an ankle sticking from the ground in a small wood some twenty miles outside Berlin.[1] Several days of heavy rain had washed away the covering of top-soil partially uncovering a shallow grave. From it, the police disinterred the corpse of a well-built male in his forties. He had been shot three times at close range. While his face, ravaged as it had been by vermin and maggots, was hard to recognise, the jacket contained two labels; one identified the tailor, Hoffman, the other the owner, Erik Hanussen.

Kriminalrat Mölders, the officer in charge of the murder enquiry, had on his desk a missing person's report filed on

March 26th by Elizabeth Heine, the clairvoyant's personal assistant. Mölders summonsed Heine to identify the body which, with difficulty due to its condition, she managed to do. More than thirty years later, she still vividly recalled that her former employer's face 'bore an expression of absolute horror'.[2]

No sooner had the body been identified, on orders from Goebbels, the police investigation was closed. No suspects were questioned and no forensic examinations carried out. As with Edmund Forster, the Nazis were diligent in removing all evidence of their crime from the records. All of which makes it hard to be certain who killed the 44-year-old and why.

Why did Hanussen Have to Die?

The most obvious answer is that he was a Jew. In Nazi Germany, no other reason was necessary and Hanussen had a high-profile. Although he had initially been able to persuade many of his S.A. friends he was a Danish aristocrat, by 1933 the truth was widely known. Several newspapers had published articles attacking the 'Rasputin of the Reich' and providing details of his ancestry. In May 1932, the Communist paper *Berlin am Morgen* ran a series of articles entitled *'Ein Scharlatan Erobert Berlin'* (A Charlatan Conquers Berlin). In it, they argued that both Hanussen and Hitler appealed to human irrationality and gullibility and they would not rest until 'Berlin is cleansed of the last bit of this clairvoyant scum.'[3]

Attacks also came from the Right. A few weeks later, *Der Angriff*, using information provided by his disgruntled former manager Erich Juhn, ran a story about the 'Czech Jew Hanussen' which detailed his parentage.

In an attempt to ingratiate himself with the Nazis,

Hanussen had not only joined the Nazis, but also had himself baptised into the Catholic church. At the same time, he was making secret arrangements to transfer his business and his wealth to Vienna. According to his daughter, Erika Steinschneider-Fuchs, known through marriage as Baroness Winspeare, he knew all the while that he was living on borrowed time.[4]

Meeting Baroness Winspeare

Despite the fact she was only with him for eight days in 1932, after he had absented himself from her life for more than a decade, his daughter Erika cherished her father's memory. Every wall in her room in the retirement home where we met was covered with his photographs. One depicted him in flannels, strolling beside the captain of his yacht, the Ursel IV. Others, in colour, show the vessel's lavish staterooms. A beautifully-framed, eight-by-ten photograph occupied pride of place on an occasional table next to her favourite armchair. Dated December 5th, 1932, it shows her father wearing an expensively-tailored three-piece suit, white shirt and dark tie with a neatly folded handkerchief protruding from his breast pocket. The handwritten inscription reads, 'To my dearest photo companion, from your father Erik'.

Hanussen's daughter, Baroness Winspeare

Erika's dedication to her late father was both sincere and, to an outsider like myself, more than a little surprising. She was, after all, four in 1924 when he moved in with another woman. The couple divorced shortly afterwards and he made no attempt to contact either of them for the next eight years.

'I feel his presence all the time,' she told me. 'But I do not feel the presence of the Jew and clairvoyant Hanussen. It is the Catholic Hermann who helps me and people who help me and destroys those who want to harm me. Towards the end, my father knew only too well, his life was in peril every moment he stayed in Germany. He talked about the three of us emigrating to the United States, but my mother and I always knew he could never live anywhere but in Berlin. There he was famous, celebrated and wealthy. In the U.S. he would revert to being a nobody'.[5]

Hanussen's Secrets

If Hanussen was not killed merely for being Jewish there are plenty of other reasons why prominent National Socialists might have wanted him dead. It is known that, following the lessons he had learned in the twenties whilst working for *Der Blitz*, he used compromising photographs and recordings made using his hidden cameras and microphones to blackmail people in power, for either financial enrichment or political favours. Perhaps one of the men he had threatened with exposure had decided to remove him and the reputational risk he posed. If he had indeed been involved with the Reichstag fire, this alone would have been sufficient to sign his death warrant. While all these are strong and credible motives for his killing, there are two other reasons why he had to die – greed and betrayal.

The S.A. and the IOUs

By 1933, several high-ranking Nazis were deeply in debt to the wealthy clairvoyant. Locked away in Hanussen's safe were promissory notes amounting to many thousands of marks, not only from Count von Helldorf but other senior Nazis including Karl Ernst, Sturmbannführer Wilhelm Ohst and even S.A. boss Ernst Röhm. According to American author Arthur Magida, what triggered a determination to have these debts written off was Hanussen's attempt to use them to extort more money from a business deal in which the S.A. were deeply involved.

Buying the *Berliner Tageblatt*

For more than three generations, the anti-Nazi *Berliner Tageblatt*[6] and *Frankfurter Zeitung* had been published by the vastly wealthy Mosse family. In the twenties, they were among Berlin's most generous philanthropists, financing orphanages and homes for the poor as well as supporting the Berlin Philharmonic. After the death of the company's founder, Rudolf' Mosse, control passed to his son-in-law

Hans Lachmann-Mosse. In March 1933, after the family were forced to flee to Paris, the running of their publishing empire was left in the hands of long-serving employee Karl Vetter. Hans, who had promoted this former publicity manager and editor to general manager, considered him honest, loyal and trustworthy. Other members of the family dismissed him as a scheming opportunist and even described him as an 'evil genius.'[7]

Determined to Aryanise the Jewish-owned publishing house, the Nazis appointed S.A. Sturmbannführer Wilhelm Ohst as administrator with orders to buy the company. To camouflage their expropriations with a veneer of legality, the Party claimed to be making the purchase on behalf of a charity that was supposed to help war veterans. It was, in fact, a front. 'A takeover which would integrate the newspapers into an emerging Nazi Party publishing empire.'[8]

Ohst was instructed to offer two million marks for the entire business. Vetter, uncertain whether to accept or ask for more, consulted an old friend from his days as a PR – Erik Hanussen. After considering the matter, he made a counter suggestion. From his safe, he produced a bulky pile of IOU's signed by senior S.A. officers, including his friend Count von Helldorf. These, he told Vetter, could be used to blackmail Helldorf into tripling the Nazi offer. All they had to do was threaten informing Hitler of these debts and the Count, to avoid the scandal, would authorise the payment of six million marks.

The two men would split the additional four million marks between them before sending the balance to Paris.‡

---

‡ *Ohst eventually expropriated the media empire in typical S.A. fashion by brandishing a revolver and ordering at Hans Lachmann-Mosse's to*

Vetter Betrays the Plan

At the time, Vetter agreed to Hanussen's scheme. But, upon reflection, he decided that attempting to blackmail the S.A. commander was not a good idea. The following morning, he called on Helldorf and informed him of Hanussen's scheme to extract money from the Party.

The news that Hanussen was prepared to jeopardise their friendship in such an underhand way came at the end of a bad week for the Count. A few days earlier, in a phone call from Hermann Göring, he had learned of his dismissal as High Commissioner of the Berlin Police, a promotion he only received a month earlier. Göring informed him of his reassignment to become Chief Commissioner of Police at Potsdam, a position which he claimed was no less as important and prestigious as his current one. It was a lie and both men knew it. At Potsdam, his main function would be to supervise the breeding of horses.

Outraged by the clairvoyant's treachery, Helldorf contacted Karl Ernst who had replaced him as head of the Berlin S.A. What should be done about Hanussen he enquired.

'Kill him,' was Ernst's curt replied.

Hanussen's Arrest

Erik left his apartment for his nightly performance at La Scala shortly before 8pm on the evening of March 24th, 1933. His act, which took up the whole of the second half, did not start until 9pm giving him time for a quick drink at the *Grüner Zweig* (Green Branch), a favourite show business meeting place. While sipping a brandy, he was approached

sign over the publishing house or die

by Toni Ott, the bar's owner and an old acquaintance from his Vienna days. Ott warned him that two S.A. men had been asking questions about his routine. This was not the first warning he had received within the past twenty-four hours. Only that morning he had bumped into one of his former mistresses, Baroness Prawitz, who begged him to leave Berlin immediately. A few hours later, another female friend telephoned him with the same urgent advice.[9]

Having finished his drink, Hanussen continued on to the theatre. He had only gone a few yards down the street when he was stopped by a man who asked if he was Erik Hanussen. Thinking it was another autograph hunter, the clairvoyant was about to move away when a car carrying two men pulled up beside him. One was Wilhelm Ohst, the S.A. Major involved in negotiating the purchase of the Mosse Verlag. Informed he was under arrest, Hanussen initially refused to take the matter seriously. Just how serious it was the clairvoyant was not long in finding out.

As the minutes ticked towards 9pm, the director of La Scala became increasingly worried by the non-appearance of his star performer. When telephone calls to the clairvoyant's apartment went unanswered the director contacted a Herr Fleischer, an old wartime friend of Hanussen. At his apartment building, they learned from the doorman that the clairvoyant had returned earlier in the company of two men. They had gone upstairs for around a quarter of an hour before driving off again in Hanussen's red Bugatti. The star, the doorman reported, looked pale and his car had been heading not for the theatre but towards General Pape-Strasse. Telephoning La Scala, the director instructed that the disappointed, and by now increasingly restive, audience was informed that Erik had suffered a nervous breakdown and been taken to a sanatorium. Anyone requiring a refund could apply to the box office, but there would be no performance that night. Nor, as it turned out, on any other.[10]

Hanussen's Interrogation

After a drive of some four miles, the car arrived at a former military barracks recently requisitioned by the S.A. for use as a temporary prison. On arrival, Hanussen was taken not to one of the thirteen squalid cells in the dank cellar but to a brightly-lit office on the first-floor. Having made a rapid but fruitless search of his apartment before taking him to prison, his interrogators were interested in only one thing – the whereabouts of the IOUs. Despite threats and beatings, he remained stubbornly silent, probably reasoning these notes were the only leverage he had. The longer they remained out of the Nazis' grasp the less likely they were to kill him.

By midnight, realising his bluff had been called, an exhausted Hanussen agreed to hand them over. Bruised and battered, he was driven back to his apartment for what he knew would only a brief reprieve. Once home, Hanussen wasted no time in retrieving the IOUs and surrendering them.[18] As soon as the S.A. men left, the clairvoyant telephoned Fritzi, an ex-wife with whom he was still on good terms and begged her to contact a lawyer. Before he could explain matters further the line went dead.[11]

An illusionist to the last, he sat down and penned a letter in invisible ink to Erich Juhn, his manager, with whom he had fallen out with, asking that they be 'friends again.'[12]

'Yesterday they beat me till I was half dead,' he wrote. 'But half isn't enough for them. I know that without going into a trance. I wasn't as shrewd as I thought, nor as stupid as you believed. But stupid enough... I always thought that business about Jews was just an election trick for the Nazis (It wasn't).

Read carefully what the prophet Daniel has to say on the subject in chapters 11 and 12. Count the days, but only after they have destroyed a hundred temples in a single day – that's the time to start counting. The first date you get will mark the fall of the man who wants to become the ruler of the world by brute force. And the second date will mark the day on which will occur the triumphal entry of the victors. This is my farewell to you.'[13]

On the same sheet, he wrote the recipient's name in ordinary ink. Because the paper appeared blank, it was ignored by the S.A. men when, as he had surmised, they returned a few hours later. The Nazis ransacked his apartment and ripped out the telephone before dragging him back to Pape-Strasse. This time he was taken not to an office but one of the filthy underground cells where three S.A. officers, Rudolf Steinle, Kurt Egger and Ohst were waiting. Before Hanussen could beg for mercy, each took it in turns to shoot him at close range. Two bullets entered his brain and he fell dead instantly. His corpse was driven out of the city and buried in a shallow grave in the Staakower woods. Ohst then telephoned his superior, Karl Ernst, to announce that the clairvoyant was no more.

Later that morning, assistant Elisabeth Heine and Ismet Aga Dzino, Hanussen's secretary and fixer, arrived at the apartment to start work. Furniture, clothes, books, papers and ornaments lay scattered around the rooms and the telephone lay torn from its socket. While Elizabeth reported their discovery to the nearest police station, Dzino remained to start tidying up. Finding the seemingly blank sheet addressed to Ernest Juhn, and recognising the document for what it was, the secretary slipped it into his pocket and later delivered it.

How News of Hanussen's Death Was Received

In her diary for April 3rd, 1933, the Jewish journalist Bella Fromm noted sourly, 'Jan Hanussen, the stargazer and astrologer, fell into the hands of the self-styled 'sizzling souls of the people'. He has been slain. Goering's order. He has paid for his treachery in lending his hand to bring about the destruction of innocent people. When they had no more use for him, he was ruthlessly liquidated. It's strange that his familiar stars did not tell him that.'[14]

Hanussen's murder received little coverage in the German media. The National Socialist *Völkischer Beobachter* reported a dead body had been found under mysterious circumstances and went on, 'The unidentified man was discovered by workmen in forest plantation between Neuhof and Baruth. The corpse, savagely mauled by game, thus unidentifiable, appears to have laid there for days and no personal papers were found on the man. The Berlin police crime squad assigned a commission to investigate the discovery. An unconfirmed rumour claims the dead body is that of clairvoyant Hanussen.'

Der Angriff (The Attack), the SS paper published by Joseph Goebbels, reported, 'The body of a Jew was found in an evergreen grove on the road from Bayreuth to Neuhof. He had been shot to death. His face was unrecognisable. At the morgue, he was identified as Hermann Steinschneider who, under the name of Hanussen had a certain Vogue in Berlin as a clairvoyant.'

Abroad, coverage was more extensive with most European newspapers blaming the killing on the Nazis. The *New York Times* described the dead man as 'an adviser to royalty' while a headline in the *Syracuse Herald* proclaimed 'Bullets End Amazing Career of Hanussen Germany's Rasputin.'

When no one claimed Hanussen's body, it was initially buried by the State in a cheap pine coffin and a pauper's grave. Only later were his remains reburied in the far more elegant Stahnsdorf cemetery outside Berlin. His grave is marked by a roughly-hewn lump of rock bearing his name but no other information, no dates of birth and death and no mention of his successful showbusiness career.

CHAPTER 17
THE DROWNED AND THE SAVED[1]

Count no man happy until the end is known. - Solon[2]

General Kurt von Schleicher, like Hitler, believed that Germany should be led by a strong man. He also believed that man should be himself, not Hitler. During the years he spent at the top of the political ladder, first as head of the Armed Forces Division of the Reichswehr Ministry and, after 1932, as Chancellor, he did all he could to undermine his two rivals – the Social Democrats and the National Socialists, both of which he held in more or less equal contempt. Prior to the April elections, he remarked to a colleague that it would be an opportunity 'to talk to this lying brood with no holds barred...After the events of the last few days, I am really glad that there is a counterweight [to the Social Democrats] in the form of the Nazis, who are not very decent chaps either and must be stomached with the greatest caution. If they did not exist, we should virtually have to invent them.'

Hearing rumours about Hitler's treatment for hysterical blindness at the end of the First World War, Schleicher ordered his military intelligence to locate and bring him the medical file. His intention was to use it, if necessary, to thwart the Fascists' bid for power. The file was located and handed over to him. Rather than exploit the damning information at once, however, the General set it aside until he felt the moment was right. This turned out to be a fatal mistake.

At the end of December 1932, he and his elegant young wife Elizabeth, together with his close friend General Ferdinand von Bredow, were having dinner with well-connected journalist Bella Fromm. Over the meal, she urged caution as high-ranking Nazis were out to destroy them. Schleicher laughed the threat off, 'You journalists are all alike. You make a living out of professional pessimism.'[3]

On the afternoon of July 30th, 1933, von Schleicher was in the study of his villa, at Neubabelsberg near Potsdam, going over household accounts with housekeeper, Marie Guntel Elizabeth, his bride of eighteen months, was knitting in a nearby armchair. The doorbell rang. When Frau Guntel opened the door, she was confronted by six plainly-clothed SS men holding revolvers. They forced her into the study where one asked the General, 'Are you Kurt von Schleicher?'

As soon as the 50-year-old confirmed his identity, the men started shooting. A screaming Marie Guntel survived by fleeing into the garden. Von Schleicher and his young wife were shot dead and the killers drove away. The whole affair had taken less than two minutes.

In the early hours of July 1st, the body of General von Bredow, who had been shown the medical file's contents by his close friend Kurt von Schleicher, was delivered to the Lichterfeld Barracks in a wooden box. He had been shot through the head at close range.

'Nazi authorities lost no time in putting down with an iron fist any such challenges to Hitler's legitimacy,' notes Aberdeen historian Thomas Weber. 'Anyone questioning Hitler's story about the First World War experience was immediately targeted and silenced.'[4]

In this final chapter, I confirm the truth of his assertion by describing those who 'drowned' in the tsunami of Nazi's terror and those who, often against all the odds, somehow survived.

The Drowned...

Ernst Weiß

Soon after 7am on Friday June 14th, 1940, the first German army motorcyclists roared into Paris. Immediately behind them came cameramen and broadcasters who set up in the Place de la Concorde to cover the arrival of Hitler's occupying troops. The previous day, the Germans had offered to treat Paris as a non-belligerent zone if it immediately surrendered. At first, the French delegates tried to haggle, proposing that only the city proper and not its immediate surroundings would surrender. The Germans responded by threatening instant bombardment unless the French agreed to their terms.

That morning, the Military Governor, Pierre Héring, ordered French and Allied troops to withdraw. A few hours later, Parisians' heard, over hastily-erected loudspeakers, proclamations delivered in French with a strong German accent. One announced a curfew was now in force and that none could leave their homes between 8pm and 5am the following day. Another warned 'in the next two days, troops of the Reich will take a solemn march to Paris, everyone must remain at home!' While a third informed them that all the clocks must be moved forward by one hour to conform with Berlin time.

An estimated two million refugees fled the city. Roads south were jammed with women, children and the elderly pushing carts loaded with their possessions. Those who remained watched notices being posted on cinemas, bars, restaurants and even brothels reserving them for German soldiers. A sign on the Chamber of Deputies read: *'Deutschland siegt auf allen Fronten.'* (*Germany wins on all fronts*).

That morning, a terrified and disconsolate Weiß had watched the heavily-armed Wehrmacht troops, many on horseback, parading along the Champs-Élysées. With tears in his eyes he saw the Swastika raised atop the Arc de Triomphe and fluttering in the breeze above the Eifel Tower. Several months earlier he had written, 'With the years going by, emptiness is growing around me. I am still living, feeling, having desires and hopes. I do not fear death itself, but I dread the hour when, out of exhaustion, there is no more hope left within me for anything.'[5]

That June evening, the hour finally came.

As dusk descended over the city he loved, Weiß returned to the Hôtel Trianon Ill with a stomach ulcer. He lay on his iron-framed bed and listened to the clatter of rifles and stamp of jackboots as German soldiers paraded in the Place de la Sorbonne below his window. In America, Eleanor Roosevelt and Thomas Mann had been working tirelessly to secure him safe passage across the Atlantic but as the months slipped by without any word, he had abandoned all hope. Taking out his pen, he wrote a farewell note to his friends, ending with the words, 'Vive la France quand-méme (Long live France). After running a bath, he swallowed some sleeping pills and, lying naked in the warm water, slashed his wrists with a cut-throat razor. In his misery, the once-skilful surgeon bungled the job. Rather than the swift and painless end he had sought, his death was, from all accounts, slow and agonising. It was also unnecessary. In the American Embassy, the visa he had longed for and a ticket to New York awaited him; they hadn't got around to notifying him.

Author with Weiß's book outside the Paris hotel where he killed himself

Julius Zádor

Known to his family as Gyula, the doctor whose research with the tipping table had caused Edmund so much trouble, was the younger of two sons from a prosperous Jewish family. At the age of eighteen, he enrolled in the University of Sciences in Kolozsvar (now Cluj, Romania), Transylvania to study medicine.[6] The arrival of the extreme Nationalist and Anti-Semitic Admiral Horthy in Budapest in 1919, literally riding a white horse, made life for its Jews increasingly precarious. After the number of Jewish students allowed to study at its university was restricted, Gyula transferred from Budapest to a medical school in Berlin where he received his medical diploma in 1926. Between 1927 and 1933, he became an assistant professor at the neurology department of Greifswald university under the leadership of Edmund Forster.

After returning from the Paris meeting with Forster in May 1933, Zádor did not stay long in Germany. That Autumn he enrolled in a Hungarian medical school in order to gain accreditation in that country. With financial help from the family, he bought a spacious apartment in centrally-located Szep utca ('Beautiful Street') and started in private practice. In 1939, he accepted the position of Departmental Chief of Psychiatry in the Jewish hospital of Budapest. The same year he married Zsofi, daughter of a German Jew and a Hungarian mother. All the evidence suggested they were a devoted couple who, to the extent it was possible in the early 40s, shared a good life together until, sometime after 1941, Gyula was drafted into Labour Service. This was the name given by the Hungarian government to military service without military training. It was, in effect, forced labour frequently under cruel and dangerous conditions. In late 1944, Zádor's unit, which included several Jewish doctors, was deported to Germany.

The collapse of the German and Hungarian armies led to the country descending into the hopeless and destructive defence of Budapest and three months of savage rule by the Hungarian Arrow Cross. For the Jewish population, this meant hunger, contagious diseases, exposure to accidental deaths from aerial bombardment and later from shells and gunfire and, worst of all, being subjected to the rabid and unpredictable violence of Nazi hoodlums. The madness finally ended in early 1945 and a year later, Zsofi realised her husband was going to come home and spent the next three years endeavouring to trace him. By volunteering as a nurse, she was finally able to track down his last known location. In March 1945, he was still reportedly alive but extremely sick and in ward 6 of a hospital in Ohrdruf, near Buchenwald concentration camp. While he is believed to have died there, no further details about the date and reasons for his death can be found.

In 1948, Zsofi took up a position at Budapest's renowned school for theatre and acting where she taught costume design. The following year, the country slipped into a gloomy dictatorship under the personality cult of a chubby, mock-Stalin called Rakosi. Following the infamous Moscow Doctors Trials in 1952, antisemitism once more raised its ugly head. In February 1953, Zsofi returned to the apartment where she had last seen Gyula and jumped to her death from the seventh floor.

Ismet Dzino, Wife Grace and Son

Not long after his employer's slaying, Ismet Dzino, his British born wife, Grace and their young son fled abroad.[7] After short stays in London and Paris, they settled in Vienna where he found work in a casino. Dzino wrote a book about Hanussen's life and violent death in which he implicated named senior Nazis. After offering the manuscript without success to foreign newspapers, he handed it to Weiser, head of the Viennese police. In 1937, Dzino allegedly shot his wife and child, in a fit of jealous rage, before turning the gun on himself. In this task he was, according to one report, assisted by 'three or four gentlemen from Germany in long leather coats.'[8]

Count Helldorf and Karl Ernst

By 1938, Count von Helldorf had become disillusioned with the Nazi cause. Involved in the July 20th 1944 plot to assassinate Hitler, he was arrested and sentenced to death. On the 15th August, 1944, he was slowly garrotted with a piano wire noose in Plötzensee Prison. Before being put to death he had, on Hitler's order, been compelled to witness his fellow conspirators suffering a similarly gruesome death.

Karl Ernst, the S.A. commander who ordered Hanussen's murder, was a former boyfriend of Captain Ernst Röhm. Despite being a habitué of such well-known Berlin gay bars as the Kleist-Kasino and Silhouette, he was terrified of being outed. To counter rumours about his sex life, he went to the extent of getting married. After the wedding, he and his bride set off for Bremerhaven at the start of a cruise to the Canaries. It was an overseas trip from which Ernst had no intention of returning. Aware the S.A. were losing out in a power battle within the Nazi party, he intended to find a new home outside Germany. To ease his finances, he had taken with him documents implicating senior Nazis, including Hitler, in the Reichstag Fire which he hoped to sell to a major overseas newspaper. As the honeymoon couple were on the road to Bremerhaven, their car was overtaken at speed by another vehicle full of armed men. Shots were fired and his driver injured. Once the cars stopped, Hauptsturmführer (Captain) Kurt Gildisch of the Gestapo arrested Ernst at gunpoint and drove him directly to

Lichterfeld Barracks where he was executed.[9]

Hanussen's Killers: Rudolf Steinle and Kurt Egger

These two died fighting during the Second World War. The third, Wilhelm Ohst, survived. In January 1934, he was arrested on charges of financial irregularity in connection with the acquisition of the Mosse Verlag and his handling of lottery money. After a few months, he was released without charge, only to be rearrested in June following the Putsch against the S.A. Once again, he was set free after several weeks of investigation. Shortly afterwards, a special board of inquiry was set up to investigate his relationship with Karl Ernst and his role in the shooting of Hanussen. On September 29th, 1934, he was dismissed on the grounds that 'his personality and deeds do not match the spirit of the S.A.'

During the war, Ohst worked as the editor of a trade newspaper for the coal industry. In 1948, he was declared dead by a District Court. It was claimed he had been shot by communists during the last days of the war. The Berlin prosecutor who, in the 1960's, attempted to track him down to answer questions about Hanussen's murder believed this to be untrue. He suspected, but was unable to prove, that the man living with Ohst's wife was the fugitive himself who had acquired a new identity after the war.

Marinus van der Lubbe

The young Dutchman was sentenced to death by beheading two days before Christmas in 1933 after judge Wilhelm Bürger found him guilty of 'arson and attempting to overthrow the government'. Nine days into the New Year, the Public Prosecutor told him that his appeal for clemency had been rejected and that he would be beheaded the following morning. 'Thank you for telling me,' Marinus replied calmly, 'I shall see you tomorrow.'

When led from his cell early the following morning, his face was peaceful and he walked steadily towards the guillotine where the executioner, dressed in tails, top hat and white gloves, was waiting.

He died without uttering another word.

After decades spent attempting to rehabilitate him, the family of Marinus van der Lubbe succeeded. In 1981, a West German court overturned the conviction on the grounds of insanity. Campaigners demanded a state pardon arguing that since it has been imposed by a Nazi court, his conviction went against the basic ideas of justice. This pardon was finally granted in January 2008.

Presumed Drowned – Eugene Oklitz

Nothing further can be discovered for certain about Oklitz, whose name does not appear on any of the National Socialist Party records. One report claims he was killed while fighting on the Eastern Front but this was impossible to confirm.

...and the Saved

Karl Kroner, his Wife Irmgard and Son Klaus

After the war, Karl Kroner, the Pasewalk doctor who confirmed the hysterical basis of Hitler's blindness, worked as a neurologist at four different Berlin hospitals in addition to running a successful private practice. The author of many medical papers, he was the first physician to point out the value of the Wassermann test for syphilis in cases of drug and nervous disorders. In 1920, he married Dr Irmgard Liebich, a colleague he had met when employed as a consultant.[10]

'After a few years, they thought there were too many doctors in the family,' recalls their son Klaus Kroner who was, for thirty years, Professor of Industrial Engineering at the University of Massachusetts. 'She returned to university to study linguistics, specializing in the Scandinavian languages. This led to friendships with university students from all over Scandinavia, especially those from Iceland.' Soon their Berlin home was hosting parties for Icelandic students. On returning home, many rose to prominent positions in the government, politics, medicine and the media.

After the Nazis came to power, Karl was obliged to remove his doctor's sign from outside their house and soon patients, under intimidation from the authorities, sought help elsewhere. On November 11th, 1938, the day after the Nazis' anti-Jewish 'Crystal Night' pogrom, he was sent to Oranienburg (later Sachsenhausen) concentration camp. Following her husband's arrest, Irmgard Kroner turned to their friend Helgi Briem, Iceland's representative at the Danish embassy for help.[11] Briem immediately set to work to secure Kroner's freedom by applying psychological pressure to von Jagow, the chief of the storm troopers in Berlin. This official was constantly boasting about how much influence he had, so the diplomat challenged him to demonstrate this power by securing Kroner's release. After twelve days imprisonment, Karl Kroner, his head shaven and his body gaunt through starvation, was brought to von Jagow's office where a deal was arranged. He would be given his freedom provided he had left the country by midnight.

The only flight out of Berlin which would meet von Jagow's deadline was on a Danish aircraft leaving at 6pm. A call to the airline's office showed that all the seats had been taken. Once again, Briem came to the rescue, using his influence to have another passenger bumped off the flight. The official then travelled with Karl Kroner to the airport where he was involved in yet another argument as Gestapo officers attempted to prevent the doctor from boarding. In the end, Briem, waving his diplomatic passport, personally escorted Kroner to his seat on the aircraft and waited on the tarmac until it took off carrying the doctor to freedom. Irmgard and their 12-year-old son, Klaus, followed by train a few days later. All they were allowed to take out of Germany were ten Reichsmark and whatever luggage they could carry. Their home and all their other possessions were confiscated. When they finally arrived in Iceland, the family found their friends had rented an apartment, stocked it with food and made interest-free loans to tide them over.

Unable to obtain a licence to practice, Karl remained unemployed while Irmgard taught languages at the university. They had applied for visas to travel to the United States and it may have been in the hope of expediting these that, in 1943, Karl prepared the report on Hitler's treatment at Pasewalk for U.S. Naval Intelligence.

After the Kroners emigrated to the United States in 1946, Karl worked as a consultant at the Professional Hospital in Yonkers. He died peacefully in August 1954. Irmgard survived him by almost twenty years, passing away in 1973. Both had asked for their ashes to be returned to Iceland and today they are interred in Fossvog cemetery.

Mila, Balduin and Ruprecht Forster

On Sunday October 1st, 1933, Mila Forster wrote to the Chancellor of the University saying she would be leaving for Munich on Tuesday October 3rd and sought further clarification of her claims for a widow's pension.

The family remained in Bavaria for two years before

returning to Berlin and moving into a comfortable block of twenty, well-appointed apartments at 30 Stübbenstrasse in the Bayrisches Viertel district.[12] They lived there for the next ten years, during which time Mila never seems to have entered into another relationship; she is officially listed as a 'widow' throughout her time in Berlin. Despite never having a job, her family could not have been poor since her apartment building was located in an expensive part of the city and her neighbours were either professional or business people. In 1939, she had a telephone installed. Up to 1940, two of the other residents in the building appear to have been Jewish – Dr H. Burlin and Israel Kaufmann – but after that date neither were listed. In early spring 1944, Mila moved back to Southern Germany. A week later, on May 16th, the apartment building was totally destroyed by an Allied bombing raid.

Relationships with the rest of the family remained strained. When Mila and Dirk did correspond, it was mostly to argue over money. In December 1940, he wrote to her brother Paul Bretschneider, 'There is nothing good to be said about Mila. The row over her inheritance (i.e. following the sale of Mina's house in Deisenhofen) is drawing to an end but what she finally gets her hands on will be only a small part of what she expected to get her hands on. As you know I was opposed to this settlement, since I am convinced that she will immediately spend all the money. But she placed me under so much pressure that in the end I agreed just to put an end to the matter...Mila is extremely difficult to deal with. So far as the inheritance is concerned it was I who bore the brunt of her strange behaviour.' [13]

In March 1941, Dirk again wrote to Paul thanking him for a letter, adding, 'I have given up worrying about Mila, although I feel sorry for the boys. But I will only make contact with her again if she adopts a different and less hostile manner towards me.'[14]

Mila died on January 27th, 1970.

Balduin Forster studied medicine in Graz and Göttingen where he gained his doctorate with a thesis on alcoholism and later became a professor at the Institute for Forensic Medicine and head of the Forensic Institute in Göttingen. He died on Tuesday December 28th, 1999, aged 79 and was buried in Bad Krozingen. After the Germans invaded Austria, Ruprecht studied medicine in Switzerland, joined the Anaesthesia Department at Basel University Clinic and worked there until his early death from cancer in August 1955.

Dirk, Lilly and Arne Forster

Although Dirk remained in the diplomatic service until 1937, because Lilly's grandmother had been Jewish, his hopes for advancement were blocked after Hitler came to power. He was suspended following a furious argument with the Führer's over the Locarno Pact.[15] During a face-to-face meeting in the Chancellery, the Führer warned him, 'If you talk about this meeting to anyone you and your family will be killed.'[16]

In making a stand, Dirk was breaking a lifetime's habits of finding compromises and avoiding confrontations. When he discovered a colleague at the Paris embassy was arranging passports for Jews to help them escape persecution, for example, he warned the man that he would get into serious trouble. Characteristically, he neither reported nor assisted him.

In 1940, Dirk retired and went to live with Lilly in Berlin until 1943 when they were bombed out. After the war, he worked with the Allies and made occasional radio broadcasts. He also applied for compensation over his shattered career. Dirk died on February 27th, 1975 and Lilly, only a few months later, on September 15th.

Edmund's youngest brother, Arne, died from pleurisy at the age of 44 as a result of gas injuries to his lungs sustained during the First War.

Konrad Zucker

Julius Zádor's colleague at Greifswald and Forster's rival in the affections of laboratory assistant Rietzkow survived because he managed to emigrate to the U.K. where he worked at the Institute of Psychiatry in South London before becoming a professor at Heidelberg.

The Pasewalk Lazarette

In 1919, the clinic became a hostelry once more, with Paul Meyer as its first landlord. Thereafter, it passed rapidly through a number of different owners until being purchased by the Nazi Party in 1934. By this time, it was in such a poor state of repair that both the wings had to be torn down and rebuilt.

Consecrated as a *Weihestätte* or shrine, with a bronze bust of the Führer in the alcove where Hitler's iron-framed bed had stood, it became a place of pilgrimage for Nazi dignitaries, especially the Pomeranian S.A. and S.S. Hitler, however, never returned to the scene of his 'vision'.[17]

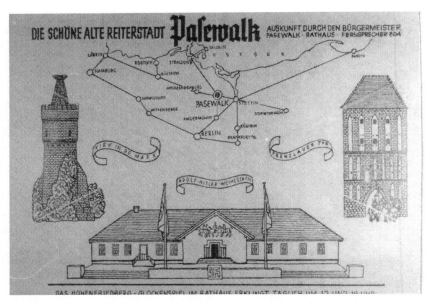

Postcard advertising the Shooting House as a Nazi shrine

The myths Hitler created around his time at Pasewalk can be judged from a book of his speeches that was published in 1923 under the title *Adolf Hitler: Sein Leben und seine Reden* (*Adolf Hitler: His Life and his Speeches*). The author's name was given as Baron Adolf-Viktor von Körber, a German aristocrat, war hero and Nazi Party supporter. In it, he describes Hitler as their nation's saviour, sent by divine providence to lead the country to glory and world domination.

'In the infirmary of the Pomeranian village Pasewalk,' says the author, 'a solitary bed stands in a darkened room... (a nurse) holds the twitching, feverish soldier of the betrayed army in her arms...a miracle comes to pass. He who was consecrated unto eternal night, who had suffered through his Golgotha in this hour, spiritual and bodily crucifixion, pitiless death as on the cross, with senses alert, one of the lowliest out of the mighty host of broken heroes – he acquires *sight*! The spasms of his features subside. And in a trance peculiar to the dying seer alone, new light fills his dead eyes, new radiance, new life!'

By comparing Hitler with Jesus, the author intended to propel this little-known and widely ridiculed right-wing politician into the public eye and establish his divine right to lead. But this 'act of shameless publicity' is even more self-serving than it first appears. That the author was Adolf-Viktor von Körber[18] has remained unquestioned for over sixty years. Only in 2016, thanks to research by Thomas Weber, was the truth revealed. Hidden away in a South African archive, he found compelling evidence, including a signed testimony by the publisher, that the fawning biography was penned by Adolf Hitler himself.

'It's 1923,' says Thomas Weber, '...and we see here a political operator who understands the political process extremely well and knows how to produce a narrative for the kind of leader only he feels he can be. So, he does not have to expressly say, 'I want to be leader.' He creates the expectation that others will call him to become the leader. The book makes some outlandish claims arguing that it should become 'the new bible of today' and uses terms such as 'holy' and 'deliverance', comparing Hitler to Jesus, likening his moment of politicisation to Jesus' resurrection.'[19]

In 1945, Pasewalk formed part of the Ucker line, a desperate last-ditch attempt to stem the rapidly advancing Soviet forces. During the intense fighting and Allied bombardment that followed, eighty percent of the ancient town was destroyed and most of the civilian population fled. Although it survived the war, the *Shooting House*, regarded as a Fascist monument, was demolished within weeks of the Soviet's taking control of the town. Later, they built a sports pavilion on the site and Herr Brose, curator of the Pasewalk museum, told me that as a child in the fifties, he had often played in its gloomy cellar – the only part of the original Schützenhaus to have survived.

Where the Shooting House once stood. The cemetery where Edmund is buried can be seen in the background

When I was in Pasewalk, on a gloomy evening in late February, the long-abandoned sports hut was shuttered and decaying. In the gathering darkness, a bitter wind blew across the wide and desolate Pomeranian plain rattling the bare branches of trees flanking the field.

Tangles of tall grass grew on the site where Edmund Forster once practiced his 'draconian' therapies, a blind soldier's sight was restored and a future dictator became convinced his divine destiny was to make Germany great again.

End

CHAPTER NOTES & REFERENCES

Chapter 1 - Hitler Lacked The Personality To Lead!

1. Garson, P. *Album of the Damned: Snapshots from the Third Reich,* page 78.
2. Meteorological records for Nürnberg on 7th September 1948. A high of 19°C with 7/8th cloud cover.
3. Albrecht Dürer born Nürnberg May 21st, 1471 died April 6th, 1528. Painter and printmaker recognised as the greatest of the German Renaissance artists, with work including altarpieces, religious paintings, numerous portraits, self-portraits and copper engravings.
4. Hans Sachs, born Nürnberg November 5th, 1494 died January 19th, 1576. A Meistersinger and poet whose work had a strongly religious influence.
5. *The Trial of German Major War Criminals. Proceedings of the International Military Tribunal Sitting at Nuremberg*

Germany. Part 1.

6. Fritz Kempner is mainly remembered today as the lawyer whose research brought to light the notorious Wannsee Protocol, a verbatim record of the 1942 meeting at which the 'Final Solution' of the 'Jewish problem' was discussed.

7. *The Trial of German Major War Criminals, op. cit.* page 50.

8. F. Wiedemann *Der Mann der Feldherr Werden Wollte*. In 1964, he published his memoirs and died, aged 78, in January 1970.

9. From an interview by journalist Julia Shearer, Regional Oral History Office, University of California.

10. Thomas Weber, *Hitler's First War*, pages 341-342.

11. Otto Friedrich *Before the Deluge*, page 309.

12. Cross-examination taken verbatim from *Das Dritter Reich im Kreuz-verhör* R. Kempner, pages 73 – 74.

13. Wiedemann, *op. cit.* page 26.

14. Neal Ascherson quoted in *Observer Magazine,* Sept 22. 1968

15. Lloyd George, who had recently met Hitler at Berchtesgaden, described him in these glowing terms in a Daily Express article written at the request of Lord Beaverbrook. Cited from *Hitler's Olympians,* Observer magazine September 291968.

16. Frederick Spotts, *Hitler and the Power of Aesthetics.*

Chapter 2 - The Hitler Of Nürnberg

1. Viktor Lutz, SA leader. From a speech delivered on Reich Labour Day September 1934.

2. Wykes, A. Quoted in David Calvert Smith, *Triumph of the Will-Original Screen Play*, page 4.

3. Shirer, W. *Berlin Diary*, page 23.
4. Pitt, B. Pageantry of Power, in Alan Wykes *The Nuremberg Rallies*, page 6.
5. Ernst von Weizäcker, cited in Piers Brendon, *The Dark Valley*, page 95. Weizäcker's father was Ribbentrop's Secretary of State between 1938 and 1943.
6. Merkl. P. *Political Violence under the Swastika*, page 539.
7. The title for the film, as with two others she made on the Reich Party Rallies, was taken from the tile of the Rally itself. Leni Riefenstahl had not planned to make a film of the 1934 rally, having directed a short one the previous year and not being interested in making another documentary. She suggested Hitler use the documentary film maker Walter Rutmann to direct. He shot some initial footage, including the title sequence that survived in the final production. Dissatisfied with his approach, Hitler demanded that Leni take over.
8. Piers Brendon *The Dark Valley: A Panorama of the 1930s*
9. From a broadcast by Joseph Göbbels, April 19th ,1945 to mark Hitler's birthday on the 20th. Quoted in the *Times* of London, 20 April 1945.
10. Martin Middlemarch. *The Nuremberg Raid.* Following the March 1944 raid, during which the RAF sustained heavy losses, they flew in strength to Nuremberg eleven times more and the Americans carried out at least three missions. On January 2nd ,1945, 521 Lancaster's dropped 1,825 tons of high explosives and 479 incendiary bombs. This was followed in February by two US Air Force raids. In total 13,807 tons of bombs were dropped on Nuremberg killing 6,369 Germans including 258 military personnel, plus 1,707 foreigners, many forced labour and prisoners of war.

11. Fest, J.C. *Hitler*, page 266

12. Wegener. Otto von. *Hitler – Memoirs of a Confidant*, page 111

13. Joachim von Ribbentrop, *The Ribbentrop Memoirs.*

Chapter 3 - A Wolf Is Born

1. George John Romanes (1848 –1894) was a Canadian-Scots evolutionary biologist who laid the foundation for comparative psychology. He believed all animals, including humans, had similar mental processes.

2. This description of Hitler's birth is based on. J. Constantinesco's, 1937 book *Hitler Secret.* Constantinesco was a journalist who, shortly after Hitler's rise to power, visited all the places associated with him and interviewed many who had known him.

3. Albert Speer, *Erinnerungen* page 313.

4. Description of Braunau-am-Inn from a booklet by Hermann Sprecht, *Ein Geschichts - Stadt und Landschaftsbild* (A History: City and Landscape) (1900).

5. Konrad Heiden, *Der Führer* page 40.

6. Hans Frank *Im Angesicht des Galgens* page 330.

7. *Ibid*

8. Bradley Smith, *Adolf Hitler: His Family, Childhood and Youth*, page 25.

9. Cited in *'Hitler as his Mother's Delegate'*, an article by Helm Stierlin, in *History of Childhood Quarterly*, Vol. 3, No. 4, 1976, page 492. Hitler uses the word 'Prügeln', which means 'beat'.

10. Hugh Trevor-Roper, *Hitler's Secret Conversations*, page 520.

11. August Kubizek, *Mein Jugenfreund op. cit.* August Kubizek, *Mein Jugenfreund* (1953). Ghosted by German writer Franz Jetzinger, a Linz archivist, this 'autobiography' is the only source of information on Hitler's youth and has been widely quoted. His account, written twenty-five years after the events, and with the aim of ingratiating himself to Hitler should, however, be approached with caution. It has many proven errors; all the dialogues are undoubtedly a fabrication and much else an invention. I have used the original German text rather than the translation with contains further mistakes.

12. *Ibid.*

13. *Ibid.*

14. *Ibid.*

15. *Ibid.*

16. Rudolph Binion, personal communication.

17. Dr Eduard Bloch, 'My Patient Hitler', *Collier's Magazine*, 15 March 1941.

18. Kubizek, *op. cit.*, page 86.

19. Binion, personal communication.

20. Heiden, K. *Der Führer*, page 81.

21. Spotts, F. (2018) *Hitler and the Power of Aesthetics* Woodstock & New York: Overlook Press.

22. Nerin Gun, *Eva Braun*, page 48.

23. Kläger, *Durch die Wiener Quartiere*, page 31.

24. The problem was simply too big for the resources available. In 1901 103,000 impoverished people were in need of food and a night's lodgings. In 1911 the asylums of just one charitable foundation, run by the Epstein family, were caring for 226,000 men and boys, 61,000 women and 46,000 children up to the age of fourteen.

25. Adolf Hitler, *Mein Kampf, op cit.*, page 20.
26. J Greiner, *Das Ende des Hitler-Mythos*, pages 13-14. As with Kubizek's 'autobiography' his account, although widely quoted, have been judged unreliable by many historians.
27. Heiden, K. op.cit., page 61.
28. J Greiner, *Das Ende des Hitler-Mythos*, pages 13-14. As with Kubizek's 'autobiography' his account, although widely quoted, have been judged unreliable by many historians.
29. Heiden, K. op.cit., page 61.

Chapter 4 – The Forsters of Nonnenhorn

1. Salman Rushdie, *Step Across the Line*. (2003) Vintage; New Ed edition.
2. The term comes from *Gottlieb Biedermeier* (*Bieder* meaning 'plain' and Meier being a common German surname), a fictitious character who featured in satirical publications during the 19th century. He personified solid but unimaginative middle-class virtues. It describes a design style popular in Germany, Austria and northern Europe between 1815 and 1860. Applied mainly to furniture, the term was also used to describe painting, sculpture, porcelain, glass and even music.
3. Deutsche Revolution (German Revolution) or Märzrevolution (March Revolution) is the term applied to events between March 1848 and 1849. Supporters and participants in the revolution are known as the *Achtundvierziger* (Forty-Eighters).
4. Karl Marx, born 1818 in Trier on the Mosel, studied law and political sciences before becoming editor of a

liberal Cologne newspaper. This was shut down by the authorities in 1843 after Marx had exposed the sufferings of agricultural workers and criticised censorship. He moved first to Paris and then to Brussels, where in February 1848, with his friend Friedrich Engels, he wrote *The Communist Manifesto*. His return to Cologne after the March Revolution was short-lived and his influence on it negligible.

5. From Switzerland, Schurz made his way to the United States, where he became an early supporter of Abraham Lincoln. Later he fought as a Union general in the American Civil War, ending a spectacular career as Secretary of the Interior. During the War, he commanded the 3rd Division of the Army of Virginia and later the 3rd Division of the Army of the Potomac, taking part in the Battles of Bull Run (July 1862), Fredericksburg (December 1862), Chancellorsville (May 1863) and Gettysburg (July 1863). By the time of his death, on 14 May 1906, Schurz had gained an international reputation for journalism and authorship. His books included *The Life of Henry Clay* (1887) and *Abraham Lincoln* (1891).

6. The equivalent of a PhD, the *Habilitation* is, in many European countries, an essential qualification for anyone wanting to become a university lecturer and professor. It is obtained via a thesis based on independent research which is reviewed by and successfully defended before an academic committee. Franz Joseph's was entitled *The Analysis of Organic Carbon Elements in Food*.

Chapter 5 – Journey into Mind

1. Garth Wood, *The Myth of Neurosis,* page 40.
2. H. Macdermott was a music-hall singer who achieved tremendous popular success with this song during the diplomatic crisis of 1878. Both the writer of the song, G.W. Hunt, and the singer saw themselves as serious commentators on foreign affairs. Ultimately Russia retreated from Bulgaria, restoring both it and Macedonia to Ottoman Turkish rule. Although hailed as a diplomatic coup for British Prime Minister Benjamin Disraeli, this meant that the Balkan Slavs suffered misrule under the Ottoman Empire for another generation. Macdermott died in 1901 and is buried in West Norwood Cemetery, south-east London.
3. Friedrich, O. *Before the Deluge, op. cit.,* page 22.
4. Marie Rose von Wesendonk Family Archive, Tuscany.
5. *Ibid*
6. *Versuche über das Verhalten des Muskels wenn Muskel und Nerv zugleich elektrisch durchströmt werden.* Inaugural - Dissertation der medizinischen Fakultät der Kaiser- Wilhelms - Universität Strassburg zur Erlangung der Doktorwürde. Strassburg 1901.
7. Garth Wood, *The Myth of Neurosis op.cit.*
8. Marie Rose von Wesendonk Family Archive, Tuscany.
9. The Suevia was built in Hamburg, by Blohm & Voss, as a cargo vessel for the Kingsin line. On 2nd June 1898, the vessel was transferred to the Hapag-Lloyd line and renamed Suevia. Until 1914 she operated on the Hamburg Eastern Asia and was in Manila when war broke out. In April 1917, she was seized by the US Shipping board and renamed the Wachusett. In

1920 the ship went to the French American line in New York and was once again renamed this time as the Margaret. In November 1923, the ship was finally sold for scrap and broken up. The Suevia was 113.2 m long and 13.4 m broad with a top speed of 11 kn.

10. Marie Rose von Wesendonk Family Archive, Tuscany.

11. *Ibid.*

12. The terms only appeared in English, French and German medical dictionaries during the mid-1880s. Before then textbooks dealing with topics in neurology, such as Moriz Benedikt's *Nerve Pathology and Electrotherapy*, published in 1874, only used such terms as 'Nerves' or 'Nervous'.

13. Cited in F.C. Rose and W.F. Bynum, *Historical Aspects of the Neurosciences*, page 8.

14. Marie Rose von Wesendonk Family Archive, Tuscany.

15. *Ibid.*

16. 'Die Klinische Stellung der Angstpsychose'.

17. Marie Rose von Wesendonk Family Archive, Tuscany.

18. Luigi Barbasetti, cited in K. McAleer, *Duelling*, page 43.

19. Stenographische Protokolle des Herrenhauses, 10th Session, 8 May 1907.

20. McAleer, *op. cit.*, page 43.

21. *Ibid.*

22. Isabel V. Hull, *The Entourage of Kaiser Wilhelm*, page 196.

23. This building survived the war and was converted into a rheumatics' clinic.

24. Robert Gaupp, 'Über den Begriff der Hysterie', *Zeitschrift für die Gesamte Neurologie und Psychiatrie*, Vol. 5, 1911, page 464.

Chapter 6 – Hitler Gets Called Up

1. *Mein Kampf op. cit.* (Manheim translation), page 148.
2. *Ibid.*
3. Aberdeen University historian Thomas Weber questions whether this famous image is an accurate record of the event or skilful propaganda. He points out that a newsreel film of the crowd shows far fewer people in the Odeonplatz than Hoffmann's picture suggests. This give rise to the suspicion that the picture was 'doctored' to support the Nazi myth of overwhelming popular support for the war. See *Hitler's First War* (Oxford: Oxford University Press)
4. *Mein Kampf, op.cit.* page 149
5. Minute no. 248, 23 January 1914, Imperial Austro-Hungarian Consulate. Cited in W. Maser, *Hitler*, page 75.
6. *Mein Kampf*, page 150.
7. BHStA/IV, RIR16/Bd,12, I Battalion/diary, 8 Sept1914.
8. Stephan von Rest & Jürgen Kraus, *Die Deutsche Armee im Weltkrieg. Uniformierung und Ausrustung – 1914 bis 1918.*
9. Heinz A. Heinz, *Germany's Hitler*, page 63.
10. A copy of the letter can be found in the files of the Institute of Contemporary History, London
11. Heinz, *op. cit.*, page 72.
12. Federal Archives, Coblenz, NS 26/4.
13. *Ibid.*
14. Together with his son and brother-in-law, Hugo

Gutmann was interned by the French in 1940. They were saved from the Holocaust by friends in the USA who arranged for their liberation and transatlantic passage.

Chapter 7 – Medicine Goes To War

1. Robert Gaupp, cited in B. Ulrich and B. Ziemann (eds), *Frontalltag*, page 102.
2. Bernd Ulrich, Krieg als Nervensache, *Die Zeit*, 22 November 1991.
3. Cited in Wolfgang Mommsen, *The Topos of Inevitable War in Germany in the Decade before 1914*, page 26.
4. Singer, *Wesen und Bedeutung der Kriegspsychosen*, page 177.
5. Robert Gaupp, *op. cit.*, page 102.
6. Lerner, P. *Hysterical Men*, page 3.
7. Robert Weldon Whalen *Bitter Wounds: German Victims of the First World War*, page 89.
8. Mendelssohn-Bartholdy, *The War and German Society*, pages 202-3.
9. P.F. Lerner, *Hysterical Men*, page 187.
10. *Ibid.*, page 6.
11. *Ibid.*
12. Nonne, M. *Anfang und Ziel Meines Lebens* (Hamburg 1971), pages 177 -178.
13. M. Nonne, *Therapeutische Erfahrungen*, page 109.
14. Duncan, B. *On Becoming a Better Therapist* American Psychological Association (2014)
15. Dan Jones (www.themindchangers.co.uk) personal communication.
16. G.M. Beard, *American Nervousness, Ibid*, page 534.
17. L.J. Rather, *Mind and Body in Eighteenth Century*

Medicine, page 191.

18. Wessely and Lutz, *op.cit.*, page 535.
19. J. Certhoux, 'De la neurasthénie aux neuroses: le traitement des neuroses dans le passe', *Annales Medico-Psychologiques*, Vol. 119, 1961, pages 913-30. A. Clark, 'Some Observations Concerning What Is Called Neurasthenia', quoted by Wessely and Lutz, *op. cit.*, page 517.
20. Shephard, *op. cit.*, page 10.
21. Schindler, 'Psychiatrie im Wilhelminischen Deutschland', quoted by Lerner, *op. cit.*, pages 40-1.
22. Willy Hellpach, quoted by Esther Fischer-Homberger, *Die traumatische Neurose*, page 133.
23. Alfred Goldschieder, 'Über die Ursachen des günstigen Gesund- heitszustandes', page 170.
24. Otto Binswanger, *Die Seelischen Wirkungen des Kriegs*, page 18. Binswanger was a psychiatrist at Jena University.
25. J. Brunner, Psychiatry, Psychoanalysis and Politics *Journal of the History of the Behavioural Sciences*, page 353,
26. Charcot, quoted by G. Guillain in *J.M. Charcot*, page 216.
27. F. Kennedy (1981) *The Making of a Neurologist: The letters of Foster Kennedy M.D., F.R.S. Edin., 1884-1952, to his wife*. Stellar Press, page 62.
28. W. Hellpach, *Lazarettdisziplin als Heilfaktor*, page 1210.
29. Lerner, *op. cit.*, page 251.

Chapter 8 – Gas Attack

1. *From a Surgeons' Journal*, 23 July 1917, page 166. Cushing first saw action in the spring of 1915, while

serving with the American Ambulance at Neuilly, France. As a surgeon and director of Base Hospital No. 5, he returned to France in May 1917 being detached from the Unit for special duties during the battles for the Messines and Passchendaele ridges. In June 1918, he was made senior consultant in neurosurgery, and participated in the three major engagements.

2. Adolf Hitler, *Mein Kampf* (1936) NSDAP publishing house, Munich.

3. *Ibid.*, page 183.

4. *Mein Kampf* was written in two volumes, the first entitled *Eine Abrechnung* (A Reckoning). It was published, on 19 July 1925, in an impression of ten thousand copies by Max Amann, who had been a sergeant-major and regimental clerk in the 16th Regiment. The second volume, *Die Nationalsozialistische Bewegung* (The Nazi Movement), was published on 11 December 1926.

5. A notable exception was historian Rudolph Binion, who first challenged many aspects of the account as long ago as 1976.

6. Sven Hedin, *With the German Armies in the West*, pages 357- 8.

7. *History of the 30th Division*.

8. *Ibid.*

9. 148th Brigade R.F.A., Sheet 28, 19th October 1918. Public Record Office, London.

10. Thermite, in use since mid-1917, was a mixture of powdered aluminium and iron oxide, which, when combined with an explosive called ophorite, doused enemy trenches in molten fragments.

11. *History of the 30th Division op.cit.*

12. Ignaz Westenkirchner, interviewed by Julius Hagemann; Harry Schultze-Wilde Collection, Ottobrunn bei München.

13. Heinz A. Heinz, *Germany's Hitler*, page 83.

14. John Terraine, *The Great War*, page 137.

15. *Ibid.*

16. C.R.M. Cruttwell, *A History of the Great War*, page 139.

17. L.F. Haber, *The Poisonous Cloud*, page 223.

18. The classification 'gas' was not introduced until 1915 by the British, January 1916 by the Germans, and January 1918 by the French.

19. In January 1916, the British government bought four and a half square miles of land at Porton, near Salisbury, in the west of England. By the time the war ended it had expanded to around ten square miles.

20. C.H. Foulkes, *Gas! The Story of the Special Brigade*, page 137.

21. W.G. MacPherson et al, *Official History of the Great War*, 'Medical Services: Diseases of the War', page 319.

22. *Ibid.*, pages 428-32.

23. *Ibid.*, page 256.

24. If the British troops were not being supplied with the gas by their own side, however, they were not averse to shelling the German troops with captured Yellow-Cross canisters well before September 1918.

25. Foulkes, *op.cit.*

26. Matthew Buck, personal communication.

27. Invented by Wilfred Stokes in 1914, it was highly mobile, relatively silent and capable of delivering projectiles at such a rate that up to fifteen, each containing around two litres of the liquefied gas,

might be airborne simultaneously.

28. The Livens mortar was invented by William Howard Livens, an officer in the Royal Engineers. It resembled a standard mortar with a three-foot-long mild steel tube attached to a base plate. Bombs were fired from a safe distance by an electric current. Projectiles would normally contain thirty pounds of pure phosgene, although almost any combination of gas could be fired over a range of up to fifteen hundred yards. As one military expert observed: 'Improved still further, the Livens projector was capable of dousing large areas with heavy concentrations of gas and was to become one of the most effective delivery systems devised.' Foulkes *op cit.*, page 162.

29. W.G. MacPherson, *op. cit.*, page 463.

30. H.R. Trevor-Roper, *Hitler's Secret Conversations*, page 177, said on the night of 16/17 January 1942.

31. By 1938, Hitler's doctors were advising him against visiting the Eagle's Nest on the Kehlstein because of a shortage of breath, but, of course, by then Hitler was well into middle age.

32. During the whole of 1918 Germany suffered some 70,000 gas casualties, around 65 per cent of their estimated total casualties. Twelve thousand occurred between 1 October and 11 November.

33. D. Winter, *Death's Men*, page 64.

34. A.G. Butler, *Moral and Mental Disorders in the War*, page 113.

35. Winter, *op. cit.*, page 64.

36. 'Bei Montagne gaskrank' (Bavarian Army HQ records); '21.10.1918 Zugang vom LKZ [Leichtkrankenzug] *Gent wegen Gasvergiftung ins Res.*

Laz. Pasewalk; Pasewalk Records; Hans Raab, 5 August 1939, to Hauptarchiv in Munich, 'Bis wir im Okt. 18 bei Werwic-Sued mit Gas . . . beschossen wurdern. Hans Bauer, 15 May 1940, *'Gas'*. Heinrich Lugauer, 5 February 1940, *'gasvergiftet'*. Regimental notice, 'gaskrank'. Mayor of Rothenburg in personal communication to Rudolph Binion, *'Gasvergiftung'*. Hermann Heer's niece in personal communication to Rudolph Binion, 'Gasangrijf; Hermann Heer, *'Gasvergiftung'*; Wilhelm Hoegner both in his book *Gaskrankheit* and in a personal communication to Rudolph Binion.

37. Köpf, G. 'Hitlers psychogene Erblindung: Geschichte einer Krankenakte' Nervenheilkunde *Zeitschrift für interdisziplinäre Forschung*, 9 (2005)

38. Weber, T. op cit. page 221.

Chapter 9 – The Shooting House

1. G. H. Estabrooks, *Hypnotism* page 52

2. In 1937 Lord Halifax, mistaking Hitler for a footman was on the point of handing him his hat. Von Neurath, the Nazi Foreign Minister, stopped him in the nick of time by frantically whispering *'Der Führer! Der Führer!'*

3. The weather report for Pasewalk on 21st October shows a clear sky and almost seven hours of sunshine with a maximum temperature of 16 °C

4. Although most biographers and historians have followed *Mein Kampf* in stating that the attack occurred on the night of October 13/14, military records confirm it occurred early on the morning of the 15th. See for example: Namentliche Verlustliste:

Ort und Tag des Verlustes La Montagne 15.10 18; Fünftaegige Meldungen der Lazarette: Oudenaarde Zugang am 15.10.18, Abzug am 16.10.18; Verlustliste des Res.Inf. Regiments 16: Am 15.10.18 bei La Montagne gaskrank ins Lazarett; Kriegsstammrolle: 15.10.18 bei Montagne gaskrank; Kriegsstammrolle 2. Regiment: 15.10.18 bei Montagne gaskrank; 23.10.18 ins Lazarett Stettin; Lazarettmeldungen: 21.10.1918 bis 19.11.1918 im preuss. Res.Laz. Pasewalk.

5. Adolf Hitler *Mein Kampf*, (Manheim translation) page 183.
6. Grosz, H.J. & Zimmerrman, J. 'Experimental Analysis of Hysterical Blindness: A Follow-up Report and New Experimental Data'. *Archives of General Psychiatry*, page 257.
7. Since no account of Hitler's journey from Ghent to Pasewalk exists, this description is based on a number of contemporary accounts together with photographs of German ambulance trains.
8. The description of Pasewalk railway station is based on a contemporary photograph.
9. The little town's only call to fame was as the birthplace, in the 19th Century, of Oskar Picht who invented the first typewriter for the blind.
10. Pasewalk museum archive
11. *Ibid.*
12. Information about Dr Karl Kroner was kindly provided to me by his son Professor Klaus Kroner.
13. Ernst Weiß, *The Eyewitness (Der Augenzeuge).* page 100.
14. *Ibid.*, page 106.
15. Rudolph Binion, *Hitler among the Germans*, pages 11-12

16. Washington National Archives of the OSS, Navy Intelligence Report 31983, Reykjavik 21 III 43.
17. Rosen, S. *My Voice Will Go With You: The Teaching Tales of Milton Erickson.*
18. Franz Polgar and Kurt Singer, pages 161-162.
19. Mona Wollheim in a letter dated 29th November 1973.
20. Jürg Zutt, in a letter to Rudolph Binion, *op.cit.* page 7.
21. Bennis, W. & Thomas, R. *Leading for a Lifetime: How Defining Moments Shape the Leaders of Today and Tomorrow*, page 17.

Chapter 10 – The Ways of The Wolf

1. Mary Wollstonecraft Shelley, *Frankenstein*, page 34.
2. Hayes-Fisher, John *(October 29, 2008) The last soldier to die in World War I, BBC News.)*
3. Hitler, A. *Mein Kampf op. cit.*, page 91.
4. *Ibid.* page 186.
5. In Heinz A. Heinz, *Germany's Hitler*, page 93.
6. *Ibid.* page 96.
7. *Ibid.* page 96.
8. *Ibid.* page 107.
9. Allan Bullock, *Hitler a Study in Tyranny*, pages 58 – 59.
10. Konrad Heiden, *Der Führer*, page 78.
11. Point 18 in the party's 25-point manifesto; cited by Robert Payne, *The Life and Death of Adolf Hitler*, page 194.
12. Konrad Heiden, *History of National Socialism*, page 31. On October 5th, the force was renamed the Sturmabteilung (Storm Detachment) or S.A., and the command of Johann Ulrich Klintzsch. The men were kitted out cheaply surplus army shirts purchased at a

government auction. Originally intended for use by troops in Africa, these were a sandy brown colour. So, by this accident of government surplus, one of the most highly organised and feared people's army in history came to be known as the Brownshirts. To counter the increasing power of the S.A., Hitler later created a new fighting force. Members of this elite palace guard swore their loyalty not to the Party but to the Führer himself. They wore black ski-caps with silver death's head buttons on them and black bordered swastika arm bands and were the nucleus of the S.S. (Schutzstaffel) which came into official existence on November 9th, 1925.

13. Quoted in Heinz, *op. cit.*, page 119.
14. Heiden, *Der Führer, op. cit.*, page 79.
15. Adolf Hitler, *Mein Kampf* (Murphy translation), page 317.
16. Kurt Ludecke, *I Knew Hitler*, page 22.
17. Heiden, *Der Führer, op. cit.*, page 113.
18. Hitler in an unsigned article for *Volkischer Beobachter*, cited by Payne, op. cit., page 200.
19. Huge Trevor-Roper, H.R. *Hitler's Secret Conversations* page 202. Said on the night of 25/26 January 1942.
20. Bleuel, H.P. *Strength through joy: Sex and society in Nazi Germany.* London: Pan Books (1976).
21. Strasser, Otto: *Hitler and I* (trans, Gwenda David and Erich Mosbacher) London: Cape (1940).
22. Huge Trevor-Roper, H.R. *Hitler's Secret Conversations op.cit.*
23. Domarus, Max, *Hitler,* Munich 1965. Page 565.
24. 24.Guida Dichl, *Die deutsche Frau und der Nationalsozialismus* Eisenach, (1933), page 42
25. Shirer, *op.cit.*, page 70.

26. 26.*Ibid.*

Chapter 11 – Babylon on Spree

1. Mel Gordon, Voluptuous Paris, The Erotic World of Weimar Berlin, page 24
2. Hoover Institution, April 1, 2001
3. Ilya Ehrenburg, *op cit.,* page 82.
4. Michael Davidson, *The World, The Flesh and Myself,* pages 150-151.
5. .Lucas, N. *Ladies of the Underworld: The Beautiful, the Damned and Those Who Get Away with It,* pages 92-93.

Chapter 12 – Hitler's Jewish Psychic

1. Spence, R. Erik Jan Hanussen: Hitler's Jewish Psychic, *New Dawn* magazine, Vo. 8. No 3, pages 21 – 29.
2. Hanussen, *Meine Lebenslinie* (orig. 1930), page 74.
3. Spence, R. *op cit.*
4. Oskar Pfungst, *Clever Hans (the Horse of Mr. van Osten).*
5. David Marks & Richard Kammann, *The Psychology of the Psychic,* pages 68-69
6. Magida, A. J. *The Nazi Séance – The Strange Story of the Jewish Psychic in Hitler's Circle,* page 55.
7. Markus Kompa (with Wilfried Kugel), 'Erik Jan Hanussen - Hokus-Pokus-Tausendsassa.' *Telepolis Magazin.*
8. Polgar and Singer, *The Story of a Hypnotist,* page
9. Hanussen, *Meine Lebenslinie op. cit.*
10. As he awaited execution by guillotine, in July of that year, he asked the prison psychiatrist: 'After my head

has been chopped off will I still be able to hear, at least for the moment, the sound of my own blood gushing from the stump of my neck?' When told he probably would Kurten replied: 'That would be the pleasure to end all pleasures.'

11. Spence, R. *op. cit.* (quoting Robin Lockhart), *Reilly: Ace of Spies.*

12. Gordon, M. *Erik Jan Hanussen: Hitler's Jewish Clairvoyant*, page 77.

13. *The Trial against Hanussen Prager Tagblatt* (Prague) December 17, 1929, in Magida *op. cit.*, pages 89 – 95.

14. 'Clairvoyant Proves Power in Czech Court,' *New York Times* 29 May 1930.

15. Polgar, F. J. & Singer, K. (1951) *The Story of a Hypnotist*, page 75.

16. Voigt, P. 'Clairvoyant Hanussen Acquitted in Leitmeritz' in Bart Collection. Magida, *op cit* page 98

17. Built in 1920 by a consortium of nine Jewish businessmen, including the Dutch aviation pioneer Anton Fokker, and situated at 22-24 Lutherstraße on the corner of Augsburgerstraße (now 12-14 Martin-Luther Straße) at the corner of Fuggerstraße. The building was heavily bombed on the night of November 22, 1943, but remained partly in use by The Voles cabaret troupe until it was finally demolished in the 1960's. Shops and apartments were built on the site of the foyer while the stage and auditorium are a car park.

18. Kurlander, E. *Hitler's Monsters: A Supernatural History of the Third Reich.*

19. A German writer famous for his horror short stories and novels Ewers began his literary career as a poet, publishing a book of satirical verses, in 1901.

20. Berlin journalist Bella Fromm, described Wessel as 'a cheap pimp; who was most likely killed by the friend of a girl whom he was pimping'. The song, which starts: 'Flag high, ranks closed, The S.A. marches with silent solid steps' was actually written by his brother. Horst merely signed his name to it. Hitler liked the song so much that he took it as the party anthem. The tune is a traditional northern Europe one and shares its melody with the Christian hymn 'How Great Thou Art'.

21. Heiden, *op. cit.*, page 577.

22. Gordon, M. *Voluptuous Berlin, op. cit.*, page 218.

23. Gordon, M. *Erik Jan Hanussen: Hitler's Jewish Clairvoyant op. cit.*, page 214.

24. Born Edward Alexander Crowley, to fundamentalist Christian parents, he rejected mainstream religion as a young man to become an occultist, ceremonial magician and prophet. His title of 'The Beast 666' was taken from the book of Revelations 13.18. 'Let him that hath understanding count the number of the beast…Six hundred threescore and six.'

25. Werner Gerson (Pierre Mariel), 'Mage ou Espion?' in *Le Nazisme: Societe Secrete.*

26. Spence, R.B. *Secret Agent 666: Aleister Crowley, British Intelligence and the Occult*, pages 210-213.

27. Neubauer, A, *Speed Was My Life* Barrie and Rockliff, (1960).

28. Quincy Howe, World Diary, 1929-1934. New York: McBride.

29. Joseph Howard Tyson, *The Surreal Reich*, page 11.

30. Mosher. J.A. *Effective Public Speaking: The Essentials of Extempore Speaking and of Gesture.* (1917), page 53.

31. Gordon, M. *Erik Jan Hanussen- Hitler's Jewish*

Clairvoyant. Op.cit.

32. Twenty-six-year-old Louis Ferdinand Victor Edward Albert Michael Hubert, Prince of Prussia was a member of the royal House of Hohenzollern and the pretender for a half-century to the abolished German throne.

33. The eldest child of Prince Heinrich XXXIV Reuss of Köstritz he was descendant of King William II of the Netherlands.

34. The youngest daughter of Tsar Nicholas II she was reported murdered, along with her family, by the Bolshevik secret police, in 1918. Persistent rumours of her escape resulted in a number of women claiming the title. DNA testing has subsequently confirmed that all four grand duchesses were killed.

35. A refugee from Nazi Germany, Riess recorded the end of Hitler's Third Reich as an American War Correspondent. Fluent in German and English he was became a prolific author, producing a stream of newspaper and magazine articles, novels, biographies, screenplays and plays. He died in Zurich, Switzerland, aged 90.

36. Kugel, *op.cit.,* page 60.

37. Paudler, M. *Auch Lachen will gelernt sein* (Berlin: Universitas (1978), pages 121 – 122.

38. *Ibid.*

39. Hett, B.C. (2014) *Burning the Reichstag: An Investigation into the Third Reich's Enduring Mystery.*

40. Fritz Tobias, *The Reichstag Fire: Legend and Truth,*

41. Rudolf Diels. Statement March 1933

42. Ian Kershaw, I. (1987). *The 'Hitler Myth': Image and Reality in the Third Reich.*

43. Van der Lubbe Statement March 1933

44. Keiteite, C. *Ich kann nicht schweigen* (*I Cannot Keep Silent*)

45. Gordon, M. *op cit.*, page 244.

46. Bella Fromm, *Blood and Banquets*, page 78.

Chapter 13 – Betrayal

1. Still held sacred by physicians, the Hippocratic oath includes the following promise: 'What I may see or hear in the course of the treatment or even outside of the treatment in regard to the life of men, which on no account one must spread abroad, I will keep to myself, holding such things shameful to be spoken about. If I fulfil this oath and do not violate it, may it be granted to me to enjoy life and art, being honoured with fame among all men for all time to come; if I transgress it and swear falsely, may the opposite of all this be my lot.' It was this section that Forster was violating when he betrayed Hitler's medical file to the anti-fascist writers.

2. Armbruster, Jan, *Edmund Robert Forster 1878 – 1933 Journey and work of a German Neuropsychiatrist* Treatises on the History of Medicine and Science No. 102, page 24.

3. Lovis Corinth (1858-1925). A prolific artist he produced some 900-works including 60 self-portraits over his lifetime. In 1925 while in Holland to look at Dutch masters he died of pneumonia in Zanvoort. After Hitler came to power much of his later work was condemned as 'Degenerate' by the Nazis and burned.

4. Marie Rose von Wesendonk Family Archive, Tuscany *op. cit.*

5. Forster, E. (1930). Selbstversuch mit Meskalin. *Zeitschrift für die gesamte Neurologie und Psychiatrie.*

6. Gleichgewichtsreaktionen bei Erkrankungen des Zentralnervensystems (Filmdemonstration) *Deutsche Zeitschrift für Nervenheilkunde,* Berlin 130 (1933) pages 25 – 43.

7. Marie Rose von Wesendonk Family Archive, *op.cit.*

8. Davidson, M. (1962) *The World, The Flesh and Myself, op. cit.* page 159.

9. Bella Fromm, *Blood and Banquets,* pages 273-274

10. *Ibid.,* page 274.

11. Ibid., page 221

12. *The Eyewitness,* page 151

13. Schofield, Victoria, *Witness to History,* pages 80 -81.

14. *Ibid.*

15. This anecdote was recounted to Rudolph Binion by a Greifswald archivist who had been at the University during Forster's time. Personal communication.

16. G. M. Gilbert *Nuremberg Diary* London: Eyre & Spottiswoode (1948) page 67. Keitel was found guilty of war crimes, sentenced to death and hanged in 1946.

17. R. Binion, *Hitler among the Germans, op.cit.* pages 11-12.

18. Ruth Lidz later became a professor of psychiatry at Yale.

19. P. Horn (1915) cited in J. Brunner, 'Psychiatry, *Psychoanalysis and Politics',* page 354.

20. Archiv der Gesellschaft fur Rassenbiologie, Berlin, 18 August 1938.

21. Marie Rose von Wesendonk Family Archive. *op. cit.*

22. UAG Kurator 449, Blatt 280 R.

23. Marie Rose von Wesendonk Family Archive. *op. cit.*

24. Unsuccessful attempts to track down this document have been made by several researchers, journalists and family members including Arne Forster, Edmund's grandson, Professor Binion, myself and reporters from *Der Spiegel*. One likely explanation for this failure is that Edmund deposited the Krankenblatt under a false name. This would be a sensible thing to do given the risks of possessing a document that was a state secret.

25. Mehring claims that this meeting took place 'in the Café Royal'. There was, however, no such café in Paris at that period. The registry of commerce for 1930 does however show a Royal Café, at 8 place de l'Opéra and Le Royal, at 12 boulevard Montmartre, of these the former seems a more likely venue.

26. Bulletin Météorologique de l'Office Nationale.

27. Nunan, T. (April 7, 2008) *Leopold Schwarzschild, Das neue Tage-Buch, and Anti-Totalitarianism in Interwar Europe, 1933-1941*.

28. The popular *Le Temps*, for example, cost only 40 centimes.

29. *Das neue Tage-Buch* 1, Vol. 1, pages 9-12.

30. Leopold Schwarzschild, '*Die Woche*,' *Das neue Tage-Buch* 1, Vol. 1, 3.

31. Nunan, T. *op cit.*

32. Jean-Michel Palmier, *Weimar in Exile: The Antifascist Emigration in Europe and America*, pages 92-95.

33. Harry Kessler, Diary Entry, February 28, 1933, in *Diaries of a Cosmopolitan*, trans. Charles Kessler, London: Weidenfeld and Nicolson, 1971. 449).

34. Gustav Regler, *The Owl of Minerva* (New York: Farrar, Straus, and Cudahy, 1960, 157-158.

35. With a weekly circulation of 20,000 copies *The New*

Diary appeared each week from July 1, 1933, until forced out of business by French regulations and Gestapo raids on May 5, 1940 issue.

36. Walter Mehring (1896-1981) quoted by Binion, *op. cit.*, page 8. Born, in Berlin, Mehring was an Expressionist poet and author of novels such as *The Infernal Comedy* (*Die hollische Komodie*, 1932), *The Night of the Tyrant* (*Die Nacht des Tyrannen*, 1937) and *The Lost Library* (*Die verlorene Bibliothek*, 1951). However, his reputation was made as the writer of the anti-bourgeois The Political Cabaret (Das politische Cabaret, 1920) and Noah's Ark SOS (Arche Noah SOS, 1931). He died in Zurich.

37. Weber, T. *Hitler's First War* Oxford, op.cit.

38. Edmund Forster, 'Das Nervensystem', in Hermann Lüdke and Carl Robert Schlayer (eds), *Lehrbuch der pathologischen Physiologie*, pages 269-334.

39. Klaus-Peter Hinze in a postscript to the 1977 American edition of *The Eyewitness*, page 202.

40. Mona Wollheim in a letter dated 29th November 1973.

41. *Ibid.*

42. *Ibid.*

Chapter 14 – The Trial of Edmund Forster

1. Remark made to Rudolf Diels, first chief of the Gestapo, in front of the blazing Reichstag on the night of 27th /28th February.

2. Shirer, W. *The Rise and Fall of the Third Reich, op. cit.*, page 248.

3. Stephen Roberts quoted in 'Is he Hitler's Successor' by Stefan Lorant. *Picture Post*, December 16th, 1939. Vol 5. No 11, pages 19-33.

4. Diels, rose to the rank of SS-Standartenführer (Colonel) and in 1943 married Ilse Göring, widow of Göring's younger brother Karl. He was eventually defeated by the combined forces of Himmler and Heydrich of the SS finishing up a prisoner in the basement of his own former headquarters. He survived the experience, and the war, only thanks to the personal intervention of his former boss Hermann Göring. Diels, who had been a member of the extreme right-wing Students' Corps in the Weimar Republic, was clever, subtle, shrewd, humourless, cynical and highly educated. Although never a card-carrying Nazi, he promised to create for his master an instrument of power the likes of which had never previously been seen in the history of Prussia. He proved as good as his word.

5. Lorant, *op.cit.*

6. *Ibid.*

7. Quoted in Adolf Klein, *Köln im Dritten Reich: Stadtgeschichte der Jahre 1933-1945*, page 136.

8. Bernholz, P. (2017) *Totalitarianism, Terrorism and Supreme Values: History and Theory (Studied in Public Choice)* Springer International Publishing.

9. Original hand-written letter on file in the Geheimes Statsarchiv 'Preussischer Kulturbesitz', Berlin. (GSA).

10. Source Geheimes Staatsarchiv. After Edmund's death, in late September 1933, the Ministry reopened the case. Luise vehemently denied the blackmail allegations despite Klara Korth, and Johanna Rätz standing by their original statements. Although the university decided that no such blackmail attempt had taken place, the Ministry was apparently less certain, criticising her 'questionable' behaviour and

decreeing that she should never be allowed to work at the clinic again.

11. This is, of course, speculation. But if we accept that the campaign to neutralise Forster's potentially highly politically damaging revelations by having him disgraced, dismissed, and probably killed originated in the highest levels within the Nazi party, then Göring is certainly the most likely candidate. He was intensely protective of Hitler's reputation and, as we have seen, utterly ruthless in pursuit of that goal. He was also sufficiently intelligent and subtle to recognise that, at that stage, it would be inappropriate merely to have Forster murdered.

12. Ernst-Moritz-Arndt-Universität Archiv UAG.

13. *Ibid.*

14. UAG PA486 Blatt 75 ru.v. Aufzeichnungen des Universität Kurators Zum Gesprach mit Forster.

15. *Ibid.*

16. Ernst-Moritz-Arndt-Universität Archiv UAG *op. cit.*

17. *Ibid.*

18. *Ibid.*

19. *Ibid.*

20. *Ibid.*

21. *Ibid.*

22. *Ibid.*

23. *Ibid.*

24. *Ibid.*

25. *Ibid.*

26. Balduin Forster, personal communication.

27. Ernst-Moritz-Arndt-Universität Archiv UAG *op cit.*

Chapter 15 – The Strange Suicide of Edmund Forster

1. Heinz Höhne, *Order of the Death's Head,* page 113.
2. Ruth Lidz later became a professor of psychiatry at Yale.
3. Jan Armbruster, *Edmund Robert Forster,* pages 91-2.
4. Forster, E. (1933) 'Wann muß der praktische Arzt Suizidneigung vermuten und wie verhalt er sich dann', *Münchener Medizinische Wochenschrift,* Vol. 80, pages 766-9.
5. While it may seem strange an insurance company would pay out in the event of a suicide, this was the case in Germany at the time.
6. Arne Forster, 2002, personal communication. This is the only source for where Edmund's body was found. No official documents relating to his death have survived.
7. Balduin Forster, interview 1973.
8. Binion, personal communication.
9. It was renamed the Ernst-Moritz-Arndt University of Greifswald in 1933.
10. Binion, personal communication.
11. Ernst-Moritz-Arndt-Universität Archiv UAG.
12. Balduin, *op. cit.*
13. Letter to Rudolph Binion.
14. Postcard from Lilly to Dirk Forster dated 15 September 1933; Marie Rose von Wesendonk Family Archive, Tuscany.
15. In a letter to Marie Rose von Wesendonk, *op.cit.*
16. Letter from Lilly to Dirk Forster, Marie Rose von Wesendonk Family Archive. *op. cit.*
17. Ernst-Moritz-Arndt-Universität Archiv UAG. 2002,
18. Höhne, H. *op.cit.*
19. *Ibid.*
20. Phil Howells archive, personal communication.

21. After the S.A. had been decimated, during the 'Night of the Long Knives'. S.S. commander Heinrich Himmler decreed a period of service in the concentration camps should form an obligatory part of SS training.
22. Max von der Grün. *Wie war das Eigentlich? Kindheit und Jugend im Dritten Reich,* page 75.
23. Pam Forster, personal communication.
24. Ernst-Moritz-Arndt-Universität Archiv UAG.
25. This building is still standing but was converted into a gymnasium under the East German regime.
26. Letter from Lilly to Dirk Forster dated 14th September 1933; Marie Rose von Wesendonk Family Archive. *op. cit.*

Chapter 16 – Death of a Psychic

1. As with so much of Hanussen's life there is an equal amount of mystery and uncertainty surrounding details of his death. In a letter to his daughter, Erika, former employee Elizabeth Heine claimed the body had been dumped in an isolated woodman's hut. Other reports say it was hastily buried and this is the version I have gone for as, on balance, it seems the more likely.
2. Elizabeth Heine, personal communication.
3. Magida, A.J. *The Nazi Séance.* Palgrave Macmillan, (2011) page 211.
4. Erika Fuchs, personal communication. Erika died in 2005.
5. *Ibid.*
6. First published by Rudolf Mosse in 1872 the *Berliner Tageblatt* 1920, the newspaper had a circulation of

245, 000 and was particularly critical and hostile to the Nazis.

7. Mosse, G. *Confronting History*, page 72.
8. *Ibid.* page 72.
9. Magida, A. *The Nazi Séance*, op cit. pages 193 – 194.
10. Tabori, P. *Companions of the Unseen*.
11. *Ibid.*
12. Bruno Frei, *Hanussen. Ein Bericht* (1934).
13. Pierre van Paassen. The Date of Hitler's Fall, *Redbook*, May 1942 pages 85 – 86.
14. Fromm, *op. cit.*, page

Chapter 17 - The Drowned and The Saved

1. The chapter's title is taken from the book of the same name by the Italian writer and Auschwitz survivor Primo Levi.
2. Solon, (*c.* 630 BCE - *c.* 560 BCE) an Athenian statesman and poet, known as one of the Seven Wise Men of Greece, introduced a more humane legal system.
3. Fromm, B. *Blood & Bouquets*, page 68.
4. Weber, T. *Hitler's First War*, op.cit., page 296.
5. Quoted by Hinze, *op. cit.* page 20.
6. Information about the life of Zádor was kindly provided by Paul and Antony Zádor, Alle Davis Harris Professor of Biology and Neuroscience at Cold Spring Harbour Laboratory in the US.
7. According to some account when Grace told Hanussen she intended to marry his secretary the clairvoyant warned her that to do so would be to sign the death warrant for her entire family. 'Beware Miss Cameron!' he is said to have told her: The man you

are going to marry will be your murderer. I... hear shots... bullets hit you... you collapse... You are dead.' Cited in Tabori, P. *Companions of the Unseen* New York: University Books. (1968), page 51.

8. *Ibid.*

9. Hancock, E. *Ernst Röhm* Palgrave Macmillan (2011) page 148, Tabori, *op.cit.*

10. Information about Dr Karl Kroner was kindly provided by his son Professor Klaus Kroner.

11. In 1938 Iceland was part of Denmark and Christian X of Denmark was also King of Iceland. Although the country was mainly self-governing it only became independent in 1944. This meant that Iceland's affairs were dealt with by the Danish Ambassador in Berlin. However, since there was a German Consul-General, Herr Gerlach, in Reykjavik there was also an Icelandic Consul-General in Berlin.

12. This building was owned, perhaps not coincidentally, by a Netherland's company the Algemeene Belegguns Maatschappy

13. Marie Rose von Wesendonk Family Archive, Tuscany.

14. *Ibid.*

15. Hitler renounced the Locarno Pact, a non-aggression treaty signed in 1925 by Germany, France and Belgium, on 7 March 1936 following his reoccupation of the Rhineland.

16. Pam Forster, personal communication. Given that Dirk only ranked 5th in the diplomatic pecking order, it is surprising that Hitler bothered to discuss the matter with him at all. Furthermore, while he was certainly capable of making such a threat he was, perhaps, too conscious of maintaining his dignity

before a subordinate to have done so.

17. NARA RG 242, T-581-3, investigation by the NSDAP party archive, 1938-1939.

18. Born in 1891 on the Island of Rugen, Adolf von Körber came from a distinguished Prussian family and served in the Air Force until invalided out in 1917. After the war, he worked as a journalist in Munich and covered the Putsch in 1923. An early supporter of Hitler, he joined the Party as member number 11640 in 1922. The was persuaded to put his name to the book which appeared the following year. After falling out with the Nazis, following the failed coup, his house was watched, his telephone tapped and his movements scrutinised. Following the failed attempt on Hitler's life, in July 1944, he was imprisoned in Sachsenhausen Concentration Camp. Liberated by the Russians he returned to journalism and enjoyed a successful career until retiring to South Africa where he died in 1969.

19. Weber, T. quoted in *The New York Times*, October 6th 2016.

REFERENCES & BIBLIOGRAPHY

Archives, Institutions, and Individuals Consulted

Akademie der Künste, Abteilung Bildende Kunst.

Archiv der Hapag Lloyd AG, Hamburg.

Archiv der Siemens-AG.

Arztekammer Berlin.

Bavarian Ministry of War, Medical Department.

Bayerisches Hauptstaatsarchiv, Abteilung IV Kriegsarchiv (BayHStA), Munich.

Bereichsbibliothek Rechtswissenschaft, Universitätsbibliothek Mannheim.

Bibliothèque Nationale de France (special thanks to Madame Monique Moulène).

Bildarchiv am Institut für Geschichte der Medizin/ZFA (HU zu Berlin).

Bildarchiv Preußischer Kulturbesitz Berlin.

Bilddatenbank Deutsches Historisches Museum.

Bundesarchiv Berlin (BArch).

Bundesarchiv Filmarchiv.

Bundesarchiv Militararchiv Freiburg.

Bundesbank Bundesrepublik Deutschland.

Bundesbeauftragte des Staatssicherheitsdienstes der ehemaligen Deutschen Demokratischen Republik.

Deputy General Command, Bavarian I. Army Corps. Sanitary Dept.

Deutsche Gesellschaft für Psychiatrie, Psychotherapie und Nervenheilkunde.

Deutscher Wetterdienst, Regionales Gutachtenbüro, Potsdam.

Ernst-Moritz-Amdt-Universität Greifswald, Universitätsarchiv (UAG).

Freie Universität Berlin, Institut für Geschichte der Medizin (special thanks to Frau Kliesch).

Geheimes Staatsarchiv Preußischer Kulturbesitz Berlin (GStA PK).

Gesamtverband der Deutschen Versicherungswirtschaft.

Haupt- und Kulturamt Anklam.

Humboldt-Universität zu Berlin, Universitätsbibliothek, Universitätarchiv.

Julius Hagemann; Harry Schultze-Wilde Collection, Ottobrunn bei München.

Karl Bonhoffer Papers Charité Nervenklinik Collection.

KZ Gedenkstätte Oranienburg.

La Bibliothèque Historique de la Ville de Paris.

Landesarchiv Berlin.

Lehrstuhl Prof Dr Luck für Bürgerl. Recht, Europäische, Deutsche und Sächsische Rechtsgeschichte, Martin-Luther-Universität Halle- Wittenberg.

Leonaris Film.

Les collections de la Documentation Française et les Collections Photographiques de la Documentation Française.

Marie Rose von Wesendonk Family Archive, Tuscany.

Militärarchiv Württemberg (MA), Stuttgart. Deputy General
    Command, XIII Army Corps.
Ministry of Labour (RAM) Collection.
Ministry of the Interior (MdI) Collection.
Musikabteilung der Staatsbibliothek zu Berlin Stiftung
    Preußischer Kulturbesitz.
Nonnenhorn Museum.
Phil Howells Family Archive.
Rudolph Binion Archive, Boston.
Sächsisches Hauptstaatsarchiv (SHSA), Dresden.
Saxon Ministry of War, Medical Department.
Schularchiv des Jahn-Gymnasiums, Greifswald.
St Jakobi Gemeinde, Greifswald (special thanks to Pastor
    Hanke).
Stadt Pasewalk, Museum (special thanks to Herr Brose).
Stadtarchiv Hansestadt Greifswald (special thanks to Frau
    Neitzel).
Standesamt Greifswald.
Universitätarchiv Heidelberg.

Documents
Bundesarchiv Berlin
BArch, NS 26/2214
BArch, NS 26/47
BArch, NS 26/17a

Geheimes Staatsarchiv Preußischer Kulturbesitz Berlin
GStA PK, I. HA Rep. 76 Va Sekt. 7 Tit. IV Nr. 21 Bd. 12: Acta
    betreffend die Anstellung und Besoldung der
    ordentlichen und außerordentlichen Professoren in der
    Medizinischen Fakultät der Universität zu Greifswald
    vom Juli 1922 bis Februar 1929.
GStA PK, HA I Rep. 76 Va Sekt. 7 Tit. X Nr. 21 Bd. 7: Acta

der Universitäts-Irrenklinik zu Greifswald vom August 1927 bis Februar.

GStA PK, HA I Rep. 76 VA Sekt. 7 Tit. IV Nr. 21 Adh. II Acta betreffend: das Disziplinarverfahren gegen den o. Prof Edmund Forster in der Nervenklinik, August 1933-November 1933,

GStA PK, HA I Rep. 76 VA Sekt. 7 Tit. IV Nr. 31 Bd. Ill: Acta betreffend die wissenschaftlichen Reisen der Dozenten von Januar 1929-November 1934.

GStA PK, HA I Rep. 76 VA Sekt. 2 Tit. IV Nr. 50 Bd. X: Acta betreffend die Privatdozenten in der Medizinischen Fakultät der Universität zu Berlin vom Juli 1908-Juni 1910.

Universitatsarchiv Greifswald

UAG Kurator 449: Registratur des Universitätskuratoriums Greifswald Psychiatrische und Nervenklinik, 1928-1934.

UAG Kurator 448: Registratur des Universitätskuratoriums Greifswald Psychiatrische und Nervenklinik, 1921-1927.

UAG MF 77: Medizinische Fakultät, Akte Zador.

UAG MF 221: Medizinische Fakultät: Beurlaubung von Dozenten.

UAG MF 571: Medizinische Fakultät, Akte Geheim 1932-1944.

UAG BM 40: Bereich Medizin 40, Fakultätsratsitzungen.

UAG PA 2393 Personalakte Vorkastner.

UAG PA 486 Personalakte Forster.

UAG Kurator 454: Die Assistenzärzte der Psychiatrischen und Nervenklinik 1926-1935.

Imperial War Museum (IWM) and Public Record Office (PRO) London

Official Diary of the 148th Brigade Royal Artillery, PRO

W095 HQ 30th Division Artillery. War Diary, PRO WO 95 2317.

War Diary of 6th Brigade Royal Garrison Artillery, PRO WO 95 297

Brief History of the 30th Division

30th Division in France and Flanders. Compiled for the Imperial War Museum (Typescript)

Unpublished Dissertations

Armbruster, J. (1999). Edmund Robert Forster (1878-1933): Lebensweg und Werk eines deutschen Neuropsychiaters. Inaugural-Dissertation zur Erlangung des akademischen Grades Doktor der Medizin, Medical Faculty, Ernst-Moritz-Arndt-Universität, Greifswald.

Lerner, P.F. (1996). Hysterical Men: War, Neurosis and German Mental Medicine 1914-1921. Graduate School of Arts and Sciences, Columbia University.

BIBLIOGRAPHY

Achille-Delmas, F. (1946). *Adolf Hitler: Essai de Biographie Psycho- Pathologique*. Paris, Librairie Marcel Rivière et Cie.

Aird, R.B. (1933). *Foundations of Modern Neurology: A Century of Progress*. New York: Raven Press.

Alexander, F.G.S. (1966). *The History of Psychiatry: An Evaluation of Psychiatric Thought and Practice from Prehistoric Times to the Present*. New York: Harper & Row.

Anonymous (1919). *A Brief History of the 30th Division*. London: War Narratives Publishing Company.

Anonymous (1919). *Military Operations - France and Belgium 1918. Vol. V 26th September-11th November*. Nashville: Imperial War Museum and the Battle Press.

Anton, J. (1987). *Korrektur einer Biographie Adolf Hitler 1908-1920*. Frankfurt/Berlin: Verlag Ullstein.

Armbruster, J. *Edmund Robert Forster 1878 – 1933 Journey and work of a German Neuropsychiatrist* Treatises on the History of Medicine and Science No. 102.Ernst-Moritz-Arndt University, page 24.

Artwinski, E. v. (1919). 'Uber traumatische Neurosen nach Kriegsverletzungen.' *Zeitschrft für die Gesamte Neurologie und Psychiatrie* Vol. 45, pages 242-60.

Aschaffenburg, G. (1915). 'Winke zur Beurteilung von Nerven- und psychisch-nervosen Erkrankungen.' *Münchener Medizinische Wochenschrift, Feldärztliche Beilage* Vol. 62, pages 931-3.

Baker, A. (2000) *Invisible Eagle*, London: Virgin

Barbasetti, L. (1896). *Ehren-Codex*. Vienna.

Barnett, C. (2000). *The Great War*. London: Penguin Books.

Beard, G.M. (1880) A *Practical Treatise on Nervous Exhaustion (Neurasthenia)*. New York: William Wood.

Beard, G.M. (1881). *American Nervousness*. New York: Putnam.

Beckett, I. and Simpson, K. (eds) (1985). *A Nation in Arms: A Social Study of the British Army in the First World War*. Manchester: Manchester University Press.

Bennis, W.G. and Thomas, R.J. (2002). *Geeks and Geezers: How Defining Moments Shape the Leaders of Today and Tomorrow*. Boston: Harvard Business School Press.

Bérard, A. (1976) *Au temps du danger allemand*, Vol. 1, Un Ambassadeur se Souvient Plon: Paris.

Bernholz, P. (2017) *Totalitarianism, Terrorism and Supreme Values: History and Theory (Studied in Public Choice)* Springer International Publishing.

Berrios, G.P. and Porter, R. (eds) (1995). *A History of Clinical Psychiatry: The Origin and History of Psychiatric Disorders*.

London: Athlone Press.

Binion, R. (1973). 'Hitler's Concept of Lebensraum: The Psychological Basis.' *History of Childhood Quarterly* Vol. 1, No. 20.

Binion, R. (1991). *Hitler among the Germans*. DeKalb: Northern Illinois University Press.

Binswanger, O. (1914). *Die Seelischen Wirkungen des Krieges*. Berlin: Deutsche Verlagsanstalt.

Birnbaum, K. (1916); 'Ergebnisse der Neurologie und Psychiatrie. Kriegsneurosen und Psychosen auf Grund der gegenwärtigen Kriegsbeobachtungen. Sammelbericht. III.' *Zeitschrift fur die Gesamte Neurologie und Psychiatrie: Referate und Ergebnisse* Vol. 12, pages 317-88.

Bleuel, H.P. (1996). *Sex and Society in Nazi Germany*. New York: Dorset Press.

Bloch, E. (1941). 'My Patient Hider, as told to J.D. Ratcliff.' *Colliers* 15 March, Vol. 11, pages 35-7; 22 March, pages 69-73.

Bonhöffer, K. (1933). 'Edmund Forster.' *Deutsche Medizinische Wochenschrift* Vol. 59, page 1516.

Brady, J.P.L. (1961). 'Experimental Analysis of Hysterical Blindness.' *Archives of General Psychiatry* Vol. 4, pages 331-9.

Braun, O. (1940) *Von Weimar zu Hitler 1930—1933*. New York: Europa.

Brazier, M.A.B. (1988). *A History of Neurophysiology in the 19th Century*. New York: Raven Press.

Brendon, P. (2001). *The Dark Valley: A Panorama of the 1930s*. London: Pimlico.

Brunner, J. (1919). 'Psychiatry, Psychoanalysis and Politics during the First World War.' *Journal of the History of Behavioural Sciences* Vol. 27, pages 352-65.

Bullock, A. (1961). *Hitler: A Study in Tyranny*. London: Bantam.

Bumke, O. (ed.) (1907). 'Über Melancholie, von Dr Edm. Forster in Berlin.' In Schmidt's *Jahrbücher der in-und ausländischen gesamten Medizin*. Leipzig.

Butler, A.G. (1943). *Moral and Mental Disorders in the War of 1914-1918*. Canberra.

Calic, E. (1968). *Ohne Maske. Hitler - Breiting. Geheimgespräche 1931*. Frankfurt: Societät Verlag.

Caplan, E.M. (1995). 'Trains, Brains and Sprains: Railway Spine and the Origins of Psychoneuroses.' *Bulletin of the History of Medicine* Vol. 69, pages 387- 419.

Caplan, J. (1977). 'The Politics of Administration: The Reich Interior Ministry and the German Civil Service 1933-1943.' *The Historical Journal* Vol. 20, pages 707- 36.

Chamberlain, H.S. (1913). *Foundations of the Nineteenth Century*. New York: John Lane Co.

Chertok, L. (1975). 'Hysteria, Hypnosis, and Psychopathy: History and Perspectives.' *Journal of Nervous and Mental Disorders* Vol. 161, pages 367-78.

Cobden, R. (1870) *Speeches on Questions of Public Policy*, Miami: Hardpress

Cocks, G. (1985). *Psychotherapy in the Third Reich*. Oxford: Oxford University Press.

Collie, J. (1913). 'Malingering.' *British Medical Journal* Vol. 2, page 647.

Constantinesco, J. (1937). *Hitler Secret*. Paris: La Societe Française de Librairie et d'Editions.

Crankshaw, E. (1956). *Gestapo: Instrument of Tyranny*. London: Putnam.

Cross, C. (1973). *Adolf Hitler*. London: Hodder & Stoughton.

Cruttwell, C.R. (1936). *A History of the Great War*. Oxford: Oxford University Press.

Cushing, H. (1917). *From a Surgeon's Journal.* Boston: Little, Brown and Co.

Davidson, E. (1966). *The Trial of the Germans: Nuremberg 1945-1946.* New York: Macmillan.

Davidson, M. (1962) *The World, The Flesh and Myself* Washington:Guild Press,

De Sales, R. de R. (1941). *Adolf Hitler - My New Order; Collected Speeches.* New York.

Dichl, G. (1933) *Die deutsche Frau und der Nationalsozialismus,* Neuland Verlag: Eisenach.

Drexler, A. (1923). *Mein Politisches Erwachen.* Munich:Deutscher Volksverlag.

Dunn, S. (1918). 'Report on the Nature of Lesions Produced in Experiments on Animals by Inhalation of Diphenyl-chlorarsine and Allied Compounds.' *MRC Chemical Warfare Medical Committee Report* No. 9, page 35.

Eksteins, M. (1989). *Rites of Spring: The Great War and the Birth of the Modern Age.* Boston: Houghton Mifflin.

Eastabrooks, G.H. (1957) *Hypnotism* New York: W.P. Dutton

Feder, G. (1932). Das Programm der NSDAP und seine weltanschaidichen Grundgedanken. Munich: Verlag Frz. Eher.

Feldman, G. (1993). *The Great Disorder: Politics, Economics, and Society in the German Inflation.* New York: Oxford University Press.

Fest, J.C. (1974). *Hitler.* (Translated by Richard and Clara Winston.) London: Weidenfeld &, Nicolson.

Fischer-Homberger, E. (1975). *Die traumatische Neurose: Vom somatischen zum sozialen Leiden.* Bern: Hans Huber Verlag.

FitzGerald, M. (2013) *The Nazi Occult War,* London: Arcturus Publishing.

Flood, C.B. (1989). *Hitler - The Path to Power.* Boston:

Houghton Mifflin.

Flower, N. (ed.) (1919). *The History of the Great War*. London: Waverley.

Flury, M. and Wieland, K. (1921). 'Ueber Kampfgasvergiftungen: Lokal reizende Arsenverbindungen.' *Zeitschrift für die gesamte experimentelle Medizin* Vol. 13, page 523.

Forster, E. (1905) *Die Klinische Stellung der Angstpsychose*, Habilitation thesis.

Forster, E. (1917). 'Hysterische Reaktion und Simulation.' *Monats-schrift für Psychiatrie und Neurologie* Vol. 42, pages 298-324,370—81.

Forster, E. (1918). 'Hysterische Reaktion und Simulation.' *Neurologisches Centralblatt* Vol. 37, pages 468-9.

Forster, E. (1930). 'Selbstversuch mit Meskalin.' In *Zeitschrift für die gesamte Neurologie und Psychiatrie*. (Edited by A.L.M. Alzheimer.) Berlin: Verlag von Julius Springer.

Forster, E. (1933). 'Für die Praxis.' *Münchener Medizinische Wochenschrift* Vol. 20, pages 766-9.

Forster, E. (1933) 'Wann muß der praktische Arzt Suizidneigung vermuten und wie verhalt er sich dann', *Münchener Medizinische Wochenschrift*, Vol. 80, pages 766-9.

Foulkes, C.H. (1934). *Gas! The Story of the Special Brigade*. Edinburgh: William Blackwood.

Frank, H. (1953). *Im Angesicht des Galgens*. München: Gräfelfing.

Freimark, H. (1920). *Die Revolution als Massenerscheinung*. Wiesbaden.

Friedrich, O. (1972). *Before the Deluge*. New York: Harper and Row.

Fromm, B. (1990) *Blood & Bouquets*, New York: Carol Publishing Group.

Fussell, P. (1975). *The Great War and Modern Memory.* New York: Oxford University Press.

Gardner, B. (ed.) (1965). *Up the Line to Death: The War Poets of 1914-18.* London: Methuen.

Garson, P. (2008) *Album of the Damned: Snapshots from the Third Reich,* Academy Chicago Publishers

Gaupp, R. (1952). 'Some Reflections on the Development of Psychiatry in Germany.' *American Journal of Psychiatry* Vol. 108, pages 721-3.

Gerson, W. (Pierre Mariel), (1972) 'Mage ou Espion?' in *Le Nazisme: Societe Secrete.* Paris: J'ai Lu, 1972, http://humanisme.canalblog.com/ archives/2010/08/22/18871564.html (10 April 2014).

Gilbert. G. M. (1948) *Nuremberg Diary* London: Eyre & Spottiswoode

Goebbels, J. (1948). *The Goebbels Diaries.* (Translated and edited by Louis P. Lochner.) London: Hamish Hamilton.

Goldschieder, A. (1915). 'Über die Ursachen des günstigen Gesund- heitszustandes unserer Truppen im Winterfeldzuge.' *Zeitschrift für Physikalische und Diatetische Therapie* Vol. 19, page 170.

Goldstein, K. (1917). 'Über die Behandlung der Hysterie.' *Medizinische Klinik* Vol. 13, pages 757-8.

Goldstein, K. (ed.) (1953). *Carl Wernicke (1848-1905).* Springfield: Thomas.

Gordon, M. (2000) *Voluptuous Panic: The Erotic World of Weimar Berlin,* Port Townsend: Feral House.

Gordon, M. (2001) *Erik Jan Hanussen: Hitler's Jewish Clairvoyant,* Port Townsend: Feral House.

Graf, O.M. (1928). *Prisoners All.* (Translated by Margaret Green.) New York: Knopf.

Greiner, J. (1947). *Das Ende des Hitler-Mythos.* Zurich/Leipzig/ Vienna: Amalthea.

Grosz, H.J. and Zimmerman, J. (1965). 'Experimental Analysis of Hysterical Blindness: A Follow-up Report and New Experimental Data.' *Archives of General Psychiatry* Vol. 13, pages 256-60.

Grün, M. von der (2007) *Wie war das Eigentlich? Kindheit und Jugend im Dritten Reich*. Deutscher Tachenbuch Verlag.

Guillain, G. (1955). *J.M. Charcot 1825-1893: Sa Vie - Son Oeuvre*.

Paris: France Masson et Cie.

Gun, N.E. (1969). *Eva Braun - Hitler's Mistress*. London: Bantam.

Haber, L.F. (1986). *The Poisonous Cloud: Chemical Warfare in the First World War*. Oxford: Clarendon Press.

Hanfstaengl, E. (1957). *Hitler: The Missing Years*. London: Eyre & Spottiswoode.

Hanser, R. (1971). *Prelude to Terror: The Rise of Hitler 1919-1923*.

London: Hart-Davis.

Hanser, R. (1971). *Putsch*. New York: Pyramid Books.

Hanussen, E. (1930) *Meine Lebenslinie*, Frankfurt a. M: Wunderkammer Verlag.

Harrison, E, (1996) *Count Helldorf and the German Resistance to Hitler (ESRI Working Papers in Contemporary History & Politics)*.

Healy, David (2000). *The Creation of Psychopharmacology*. Cambridge, Massachusetts: Harvard University Press.

Hedin, S. (1915). *With the German Armies in the West*. London: John Lane, Bodley Head.

Heiber, H. (1972). *Goebbels*. New York: De Capo.

Heiden, K. (1935). *History of National Socialism*. New York: Knopf.

Heiden, K. (1939). *One Man against Europe*. Harmondsworth, Penguin.

Heiden, K. (1944). *Der Führer: Hitler's Rise to Power*. London: Victor Gollancz.

Heinz, H.A. (1934). *Germany's Hitler*. London: Hurst & Blackett.

Hellpach, W. (1915). 'Lazarettdisziplin als Heilfaktor.' *Medizinische Klinik* Vol. 11, pages 1207-11.

Heston, L.L.H.R.N. (2000). *The Medical Casebook of Adolf Hitler: His Illnesses, Doctors and Drugs*. New York: Cooper Square Press.

Hett, B.C. (2014) *Burning the Reichstag: An Investigation into the Third Reich's Enduring Mystery* Oxford: Oxford University Press

Hinton, D.B. (2000). *The Films of Leni Riefenstahl*. Lanham, Md: Scarecrow Press.

Hitler, A. (1933). *My Battle (Mein Kampf)*. (Translated by Captain E.S.

Dugdale) Boston: Houghton Mifflin.

Hitler, A. (1933). *My Struggle*. London: Paternoster Library.

Hitler, A. (1936). *Mein Kampf*. München: Centralverlag der NSDAP.

Hitler, A. (1939). *Mein Kampf*. (Translated by James Murphy.) London: Hurst and Blackett.

Hitler, A. (1969). *Hitler's Mein Kampf*. (Translated by Ralph Manheim.) London: Hutchinson.

HMSO (1946). *'The Trial of German Major War Criminals: Part 1.' Proceedings of the International Military Tribunal Sitting at Nuremberg Germany*. London.

Höhne, H. (1969). *The Order of the Death's Head: The Story of Hitler's SS*. London: Secker & Warburg.

Holden, W. (1998). *Shell Shock: The Psychological Impact of War*. London: Channel 4 Books.

Holland, B. (2003) *Gentlemen's Blood: A History of Dueling from Swords at Dawn to Pistols at Dusk*, New York:

Bloomsbury.

Howe, Q. (1934) World *Diary* New York: Robert McBride & Company.

Hull, I.V. (1982). *The Entourage of Kaiser Wilhelm II 1888-1918.* Cambridge: Cambridge University Press.

Infield, G. (1978). *Eva and Adolf.* New York: Grosset & Dunlap.

Jenks, W.A. (1960). *Vienna and the Young Hitler.* New York: Columbia.

Jetzinger, F. (1958). *Hitler's Youth.* Westport, Conn: Greenwood.

Joachimsthaler, A. (1992). *Hitler in München: 1908-1920.* Berlin: Ullstein.

Jones, N. (1999). *Rupert Brooke: Life, Death and Myth.* London: Richard Cohen.

Kater, M. (1985). 'Professionalization and Socialization of Physicians in Wilhelmine and Weimar Germany.' *Journal of Contemporary History* Vol. 20, pages 677-701.

Kaufmann, F. (1917). 'Zur Behandlung der motorischen Kriegsneurosen.' *München Medizinische Wochenschrift* Vol. 64, pages 1520-3.

Kehrer, F. (1917). 'Behandlung und ärztliche Fürsorge bei Kriegsneurosen.' *Die Kriegsbeschädigtenfürsorge* Vol. 2, pages 158-64.

Kehrer, F. (1917). 'Zur Frage der Behandlung der Kriegsneurosen.' *Zeitschrift für die Gesamte Neurologie und Psychiatrie* Vol. 36, pages 1-22.

Kempner, R.M.W. (1969). *Das Dritte Reich im Kreuzverhör, Aus den unveröffentlichten Vernehmungsprotokollen des Anklägers.* München /Esslingen: Bechtle Verlag.

Kendell, R.E. (1983). 'Hysteria.' In *Handbook of Psychiatry: The Neuroses and Personality Disorders.* Cambridge: Cambridge University Press.

Kennedy, F and Butterfield. I.K. (1981). *The making of a neurologist: The letters of Foster Kennedy M.D., F.R.S. Edin.1884-1952, to his wife, from Queen Square, London 1906-1910, New York City 1910-1912, British Expeditionary Force 1915-1918.* London: Stellar Press.

Kershaw, I. (1987). *The 'Hitler Myth': Image and Reality in the Third Reich.* Oxford: Oxford University Press.

Kershaw, I. (1998). *Hitler: 1889-1936* Hubris: London, Penguin Press.

Kessler, H. (1971) Diary Entry, February 28, 1933, in *Diaries of a Cosmopolitan,* (trans. Charles Kessler) London: Weidenfeld and Nicolson.

Kläger, E. (1910): *Durch die Wiener Quartiere.* Vienna.

Klein, A (1983), *Koln im Dritten Reich: Stadtgeschichte der Jahre 1933-1945.*

Koestler, A. (2005) *Arrow in the Blue* London: Random House.

Köpf, G. (2005) 'Hitlers psychogene Erblindung: Geschichte einer Krankenakte' Nervenheilkunde *Zeitschrift für interdisziplinäre Forschung,* 9 (2005) 783-790. NARA, RG242, T-581/1A. Köln: Gauverlag Westdeutscher Beobachter.

Klein, A. (2000). 'Zum Tod von Herr Prof. Dr E. Forster.' *Rechtsmedizin: Organ der Deutschen Gesellschaft fur Rechtsmedizin* Vol. 10 (3), page 14.

Kocka, J. (1984). *Facing Total War. German Society, 1914-1918.* Leamington Spa: Berg.

Kompa, M. (with Wilfried Kugel), 'Erik Jan Hanussen - Hokus-Pokus-Tausendsassa'. *Telepolis Magazin,* eww.heise.de /tp/artikel/27/27562/1.html (10 April 2014).

Kraepelin, E. (1904). *Psychiatrie: Ein Lehrbuch für Studierende und Ärzte.* Leipzig: Barth.

Kretschmer, E. (1917). 'Hysterische Erkrankung und

hysterische Gewohnung.' *Zeitschrift für die Gesamte Neurologie und Psychiatrie* Vol. 37, pages 69-91.

Kubizek, A. (1953). *Mein Jugenfreund*, Graz-Stuttgart: Leopold Stocker Verlag.

Kurlander, E. *Hitler's Monsters: A Supernatural History of the Third Reich.* New Haven: Yale university press (2017)

Lemer, P. (1996). *'Hysterical Men: War, Neurosis and German Mental Medicine, 1914-1921.'* Unpublished PhD thesis. Columbia University, Graduate School of Arts and Sciences.

Levi, P. (1988) *The Drowned and the Saved* London: Michael Joseph.

Lockhart, R. (1984) *Reilly: Ace of Spies.* New York: Penguin Books.

Lorant, S. (1939). 'Is He Hitler's Successor?' *Picture Post* Vol. 5, pages 19-33.

Lucas, N. (2007) *Ladies of the Underworld: The Beautiful, the Damned and Those Who Get Away with It.* Kessinger Publishing.

Ludecke, K.G.W. (1938). *I Knew Hitler.* London: Jarrolds.

Lüdke, H. and Schlayer, C.R. (eds). (1922). *Lehrbuch der Pathologischen Physiologie. Für Studenten und Ärzte* Leipzig:Engelmann.

Lutz, T. (1995). 'Neurasthenia and Fatigue Syndromes.' In *A History of Clinical Psychiatry: The Origin and History of Psychiatric Disorders.* (Edited by G. Berrios and R. Porter.) New York: New York University Press.

McAleer, K. (1994). *Duelling: The Cult of Honour in Fin-de-Siècle Germany.* Princeton: Princeton University Press.

Mackintosh, W. (1919). 'Mustard Gas Poisoning.' *Quarterly Journal of Medicine* Vol. 13, page 201.

Macpherson, W.G., Herrington, W.P., Elliott, T.R. and Balfour, A. (eds) (1923). *Official History of the Great War,*

Vol. II. London, HMSO.

Magida, A. J. (2011) *The Nazi Séance – The Strange Story of the Jewish Psychic in Hitler's Circle*. Palgrave Macmillan.

Manvell, R and Fraenkel, H. (1960). *Doctor Goebbels: His Life and Death*. London: Heinemann.

Marks, D. and Kammann, R. (1980) *The Psychology of the Psychic*. New York: Prometheus Books.

Markus Kompa (with Wilfried Kugel), 'Erik Jan Hanussen - Hokus-Pokus-Tausendsassa.' *Telepolis Magazin*, 10 April 2014.

Martin, J.P. (1981). 'Reminiscences of Queen Square.' *British Medical Journal* Vol. 2, pages 1640-2.

Maser, W. (1965). Der Sturm auf die Republik: Frühgeschichte der NSDAP. Frankfurt, DVA, Rev. und erg. Neuausg.

Maser, W. (1971). *Adolf Hitler: Legende, Mythos, Wirklichkeit*. München und Esslingen: Bechtle Verlag.

Maser, W. (1973). *Hitler*. London: Allen Lane.

Mehring, W. (1952). *Die verlorene Bibliothek: Autobiographie einer Kultur*. Hamburg: Ronholt.

Mendel, K. (1917). 'Die Kaufmannsche Methode.' *Neurologisches Zentralblatt*. Vol. 36, pages 181-93.

Mendelssohn-Bartholdy, A. (1937). *The War and German Society: The Testament of a Liberal*. New Haven: Yale University Press.

Merkl, P.H. (1992). *Political Violence under the Swastika*. Princeton: Princeton University Press.

Meyer, A. (1934). Mit Adolf Hitler im Bayerischen Reserve-Infanterie-Regiment 16 List. Neustadt: Aisch.

Micale, M.S. (1989). 'Hysteria and its Historiography: A Review of Past and Present Writings.' *History of Science* Vol. 27, pages 223-61, 319-51.

Micale, M.S. (1990). 'Charcot and the Idea of Hysteria in the

Male: Gender, Mental Science, and Mental Diagnosis in Late Nineteenth-Century France.' *Medical History* Vol. 34, pages 363-411.

Micale, M.S. (1995). *Approaching Hysteria, Disease and its Interpretations*. Princeton: Princeton University Press.

Middlebrook, M. (1983). *The Kaisers Battle*. London: Penguin Press.

Middlemarch, M. (1980). *The Nuremberg Raid*. London: Allen Lane.

Mommsen, W. (1981). 'The Topos of Inevitable War in Germany in the Decade before 1914.' In *Germany in the Age of Total War*. (Edited by Volker Berghahn and Martin Kitchen.) London: Croom Helm.

Mosher. J.A. (1917) *Effective Public Speaking: The Essentials of Extempore Speaking and of Gesture*. New York: The Macmillan Company.

Mosse, G.L. (1998). *The Crisis of German Ideology: Intellectual Origins of the Third Reich*. New York: Howard Fertig.

Mosse, G.L. (2000) *Confronting History*, Wisconsin: University of Wisconsin Press.

Muck, O. (1917). 'Über Schnellheilungen von funktioneller Stummheit und Taubstummheit nebst einem Beitrag zur Kenntnis des Wesens des Mutismus.' *Münchener Medizinische Wochenschrift Feldärztliche Beilage* Vol. 64, pages 165-6.

Myers, C.S. (1940). *Shell Shock in France 1914-1918*. Cambridge: Cambridge University Press.

Neubauer, A, (1960) *Speed Was My Life* London: Barrie and Rockliff.

Nicholls, A.J. (2000) *Weimar and the Rise of Hitler*, New York: St. Martin's Press.

Nonne, M. (1915). 'Soll man wiedertraumatische Neurosen diagnostizieren?' *Archiv für Psychiatrie* Vol. 56, pages

337-9.

Nonne, M. (1922). 'Therapeutische Erfahrungen an den Kriegsneurosen in den Jahren 1914-1918.' In *Geistes -und Nervenkrankheiten*. (Edited by Karl Bonhoeffer.) Vol. 4. Leipzig: Barth.

Nonne, M. (1971). *Anfang und Ziel Meines Lebens*. Hamburg: Hans Christians Verlag.

Nunan, T. (April 7, 2008) *Leopold Schwarzschild, Das neue Tage-Buch, and Anti-Totalitarianism in Interwar Europe, 1933-1941*. Senior thesis submitted to the Department of German in partial fulfilment of the requirements for the degree of Bachelor of Arts, Princeton University, Princeton, New Jersey.

Olden, R. (1936). *Hitler*. New York: Covici, Friede Inc.

Oppenheim, H. (1915). 'Der Krieg und die traumatischen Neurosen.' *Berliner Klinische Wochenschrift* Vol. 52, pages 257-61.

Oppenheim, H. (1916). Die Neurosen infolge von Kriegsverletzungen. Berlin: Karger.

Overy, R. (1984). *Goering*. London: Routledge & Kegan Paul.

Owen, H. and Bell, J. (eds) (1967). *Wilfred. Owen: The Collected Letters*. Oxford: Oxford University Press.

Owen, W. (1963). *The Collected Poems of Wilfred Owen*. (Edited by C. Day Lewis.) New York: New Directions.

Palmier, J-M. (2007) *Weimar in Exile: The Antifascist Emigration in Europe and America* (trans. David Fernbach) New York: Verso

Paudler, M. (1978) *Auch Lachen will gelernt sein* (Laughter Too Must Be Learned) Berlin: Universitas.

Payne, R. (1973). *The Life and Death of Adolf Hitler*. London: Jonathan Cape.

Pfungst, O. (1965) *Clever Hans (the Horse of Mr. van Osten)* New York: Holt, Rinehart and Winston.

Pick, D. (1993). *War Machine: The Rationalization of Slaughter in the Modern Age.* New Haven: Yale University Press.

Polgar, F. J. & Singer, K. (1951) *The Story of a Hypnotist.* New York: Hermitage House.

Post, D.E (1998). 'The Hypnosis of Adolf Hitler'. *Journal of Forensic Science* Vol. 43, pages 1127-32.

Pridham, G. (1973). *Hitlers Rise to Power: The Nazi Movement in Bavaria, 1923-1933.* London: Hart-Davis, McGibbon.

Priestley, M. (1918). *Report on the Length of Stay in Hospital in the United Kingdom and the Disposal of Gas Casualties.* Chemical Warfare Medical Committee Report No. 16, London.

Proctor, R. (1988). *Racial Hygiene: Medicine under the Nazis.* Cambridge, Mass: Harvard University Press.

Raether, M. (1917). 'Neurosen-Heilungen der 'Kaufmann-Methode'.' *Archiv für Psychiatrie* Vol. 57, pages 489-502.

Rather, L.J. (1965). *Mind and Body in Eighteenth Century Medicine.* London: Wellcome Historical Medical Library.

Rauschning, H. (1939). *Hitler Speaks.* London: Thornton Butterworth.

Read, C.S. (1918). 'A Survey of War Neuropsychiatry.' *Mental Hygiene* Vol. 2, page 60.

Redlich, F. (1998). *Hitler: Diagnosis of a Destructive Patient.* Oxford: Oxford University Press.

Regler, G. (1960) *The Owl of Minerva* New York: Farrar, Straus, and Cudahy.

Repfennig, E. (1933). Zehn Jahre Kampf um Pasewalk, die Lazarettstadt Adolf Hitlers, Pasewalk. (Ten years' struggle at Pasewalk, the hospital town of Adolf Hitler. An account of the local branch of the NSDAP, published to celebrate the tenth anniversary of the Pasewalk branch.)

Rest, v. S. & Kraus, J. (2004) *Die Deutsche Armee im Weltkrieg.*

Uniformierung und Ausrustung – 1914 bis 1918 Vienna: Verlag Militaria.

Ribbentrop, J. von. (1954). *The Ribbentrop Memoirs.* (Translated by Oliver Watson.) London: Weidenfeld & Nicolson.

Rice, F.A. (1939). 'We Hadn't Heard of Hitler.' *Picture Post* Vol. 2, pages 75-6.

Richter, D. (1992). *Chemical Soldiers: British Gas Warfare in World War I.* Kansas: University Press of Kansas.

Ritter, G. (1958). *The Schlieffen Plan: Critique of a Myth.* London: Wolf.

Rose, F.C. and Bynum, W.F. (1982). *Historical Aspects of the Neurosciences: A Festschrift for Macdonald.* Critchley, NY: Raven Press.

Rosen, S. (1982) *My Voice Will Go With You: The Teaching Tales of Milton Erickson.* New York: W.W. Norton & Co.

Rosenbaum, R. (1998). *Explaining Hitler: The Search for the Origins of his Evil.* New York: Random House.

Roth, E. (1915). 'Kriegsgefahr und Psyche.' *Ärztliche Sachverständigenzeitung* Vol. 21, pages 1-3.

Rothmann, M. (1916). 'Zur Beseitigung psychogener Bewegungs-störungen bei Soldaten in einer Sitzung.' *Münchener Medizinische Wochenschrift Feldärztliche Beilage* Vol. 63, pages 1277-8.

Rürup, R. (1984) 'Der Geist von 1914 in Deutschland. Kriegsbegeisterung und Ideologisierung des Kriegs in Ersten Weltkrieg.' In *Ansichten vom Krieg. Verleichende Studien zum Ersten Weltkrieg in Literatur und Gesellschaft.* Hain: Ferum Academicum.

Sänger, A. (1915). 'Uber die durch den Krieg bedingten Folgezustände am Nervensystem. Vortrag im ärztlichen Verein in Hamburg am 26.1. und 9.11.15.' *Münchener Medizinische Wochenscrift. Feldärztliche Beilage 62:*

522-3; 564-7

Schacht, H. (1949). *Abrechnung mit Hitler*. Berlin: Michaelis-Verlag.

Schjerning, O. v. (1920). *Die Tätigkeit und die Erfolge der deutschen Ärzte im Weltkriege*. Leipzig: Barth.

Schmidt, W. (1915). 'Die psychischen und nervösen Folgezustände nach Granatexplosionen und Minenverschüttungen.' *Zeitschrift fur die Gesamte Neurologie und Psychiatrie* Vol. 29, pages 514-42.

Schneck, P. (1993). 'Die Berufungs- und Personalpolitik an der Greifswalder Medizinischen Fakultät zwischen 1933 und 1945.' In *Akademische Karrieren im 'Dritten Reich'. Beitrage zur Personal- und Berufungspolitik an Medizinischen Fakultäten*. (Edited by G. Gau and P. Schneck) Institut für Geschichte der Medizin Universitatsklinikum Charité, Medizinische Fakultät Humboldt-Universität, Berlin.

Schofield, V. (2012) *Witness to History: The Life of John Wheeler-Bennett* New Haven: Yale University Press.

Schuller, L. (1917). 'Heilung der Erscheinungen der Kriegshysterie in Wachsuggestion.' *Deutsche Medizinische Wochenschrift* Vol. 43, pages 652-4.

Schwalbe, K. (1969). *Wissenschaft und Kriegsmoral: Die Deutschen Hochschullehrer und die Politischen Grundfragen des Ersten Weltkrieges*. Gottingen: Musterschmidt Verlag.

Schwarzschild, L. (1933). 'Die Woche.' *Das neue Tage-Buch*, Issue 1, pages 271-5.

Shakespear, L.C.J. (1921). *History of the 30th Division 1915-1918*. London: Imperial War Museum.

Shelley, M.W. (1921) *Frankenstein*, New York: Dover Publications.

Shephard, B. (2000). *A War of Nerves: Soldiers and Psychiatrists 1914-1994*. London: Jonathan Cape.

Shirer, W. (1941) *Berlin Diary*. London: Hamish Hamilton.

Shirer, W. (1962). *The Rise and Fall of the Third Reich*. London: Secker &. Warburg.

Shorter, E. (1992). *From Paralysis to Fatigue: A History of Psychosomatic Illness in the Modern Era*. New York: Free Press.

Singer, A. (1915). 'Über die durch den Krieg Bedingten Folgezustände am Nervensystem. Vortrag im ärztlichen Verein in Hamburg am

und 9.11.1915.' *Münchener Feldärztliche Beilage* Vol. 62, page 567.

Singer, K. (1915). 'Wesen und Bedeutung der Kriegspsychosen.' *Berliner Klinische Wochenschrift* Vol. 52, pages 177-80.

Singer, K. (1919). 'Die zukünftige Begutachtung traumatischer Nervenkrankheiten.' Ärztliche Sachverständigen-Zeitung Vol. 25, pages 330-49.

Smith, B.F. (1967). *Adolf Hitler: His Family, Childhood and Youth*. Stanford: Stanford University Press.

Smith, D.C. (1990). *Triumph of the Will: The Reich Party Rally of 1934*. Richardson, Tex: Celluloid Press.

Sombart, N. (ed) (1982). *The Kaiser in his Epoch: Some Reflections on Wilhelmine Society, Sexuality and Culture*. Cambridge: Cambridge University Press.

Sommer, R. (1916). *Krieg und Seelenleben*. Leipzig: Nemnich Verlag.

Sommer, R. (1917). 'Beseitigung funktioneller Taubheit, besonders bei Soldaten, durch eine experimentalpsychologische Methode.' *Schmidts Jahrbucher der in- und ausländischen Gesamten Medizin* Vol. 84, page 68.

Speer, A. (1969) *Erinnerungen*. Berlin: Propylaeen Verlag.

Spotts, F. (2018) *Hitler and the Power of Aesthetics* Woodstock

& New York: Overlook Press.

Spence, R.B. (2008) *Secret Agent 666: Aleister Crowley, British Intelligence and the Occult*. Port Townsend: Feral Press.

Spence, R. B. Erik Jan Hanussen: Hitler's Jewish Psychic, *New Dawn*, Vo. 8. No 3. Pages 21 – 29.

Sprecht, H. (1900). *Ein Geschichts - Stadt und Landschaftsbild*. Braunau-am-Inn, Austria.

Stierlin, H. (1976) *Hitler as his Mother's Delegate'*, *History of Childhood Quarterly*, Vol. 3, No. 4.

Stone, M. (ed.) (1985). *Shell Shock and the Psychologists: The Anatomy of Madness*. London: Tavistock.

Störring, E. (1938). *Die Psychiatrie in Greifswald*. In H. Loeschke and A. Terbrüggen (eds.) 100 Jahre medizinische Forschung in Greifswald. Festschrift zur Feier des 75jährigen Bestehens des Medizischen Vereins. Greifswald 1938, pages 181-200.

Stromberg. R.N. (1982) *Redemption by War: The Intellectuals and 1914*. University Press of Kansas.

Tabori, P. (1968) *Companions of the Unseen*, New York: University Books.

Terraine, J. (1965). *The Great War 1914-1918*. London: Hutchinson.

Tobias, F. (1963) *The Reichstag Fire: Legend and Truth*, London: Secker & Warburg

Toland, J. (1976). *Adolf Hitler*. New York: Doubleday.

Trevor-Roper, H.R. (1976). *Hitlers Secret Conversations*. London: Octagon Press.

Trillat, E. (1986). *Histoire de l'hysterie*. Paris: Seghers.

Trimble, M. (1981). *Post-traumatic Neuroses: From Railway Spine to the Whiplash*. Chichester: Wiley.

Tuchman, B.W. (1962). *August 1914*. London: Constable.

Tyson, J. H. (2010) The Surreal Reich, New York: iUniverse Inc.

Ulrich, B. (1991) Krieg als Nervensache, *Die Zeit*, 22 November.

Ulrich, B. and Ziemann, B. (eds) (1992). *Frontalltag im Ersten Weltkrieg: Wahn und Wirklichkeit.* Frankfurt: Fischer.

Ulrich, B. and Ziemann, B. (eds) (1992). 'Nerven und Krieg. Skizzierung einer Beziehung'. In *Geschichte und Psychologie. Annäherungsversuche.* (Edited by B. Loewenstein) Pfaffenweiler: Centaurus.

Van den Bussche, H. (1999). 'Rudolf Degkwitz: Die politische Kontroverse um einen außergewöhnlichen Kinderarzt.' *Kinder- und Jugendarzt* Vol. 30, pages 425-31, 549-56.

Veith, I. (1965). *Hysteria: The History of a Disease.* Chicago: University of Chicago Press.

Waters, T. A. (1993) *Mind, Myth and the Magik.* Seattle: Hermetic Press.

Watkins. J.G. (1048) *Hypnotherapy of War Neuroses,* The Roland Press

Weber, T. (2010) *Hitler's First War* Oxford: Oxford University Press.

Wegener, Otto von (1985). *Hitler - Memoirs of a Confidant.* (Edited by H.A. Turner, Translated by Ruth Hein.) New Haven: Yale University Press.

Weichbrodt, R. (1917). 'Zur Behandlung Hysterischer Störungen.' *Archiv für Psychiatrie* Vol. 57, pages 519-25.

Weichbrodt, R. (1918). 'Einige Bemerkungen zur Behandlung von Kriegsneurotikern.' *Monatsschrift für Psychiatrie und Neurologie* Vol. 43, page 266.

Weiss, E. (1986; written 1938; first published 1963). *Der Augenzeuge.* Berlin: Aufbau-Verlag.

Weiss, E. (1977). The Eyewitness. (Translated by Ella R.W. McKee.) Boston: Houghton Mifflin.

Weller, W. (1920). *The Medical Aspects of Mustard Gas*

Poisoning. London: Henry Kimpton.

Wessely, S. and Lutz, T. (1995). 'Neurasthenia and Fatigue Syndromes.' In *A History of Clinical Psychiatry: The Origin and History of Psychiatric Disorders*. (Edited by G. Berrios and R. Porter.) New York: New York University Press.

West, F. (1921). *Chemical Warfare*. New York: McGraw-Hill.

Wexberg, E. (1916). 'Neurologische Erfahrungen im Felde.' *Wiener Medizinische Wochenschrift* Vol. 66, pages 1410-11.

Whalen, R.W. (1984). *Bitter Wounds: German Victims of the First World War*. Ithaca: Cornell University Press.

Whitlock, F.A. (1967). 'The aetiology of Hysteria. '*Acta Psychiatrica Scandinavica* Vol. 43, pages 144-62.

Wiedemann, F. (1964). *Der Mann der Feldherr Werden Wollte*. Berlin: Blick und Bild Verlag.

Wilson, R. (1918). *Robert Wilson Diary, January—March 1918*. London: Imperial War Museum.

Wiltshire, H. (1916). 'A Contribution to the Aetiology of Shell Shock.' *Lancet* Vol. 1, pages 1208-9.

Winter, D. (1988). *Death's Men: Soldiers of the Great War*. London: Penguin.

Winter, J.M. (1988). *The Experience of World War 1*. Oxford: Macmillan.

Winternitz, M.C. (1920). *Collected Studies on the Pathology of War Gas Poisoning*. New Haven: Yale University Press.

Wittkower, E. and Spillane, J.P. (eds) (1940). *The Neuroses in War*. New York: Macmillan.

Wollenberg, R. (1926). 'Hysterie oder Simulation.' *Psychiatrisch Neurologische Wochenschrift* Vol. 28, pages 211-12.

Wood, G. (1983). *The Myth of Neurosis*. London: Macmillan.

Wykes, A. (1970). *The Nuremberg Rallies*. London: Ballantine.

Zádor, J. (1933). 'Gleichgewichtsreaktionen bei Erkrankungen des Zentralnervensystems.' *Deutsche*

Medizinische Zeitschrift Vol. 130, pages 25-43.

Zádor, J. (1938). *'Les Réactions D'Équilibre Chez L'Homme'* Paris: Masson et Cie.

Zilboorg, K. (1941). *A History of Medical Psychology*. New York: W.W. Norton.

Zitelmann, R. (1998). *Hitler: The Politics of Seduction*. London: London House.

Zucker, K. (1928). 'Experimentelles über Sinnestäuschungen.' *Archiv für Psychiatrie* Vol. 33, pages 706-54.

INDEX